See page

143
159   } c
169

9 — Black Country.

The Economic Emergence
of the Black Country

THE
ECONOMIC EMERGENCE
OF THE
BLACK COUNTRY

A Study of the
Dudley Estate

T. J. Raybould

DAVID & CHARLES
NEWTON ABBOT

0 7153 5995 9

Set in 11 on 13-point Plantin
and printed in Great Britain
by W J Holman Limited Dawlish
for David & Charles (Holdings) Limited
South Devon House Newton Abbot Devon

Contents

CONTENTS

List of Maps

Introduction

Coal stands not beside but entirely above all other commodities. It is the material source of the energy of the country—the universal aid—the factor in everything we do.[1]

The abundant presence of coal brought the region known as the Black Country into existence between 1760 and 1830. Its exact boundaries are controversial, but in general the name is applied to an area of south Staffordshire and north Worcestershire with its centre, Dudley, approximately ten miles north-west of Birmingham. The Black Country consisted of those areas where iron production became concentrated in relation to the thick, thirty-foot coal seam which outcropped or lay at shallow depths up to 400ft below the surface. This resulted in extensive working of the seam almost to exhaustion by 1830. Such areas would include parts of the modern towns of Dudley, Tipton, Wednesbury, Darlaston, Bilston, Sedgley, Netherton, Cradley Heath and Brierley Hill. Deeper seams were also worked around the periphery of this nucleus, in districts such as Stourbridge, Kingswinford, Himley, Wolverhampton, Walsall, West Bromwich, Oldbury, Halesowen and Rowley Regis. Related trades evolved in these towns because of the concentration of pig- and wrought-iron production in the older central areas. Approximately ten miles square and lying within the quadrilateral Stourbridge, Wolver-

hampton, Walsall and Halesowen, the Black Country contained a
greater volume of coal at shallow depths than any comparable
area of Great Britain.² Intensive exploitation began after the
spread of mineral smelting into the area from Shropshire in 1766,
and the coal and iron trades flourished to the extent that the
region became the leading producer of wrought iron by 1830,
surpassing both Shropshire and South Wales.

At the end of the eighteenth century, the Dudley estate lay
mainly in the western half of the Black Country and was concentrated in Dudley, Sedgley and Brierley Hill. Dudley Castle had
been the home of the Dudleys until the development of Himley
Hall as the main family seat after the Civil War. This was situated
at Himley, approximately six miles west of Dudley on the western
edge of the Black Country. As the regional economy expanded
during the period of the eighteenth-century Industrial Revolution
the estate developed a wide range of economic activities including
agriculture, extensive mining and quarrying operations, the
manufacture of bricks, pig-iron and finished iron goods, and also
constructed its own canal and railway systems. Inevitably, the
family fortunes became closely linked to those of the Black
Country in general and to the iron trade in particular. Furthermore, Lord Dudley's position as the leading land and mineral
owner and, in many areas, lord of the manor, had wider re-
percussions for the political, social and economic development
of the area. In the eighteenth century, the bulk of Lord Dudley's
economic interests and property lay within the central and western sectors of the Black Country where he also held the lordship
of the manors of Himley, Kingswinford, Wombourne, Sedgley
and Dudley. During the various phases of subsequent economic
development, there was a close interplay between the activities of
the estate and the region in general.

It would be erroneous to suggest that industrial activity only
developed from the eighteenth century onwards. There was already a long-established tradition of mineral and iron working
both in the area and on the estate before the Industrial Revolution

of the eighteenth century.[3] But intensive exploitation of the area
began after John Wilkinson's decision to construct a mineral blast
furnace at Bradley, near Dudley, in 1766. This quickened the
pace of change and, in the period from 1766 to 1860, industrialisation and urbanisation created the Black Country and secured its
position as a major coal- and iron-producing district of national
importance. Total pig-iron production in the area increased from
2,000 tons in 1717 to 4,500 tons by 1788 and 216,000 tons in
1827. The Crimean War lifted local iron production to a peak in
1854 when 743,000 tons were produced.

Within this period, 1766-1860, the Dudley estate experienced
two distinct phases of economic expansion. The first, from 1774
to 1833, was a period of rapid growth initiated by the second
viscount to take advantage of the various factors making for expansion in the iron and mineral trades. This, perhaps, corres-
ponds to Rostow's stage three—the 'take-off'—in his model for
economic growth in which one or more substantial sectors develop a high growth rate and the impulses to growth are exploited
through the emergence of a political, social and institutional
framework. Lord Dudley, as lord of the manor with access to
Parliament, was able to exploit the situation which he found on
succeeding to the title in 1774. By 1833, a rapid increase in the
number and scale of estate activities had taken place, but profitability and efficiency were adversely affected by old-fashioned
managerial attitudes and the absence of long-term planning. On
the death of John William, Fourth Viscount and First Earl of
Dudley in 1833, the estate was held in trust until 1845 for his
nephew William. These twelve years mark the second phase of
estate development within the period of rapid growth which produced the Black Country between 1766 and 1860. The four
trustees initiated a massive expansion in the level of economic
activity, which together laid the foundations for the continuing
high profitability of the Dudley estate down to the twentieth
century. The earldom was revived in 1860, when William was
created First Earl of Dudley.

The work and contribution of these trustees during the trust period, 1833-45, will be considered elsewhere, but their reputations and contrasting careers before 1833 are of interest. John Benbow, a partner in the firm of Messrs Alban and Benbow of Lincoln's Inn, had been employed since 1800 by the Dudley estate in the capacity of chief legal adviser. By the 1820s he was evidently acting as a general supervisor of all the business of the estate and, as such, he stood condemned by the various reports made to the trustees after 1833 which revealed numerous deficiencies in management and administration. As the earl had nominated him a trustee, this was to produce considerable disharmony. Equally, Francis Downing, the chief land and mineral agent, was also condemned. He had been employed as a clerk in the chief steward's office as long ago as 1796. His actions as a trustee produced numerous crises over policy decisions. These two men had obviously been nominated by the earl as employees whom he could trust and who would maintain continuity in the management of affairs while consideration was given to the changes of policy permitted by his will.

The other two trustees were personal friends. One of them, Henry Phillpotts, Bishop of Exeter, could be trusted for his integrity and be expected to work unselfishly to carry out the tasks entrusted to him. In fact, as a reactionary Tory, his attitudes towards liberal and social reform were to harm the good relationships between the Dudley estate and the working population of the area. In addition his attempts to use his influence over trust affairs in the interest of his son were to create considerable difficulties.

It was the fourth trustee, Edward John Littleton, a close personal friend of the late earl, whose career and experience were to prove most beneficial of all to the future prospects of the Dudley estate. His residence at Teddesley Park near Wolverhampton, and his estates in the Cannock area, gave him first-hand experience of conditions in Staffordshire and in the management of a large landed estate with mineral interests. He had been a

Whig MP for Staffordshire since 1810 and demonstrated his progressive sympathies by supporting the cause of parliamentary reform from 1828 onwards. Since 1825 he had advocated a catholic emancipation Bill for Ireland and, in 1830, after close collaboration with Huskisson, he presented the anti-truck Bill as a private member's Bill: this became law in 1831. At that time, Littleton owned eight brickfields, two stone quarries, two lime works, and three collieries. His reputation stood high in Staffordshire where he was known as 'The Man of the People'. Shortly after the commencement of the trust, Littleton was appointed Chief Secretary to the Lord Lieutenant of Ireland but, after his resignation in July 1834, following a political indiscretion over the Wexford election which incurred him the criticism of O'Connell, he was able to concentrate his attention on the management of his own affairs and the Dudley estate. Created Lord Hatherton in May 1835, he emerged as the most satisfactory of the Dudley trustees, not least in his efforts to mould the character of William Ward, heir to the Dudley estate.

Although not nominated as a trustee, the appointment of James Loch, under the terms of the will, as auditor to the trust was to prove almost as valuable to the interests of the estate as the choice of Littleton. His experience of business management was vast: since August 1812 he had been chief agent to the Duke of Sutherland—a position he was to retain until 1855. As a law student at Edinburgh in 1798, Loch mixed with a talented group of progressive thinkers known as the Speculative Society, including such men as John Murray and Henry Brougham. Brougham was a friend of the late Earl of Dudley and as he too had been tutored by Dugald Stewart of Edinburgh in 1798, it is possible that the earl had been acquainted with Loch from that date. Loch's high standards of personal conduct earned him the gratitude of his employers and also the criticism of some colleagues and acquaintances. He was closely connected with the Highland Clearances and earned himself the titles of 'The Duke's Premier' and 'The Sutherland Metternich'.[4] Nevertheless, Loch established such a reputation that he was employed not only by the Duke of Sutherland but also by the Earl of Ellesmere, the Howards of Castle Howard and, after 1837, as superintendent by the Bridgewater trust. The Dudley trust was fortunate enough to have Loch as its auditor between 1835 and 1845. Although not in a position to act as the prime mover of affairs, as he could in his capacity as chief agent to the Sutherland estates, Loch's standing and character involved him closely in policy-making. Together with Littleton, theirs was the most valuable contribution to the improvement and retrenchment of the Dudley estate which laid the foundation for its future profitability on a short- and long-term basis.

In the short run, the work of the trust enabled the estate to benefit fully from the iron and mineral trades which continued to expand in the Black Country, particularly during the mid-1830s and 1840s, until the late 1850s. From that time until 1885, the iron trade experienced a relatively rapid decline which virtually destroyed the traditional basis of the regional economy as a leading producer of pig and wrought iron. As production fell, from 396,000 tons in 1861 and 326,000 tons in 1879 to 190,000 tons in 1905, there was a corresponding decline in production within the mineral and secondary iron trades. In part, this decline was linked to falling demands for wrought iron on a national scale as technological advances increased the supply of cheap steel. Within the Black Country, additional factors intensified the problems which falling demand created for local ironmasters. These were mainly related to high transport costs, the increasing cost of mineral production and the relative unsuitability of local raw materials for use in the new processes of steel production. In the short term, the collapse of the iron trade intensified labour unrest among colliers and ironworkers and increased the opportunities for their exploitation in sweated workshop and cottage industries such as the nail and chain trades. Changes in the basic structure of the regional economy also worked to produce a change in the relationship between Birmingham and the

Black Country. Traditionally, industries producing highly manufactured goods were concentrated in Birmingham, while the
Black Country produced pig and wrought iron and semi-
manufactured goods.

In contrast to the general decline of the region in the period
1860-85, the Dudley estate attained its peak prosperity from
the iron and coal trades and established a national and world-
wide reputation as a manufacturer of high-grade wrought iron.
These developments were accompanied by a further expansion
in the capital invested by the estate in the iron and colliery
trades, canals and railways, and property speculation within the
area. It may be argued that policies adopted by the estate
probably retarded the general decline of the Black Country as an
iron-producing area.

As the wealth and importance of the estate increased, further
honours and titles were accorded to the family. William Ward,
heir to the title during the period of the Dudley trust, received
the earldom of Dudley in 1860 and was attached to Earl Gran-
ville's special mission to Russia in 1855. In 1883, William's net
income from an estate of 25,554 acres was £123,176. This was
all the more remarkable as his income was exceeded by only six
members of the landed aristocracy, each of whom possessed over
100,000 acres.[5] Nevertheless, regional factors and the decline of
the wrought-iron trade in general, forced the estate to revise its
policies and the period ended with the sale of a number of ironworks and mineral properties after 1880.

The final phase in the evolution of the Black Country
economy began in the mid-1880s with the growing diversification of industry as iron and coal production declined. In particular there was an expansion in a wide range of manufactured iron
goods, engineering and allied trades connected with the motor
industry. By 1918, the production of coal and wrought iron had
virtually ceased although mineral production continued to
flourish in the fringe areas of West Bromwich and Cannock.
Within this period the estate derived a considerable income from

traditional sources until the nationalisation of the coal and steel industries after World War II. However, by the 1920s, policy and structural changes had transformed the estate as an administrative and economic unit in response to developments in the local economy and the mounting pressures to which the landed aristocracy and the mining industry in general were subjected. These changes took the form of an influx of outside capital after 1890, and the sale of landed property between 1918 and 1947. In addition, the estate relinquished its entrepreneurial role after 1924 and became a supplier of capital in a wide range of industrial and commercial undertakings. In 1947, the long connection between the Dudley family and the area was severed when the bulk of the local landed properties of the Dudley estate were sold, including the family residence at Himley Hall. The present earl retains a number of business interests and isolated properties within the district, but the traditional relationship between the Earl of Dudley and the affairs of the Black Country, while still prominent in the minds of the older generation, holds little meaning for the young.

After the death of William, First Earl of Dudley in 1885, subsequent holders of the title achieved further political and administrative distinction. His son was Parliamentary Secretary to the Board of Trade, 1895-1902, and was Lord Lieutenant of Ireland, 1902-5, during which time he incurred criticism at home by his support of Wyndham's scheme for the devolution of power in Ireland. After this he served as Governor General of the Commonwealth of Australia from 1908 to 1911. The late earl,[6] a close friend of the Duke of Windsor, was elected MP for Hornsey, 1921-4, and for Wednesbury, 1931-2. His connection with industry earned him the presidencies of the Society of British Gas Industries, 1926-7, the British Iron and Steel Corporation, 1945-6, The Federation of Chambers of Commerce of the British Empire, 1937-45, the Birmingham Chamber of Commerce, 1937-9, the British Iron and Steel Institute, 1938-40, and the vice-presidency of the Institute of Directors, when it was revived in 1949. On this occasion, the local press remarked that 'though his lordship's interests in coal and railways have been nationalised, he is still a power in iron and steel'.[7] In addition to these commitments, he was also active in the management of numerous companies with which the estate was closely connected, such as the Round Oak Steel Works Ltd. During World War II, the earl was Regional Commissioner for the Midlands, a post which he held until 1946.

*   *   *   *

The value of regional studies is frequently called in question although others would argue that our knowledge and understanding of national themes can only be thus clarified. Apart from reflecting the interaction of general regional and national economic factors on the development of the estate, which emerged from relative insignificance in the eighteenth century to national prominence by the mid-nineteenth century, the history of the Dudley estate has particular significance in numerous other respects. The changing economic role of the landed aristocracy, developments in agriculture, mining, the iron industry and transport systems, are all reflected in estate affairs. In particular, the eighteenth-century Industrial Revolution in the key area of the industrial West Midlands—the 'cradle of the Industrial Revolution'—is central to the theme of the estate's early development. Technological change and the impact of railway expansion are closely connected with the changing fortunes of the wrought-iron trade in which the Black Country was the leading national producer until the mid-nineteenth century.

Apart from the broad range of its economic activities, the history of the Dudley estate is untypical of the landed aristocracy in many other respects and differs also in matters of detail and timing. After the late eighteenth century, the bulk of its revenue was drawn from mineral and industrial enterprise rather than land or property rents. Of the landed aristocrats who pursued

B

an entrepreneurial role in mining, the vast majority had assumed
the position of rentiers by the 1880s, and were thus cushioned
from the direct impact of economic and labour problems within
the industry. The Dudley estate persisted with the direct
management of its colliery undertakings until 1924, and in other
extractive industries did not relinquish this role until 1947. The
evil resulting from harmful managerial practices and working
conditions in the mines, particularly in the Black Country, is well
established. In both respects, the administration of the Dudley
estate differed from the general pattern. Furthermore, the break-
up of the landed estates of the aristocracy in the late nineteenth
century did not commence on the Dudley estate until after 1918.

After an examination of the physical characteristics of the
region and the development of the estate before the succession of
the second viscount, the main body of the book is set within the
period 1774-1947. The local enclosure Acts and awards, employed as an agent of economic change by Lord Dudley, are
analysed. Aspects of the estate's main economic activities and
their relationship with the Black Country are then considered
through the principal phases of local economic development.

Within these phases—1766-1860, a period of regional expansion; 1860-85, when the Black Country iron trade declined; and
from 1885 to 1950, a period of transformation and recovery—
the significant periods for the estate were: 1774-1833, a period
of rapid and haphazard development, and 1833-45, the period
of retrenchment and reform; 1854-85, peak profitability from the
iron and coal trades; and 1890-1947, when restructuring, diversification of economic interests and the disposal of landed
property changed not only the basis of the estate's activities as
an economic unit, but also its relationship with the area as a
whole. These themes are set against the background of national
factors as they affected the regional economy and the landed
aristocracy in general. Finally, the problems of estate management and administration are considered. This aspect of industrialisation has, on the whole, been neglected. In the coal trade,

particular problems existed because of the scale and complexity of the industry. These problems were intensified for the Dudley estate by the range of its economic activities in addition to mineral exploitation.

The text is based almost entirely on the Dudley MSS deposited by the late earl at Dudley Public Library. These unpublished sources provide a comprehensive record of the estate's activities over the last 200 years. Additional sources contained in the Hatherton Collection at Stafford Record Office and in the Chancery Master's Exhibits at the Public Record Office have also been consulted. These are of particular value for the period 1833-45 when Lord Hatherton acted as a trustee to the estate, and for 1797-8 when the third viscount was involved in a lawsuit with his mineral agent. In general, the documents relate to the management of landed and cottage properties, various local canal, railway and enclosure Acts, manor court proceedings and the conduct of iron and mineral undertakings. Specific references are given in the text except in the case of documents consulted from the last deposit of manuscripts made by the late earl. These are still being catalogued.

Notes to the Introduction are on page 244

CHAPTER ONE

The Dudley Estate in its Regional Setting, 1774

Physical Characteristics of the Region

The two main characteristics of the Black Country were in direct contrast to each other in that the abundance of minerals was matched by an absence of natural water communications. This latter feature played a determining role in the location of industry every bit as important as the presence of the mineral outcrop.

The south Staffordshire coalfield (excluding the Cannock area lying to the north of the Bentley Faults which was developed later than the traditional Black Country areas) is small, clearly defined, and contains a number of peculiar features. It runs roughly in a north-south direction over a distance of approximately 15 miles, decreasing from 8 miles in the north to 5 miles in the south. The earlier nucleus covered an area within a radius of 3 miles of Dudley Castle. It is bounded in the west by the Western Boundary Fault running roughly north-south through Wolverhampton, Himley, Kingswinford, and Stourbridge. To the east, coal lies at a shallow depth, or outcrops, but plunges to much greater depths below the sandstone measures to the west. To the south it is bounded by a fault running west-east between

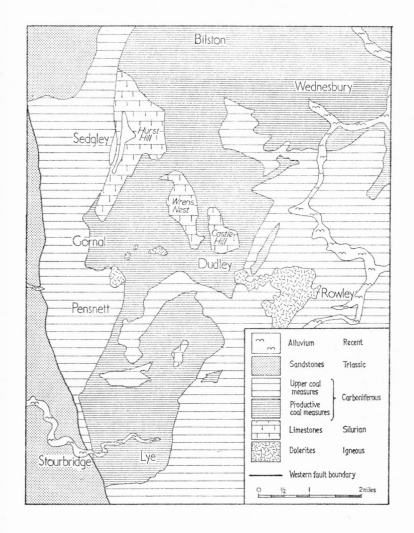

Figure 1 Solid geology of the Black Country

Stourbridge and Halesowen. The field terminates in the east along the Eastern Boundary Fault which runs roughly in a north-easterly direction through Halesowen, Oldbury and West Bromwich to Walsall; while the northern boundary is defined by the Bentley Faults between Walsall and Wolverhampton. The coalfield itself falls into two divisions lying to the north or south of the Russell's Hall Fault which runs in an easterly direction from Gornal to Rowley Regis. In the northern section the thick coal outcrops along a line from Dudley through Gornal, Coseley, Bilston, and Darlaston to Wednesbury and rarely lies more than 400ft from the surface. South of the fault, the thick coal outcrops along a shorter line in the Level area of Brierley Hill or, because of minor faults, lies somewhat deeper between 500ft and 800ft. The thick coal north of the Russell's Hall Fault was intensively exploited after 1760 and was largely exhausted in Tipton and Wednesbury by 1830, when the southern part was brought into more intensive production. Organisation of mineral enterprise and the techniques of extraction were particularly influenced by the advantages and problems created by the presence of the thirty-foot seam.

In addition to the thick coal, which actually consists of about fourteen layers interspersed with thin strata of clay and ironstone, there are eight other seams of coal. Thicker seams of clay and ironstone lie between the coal measures below the thick coal. The main ironstone seam, known as gubbins ironstone, lies directly under the thirty-foot coal. At a greater depth lies the valuable fireclay used extensively in the refractory industries of the Stourbridge area where it lies at a relatively shallow depth. As a result of this geological formation, various grades of coal, clay and ironstone could be raised from the same shaft. The thirty-foot coal was a high-grade coal used in the production of good-quality iron. Heathen coal was particularly suitable for coking and iron-smelting, while brooch coal, because of its quick-burning qualities, was particularly in demand as a domestic fuel.

The main mineral seams in order of depth are:

	thickness
Brooch Coal	2ft 9in—3ft 6in
Flying Reed Coal	2ft—3ft
Thick Coal	18ft—30ft
Gubbins Ironstone	2ft—8ft
Brick Clay	
Heathen Coal	3ft 6in—5ft
Fireclay	
White Ironstone	2ft—10ft
Sulphur or Stinking Coal ...	4ft—6ft
New Mine Coal	4ft—6ft
Fireclay Coal	4ft
Bottom Coal	2ft—12ft
Singing Coal	2ft—4ft

The ridge which divides the Black Country along a line running from the north-west to the south-east consisting of Sedgley
Beacon, Hurst Hill, Wren's Nest and Dudley Castle Hill, contains extensive outcrops of Silurian limestone. These were all
worked for limestone which, after burning, was used for building
and agriculture. With the development of the mineral smelting
of iron ore in the area, increasing quantities were used as flux
for the furnaces. The richest deposits were at the Wren's Nest
where two beds, the Upper and Lower Wenlock Limestone,
outcrop at a steep angle on both sides of the hill. The core of
the hill consists of older rocks—Wenlock Shale—while the Upper
Limestone, 25ft thick, is separated from the Lower Limestone
by a layer of impure limestone and shale known as the Nodular
Beds. Too impure for industrial use, this was left as a ridge
between the two worked bands of limestone although some parts
were quarried for road-stone during the early part of this century.

Two other distinctive features are the presence of igneous
rocks and sandstones. At its southern end the dorsal ridge divid-
ing the Black Country terminates at Rowley Hill where basalt or
Rowley Rag has been extensively quarried since the last decades
of the nineteenth century. Other isolated outcrops occur, such

as at Barrow Hill between Dudley and Kingswinford. West of the boundary fault which runs from Wolverhampton to Stourbridge, the Keuper and Bunter sandstones have been quarried for building material, and sand for moulding and building purposes.

The last major natural feature of the area, its elevated position and lack of water communications, also influenced the economic development of the region. No navigable rivers flow through or within easy reach of the Black Country as it lies on the main watershed between the Bristol Channel and the North Sea. Its rivers and streams, the Smestow, Stour, and Tame, do flow into the Severn and Trent but were not navigable, even in the eighteenth century. The hilly nature of the district and its numerous streams did provide ample water power for industry but full development of the area was only possible after canals linked it to the navigable rivers, although canal construction and maintenance proved to be expensive and difficult. Whereas the northern coalfield was able to use the Tyne, Wear and Tees to reach the ports of Newcastle and Sunderland, Black Country pits had no such advantages in the search for wider markets. The region as a whole is a plateau lying 400ft above sea level. The main dorsal ridge rises to a height of 876ft at Rowley and is nowhere less than 600ft high. Topography and lack of water posed particular problems for the early canal builders, while mining subsidence added to the difficulties of Telford and other nineteenth-century canal engineers in this locality. Because of its natural resources, the potential wealth of the Black Country was enormous, particularly after the beginning of increased economic activity in the iron and mineral trades towards the end of the eighteenth century. The Dudley estate possessed land containing all of these minerals, much of it concentrated south and west of the Dudley-Sedgley ridge, including all of the limestone outcrops at Dudley Castle and the Wren's Nest. Factors combined after 1774 to ensure that the estate derived considerable benefit from this advantageous position.

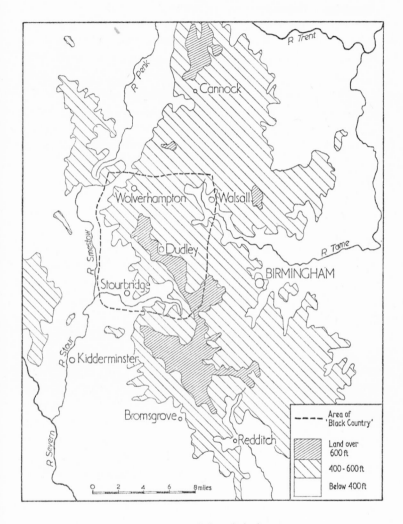

Figure 2   Relief and drainage

Economic Developments Before 1774

When the effects of the technological revolution in iron production began to make an impact on the region after the 1760s, there already existed a firm tradition of mineral and iron working on which the entrepreneurs of the eighteenth-century Industrial Revolution could base expansion. As early as 1600, the Black Country district had economic links with older developed areas and local manufacturers used coal and iron from Shropshire and the Warwickshire coalfield. Agriculture was predominant but a growing number of trades existed in addition to the usual rural crafts. Quarter sessions records for the early seventeenth century indicate that iron slitting, lock-making, and nailing were extensively developed, with nailers outnumbering all other trades.[1] A degree of local specialisation was also apparent with lorimers at Walsall and lockmakers at Willenhall. Ironmongers were active in the Birmingham and Black Country area as early as the mid-sixteenth century, supplying iron to local craftsmen and buying their finished products. Nevertheless, older market towns such as Coventry, Lichfield, and Bridgnorth still dominated the West Midlands. Birmingham, with a population of 2,000 in 1600, was the only area where inhabitants were divorced from the soil while the villages and townships of the Black Country area represented 'a countryside becoming industrialised'.

Immigration into the district, particularly heavy in the early nineteenth century, became a factor of increasing significance after 1600, together with the concentration of population and industry in specific areas. In 1600, the population per square mile was 100 in Worcestershire, 82 in Warwickshire, and 74 in Staffordshire. Corresponding figures for 1700 were 141, 112, and 111. This demonstrates a considerable increase in the total population but does not fully reflect the fact that much of the increase would be concentrated in Birmingham and the Black Country rather than throughout the three counties.

Perhaps the major impetus to the development of the Black Country was the introduction of the blast furnace into the area in the sixteenth century. Medieval bloomeries, producing bar iron forged directly from a bloom on the anvil, had been established throughout the area where charcoal and iron ore existed with water power to drive the bellows. By this process, production was laborious and output was limited to about 1cwt in a 12 hour period. Production of pig iron by blast furnace required considerable quantities of fuel and this was readily available in the wooded district north and west of Birmingham, together with ironstone. The separation of processes in iron production also required water power for the bellows and the tilt hammer of the forge—this, too, was available on the slopes of the plateau between Wolverhampton and Birmingham. The first blast furnace to be erected in the West Midlands was at Cannock Chase in 1561.[2] As other furnaces were erected and the quantity of iron to be re-heated and worked at the forge increased, there was a corresponding rise in the consumption and output of coal. By 1665, there were relatively few open pits and shafts had been sunk to a depth of 120ft. Production was from 25,000 to 70,000 tons of coal a year in the area between Wolverhampton and Birmingham. The whole of Staffordshire was producing 150,000 tons of coal and ironstone annually by 1720 and 'fully two-thirds of this must have come from the pits of South Staffordshire'.[3] It is likely that the iron trade of South Staffordshire produced only half of the total of 4,000 tons of pig iron consumed annually in the area by 1717, when the total English output was 17,350 tons. These figures reflect the growth of the coal and iron trade in the area; inevitably such developments influenced the Dudley estate.

Coal and ironstone deposits had been worked for many years on the estate. An inquisition taken on the death of Roger de Somery[4] (Baron Dudley) in December 1272, records 'four coal-pits of sea-cole' (*quattor putei de carbone maris*)[5] in the manor of Kingswinford. Another inquisition of 1291 states that 'there are iron mines worth yearly £8 ... the mines of sea coal are worth yearly 26s. 8d.'[6] The will of Edward, Lord Dudley in 1586 reflects the early involvement of the family in the local iron trade:

I wyll and bequeathe my hoole yron workes, with all my owre [ore] fytt for to mainteyne the same and underwoodes for the thoroughe mainteyninge of the same which I doe gyve and bequeathe unto Mary ladie Dudley my wyfe.[7]

The reference to 'owre' may imply that a blast furnace existed at this time, although it has been suggested that the first blast furnaces in this part of the Midlands were at Gornal Wood (c 1595) and Halesowen (1602-5).[8] Edward, Lord Dudley, who succeeded his father in 1586, built the Gornal Wood furnace and also owned Cradley furnace in 1610. It was during his lifetime that the industrial interests of the Dudley estate first achieved national prominence through the activities of his illegitimate son, Dud Dudley. His book, *Metallum Martis*, published in 1665,[9] reviewed his attempts to smelt iron ore with coal. This was part of an abortive effort to secure a renewal of a royal patent first issued to him in 1621:

...I [was] fetched from Oxford, then of Bayliol Colledge, Anno 1619, to look and manage 3 Iron Works of my Fathers, 1 Furnace, and 2 Forges, in the Chase of Pensnet, in Worcestershire, but Wood and Charcole growing then scant, and Pit-coles, in great quantities abounding near the Furnace, and to attempt by my new invention, the making of Iron with Pit-cole ... I found such success at first tryal animated me, for at my tryal or blast, I made Iron to profit with Pit-cole ...[10]

James I had granted Dud Dudley a patent in 1621 to make iron with pit coal—this was renewed in 1638. The opposition of local charcoal iron manufacturers and the destruction of family property during the Civil War prevented Dudley from developing an established market for his iron.[11] After Charles II declined to renew the patent, the secrets of his invention went with Dud Dudley into obscurity. It was not until 200 years later that the Dudley estate again manufactured iron on its own account.

Mineral enterprise continued to flourish as indicated by the estate's rent rolls for 1701. Out of a total income of £5,014 4s 4d, no less than £2,191 16s 10½d was derived from minerals:

	£	s	d
Coalworks, Knowle Hill, Netherton (Dudley)	£858	1s	9½d
„ The Paddock (Coneygre)	443	0	3
„ New Park (Parkhead, Dudley?)	540	14	10
Ironstone Mines	100	0	0
Limeworks (Dudley)	250	0	0
Land and Chief Rents, Himley, Swindon and Kingswinford	403	19	10½
Hall and Lands, Himley	74	0	0
Castle and Lands, Dudley	1,607	0	1
Manor Admittances, Rowley Regis	12	0	0
Manor Small Tenements and Cottages, Kingswinford (60)	16	0	0
Dudley Foreign (40)	6	10	0
Rowley Regis (23)	3	10	0
Tolls of Market and Fairs, Dudley	4	0	0
Manor Fees, Kingswinford	213	7	6
Woodlands, Gornal	80	0	0
„ Baggeridge	200	0	0
„ Pensnett Chase	200	0	0
[sic]	£5,014	4s	4d[12]

The exact location of the mines is uncertain but all would probably be on the line of the thick-coal outcrop around the Dudley ridge. On coming of age in June 1725, Lord Dudley took possession of a considerable amount of annuities, stock and other investments:

Southsea Capital	£6,080
Southsea Annuities	6,080
Lottery Orders, 1714	340
Queen's Lottery	2,610
Civil List	1,000
Bank Stock	2,000
Bank Annuities	1,000
Million Bank	2,000
	£21,110[13]

This apparently healthy state of affairs had been largely occasioned by the judicious choice, in 1628, of Humble Ward as a husband for Frances, heir to the Dudley estate. Ward, who succeeded to the estate in 1643, was the son of William Ward, a wealthy London goldsmith and jeweller to Queen Henrietta Maria. His wealth undoubtedly assisted the Dudley estate to recover from the ravages of the Civil War in the area.

Further evidence of existing mineral enterprise in the early years of the century is provided by a Chancery suit of 1740.[14] One deposition shows that three steam engines existed on the Dudley estate in 1731, 'one at Tipton [Coneygre], one at Dudley Wood [Netherton?], and one at the Parks [Parkhead, Dudley?]'.[15] Another records that

> The late William, Lord Dudley and Ward kept several collieries, one at Tipton upon which two fire engines for the drawing of water were employed, and one other at the Park near Dudley and another at Dudley Wood ... upon each of which a fire engine was employed. The said first mentioned fire engine ... cost ... £450 ... the other engine at Tipton ... £700 and the engine at the Park ... £500 and the engine at Dudley Wood ... £700.[16]

The engine erected near Dudley Castle in 1712 has been described as the first successful Newcomen engine;[17] this was the engine erected at Coneygre Colliery by Lord Dudley. Drainage problems were considerable in the area because of the nature of the 30ft seam and the accompanying clay measures. Four steam engines by 1740 would represent a considerable proportion of the total number of Newcomen engines erected in this area. Professor J. R. Harris[18] has estimated that eleven Newcomen engines were built by 1716 and fifty more in the period 1716-33. Three of these were at work near Wolverhampton in 1733 (these would all be on the Dudley estate) and four more were constructed in the area by 1781. Towards the end of the eighteenth century, a number of factors combined to produce a considerable expansion in the existing mineral and industrial activities of the Dudley estate and the area in general.

Factors for Expansion
Economic trends were moving undeniably in favour of the landed

interest by the late 1760s because of rising population and industrialisation. In addition to the general economic situation, a number of specific developments influenced the Dudley estate at this time. Of particular importance was the technological advance in the successful mineral smelting of iron ore at the Coalbrookdale Works of Abraham Darby by 1735. This process had originally been attempted at Coalbrookdale by Abraham Darby I in 1709. Darby had been born in Dudley in 1676 and it is possible that he first encountered the idea of mineral smelting in his home district where many would be familiar with the work and claims of Dud Dudley. Coke-smelted pig iron released the iron trade from dependence on a dwindling supply of charcoal and resulted in increased output and the concentration of blast furnaces on the coalfields. The process was introduced into the Black Country area by John Wilkinson who constructed the Bradley Ironworks at Bilston in 1766. He had used the coke-smelting process at his ironworks, formerly owned by Abraham Darby, at Broseley in Shropshire and at Bersham in Denbighshire. Because of the shortage of good furnace coke, Wilkinson also charged his furnaces with local thick-coal and improved the quality of pig iron by the use of a steam blast engine. This application of Watt's engine to the blowing cylinders made the Bradley furnace relatively independent of water power and, by achieving higher temperatures, removed a greater proportion of impurities.

The problem of converting pig into good malleable iron was not effectively solved until 1783 when Cort's patent consolidated a number of existing processes into one continuous operation. This provided the basis for the British wrought-iron industry in general and resulted in its concentration on the Black Country coalfield in particular.[19] By this process, pig iron was heated, then forged or rolled, re-heated in a balling or puddling furnace for decarburisation, and finally consolidated in a rolling process. The problem of removing impurities from pig iron had not existed when wrought iron had been produced directly from ore in the bloomery process. Of particular importance was the fact that, whereas it had been necessary to use charcoal in the conversion of coke-smelted pig to the malleable form, Cort's process enabled the cheaper fuel, coal, to be used. His success reduced production costs and increased the demand for mineral-smelted pig iron from manufacturers of iron and finished goods. Improvements in the application of steam power also influenced developments in the area after the installation of the first Watt engine at Bloomfield (Tipton) and the perfection of the rotative principle in 1782-4.

Transport improvements, especially in the form of canal construction, opened up the area after 1766. The Staffordshire and Worcestershire Canal, cut by Brindley between 1766 and 1772 to link the rivers Severn and Trent, was intended primarily to serve the interests of the Potteries, but a branch was cut from Aldersley, near Wolverhampton, through Bilston and Tipton to Birmingham. For the first time, the coal trade of the area could reach wider markets. Much of the land was still unenclosed commons and waste in the manors of Dudley, Sedgley, Kingswinford, and Rowley Regis. To facilitate exploitation, mineral rights and boundaries were clarified by a number of parliamentary Bills of enclosure.

These factors—general economic trends, technological advances, and transport improvements—would all have influenced the economic development of the Dudley estate in the long run, but they assumed a greater and more immediate significance because of the policies of John, Second Viscount Dudley and Ward, who succeeded to the title in 1774. He introduced many of the local Bills of enclosure into Parliament, and was directly responsible for two of the three additional canals which were to provide the basic transport system of the Black Country until the mid-nineteenth century.

Regional and national economic trends were undoubtedly developing to the advantage of the Dudley estate because of its geographical situation. However, it was the tradition of mineral enterprise, the availability of capital from a variety of sources, and, above all, the initiative of the second viscount, which enabled the estate to achieve such an expansion of economic interests and wealth out of these circumstances in the years after 1774.

In the debate on the causes and course of the eighteenth-century Industrial Revolution, Black Country developments reflect many of the major lines of argument. It may be that by 1772, existing factors satisfied the conditions envisaged in the second stage of Rostow's[20] model for economic growth. The advent of canal transport and technological innovation expanded the iron trade as the leading sector, and produced a multiplier effect on the level of local economic activity which became characterised by rapid sustained growth by 1800. Those who regard the entrepreneur as the agent of change, may find evidence in the activities of such local industrialists as Wilkinson, Gibbons, Boulton, and Lord Dudley himself.[21]

The sociological interpretation may also derive support from the existence of a social structure within the area which contained both an adequate labour force on which to launch expansion and a class of people willing to exploit the impulses to expansion.

However, whereas the dynamic forces which determined the timing and pace of industrial expansion within the area as a whole may be open to debate, there is no doubt as to the development of the Dudley estate. In this case, the second viscount acted as the agent of change motivated by a desire to exploit the general impulses to expansion. To this extent, the estate was a microcosm of eighteenth-century society in which a combination of factors worked to produce an economic revolution at that time. These were capital availability, transport improvements, technological innovation, growing demand, and the development of the iron trade as the leading sector of the regional economy. As lord of the manor with access to Parliament, Lord Dudley enjoyed a position of power from which to effect changes

c

within the area by personal action and parliamentary legislation. This he proceeded to do in the years 1774-88 through a co-ordinated policy of enclosure, road and canal construction, estate mineral undertakings and the granting of leases to iron and coal masters. In this process, local enclosures played a significant role.

Notes to Chapter 1 are on pages 244-6

CHAPTER TWO

Enclosure: the Cornerstone

The Acts and Awards

During the first phase of Black Country expansion between 1766 and 1860, the Lords Dudley derived two particular advantages from the enclosure of local commons and waste. Their estates were considerably increased in area and particular rights, reserved to them by a number of the enclosure Acts, contributed directly to the expansion of mineral and industrial enterprise. Although enclosure created problems involving litigation, the overall effect was overwhelmingly favourable to the financial interests of the estate. A further result of local enclosures was the extension of agricultural activity on the estates during the late eighteenth century.

Allotments to Lord Dudley by
Local Enclosure Acts and Awards, 1776-1807

Manor	Act	Area	Award	Total Area	Area Allotted to to Lord Dudley	
Ashwood Hay,		1,400			638	
Kingswinford	1776	acres	1777	1,594	acres	(40.2%)
Pensnett Chase,						
Kingswinford	1784	1,300	1787	1,433	679	(47.3%)

Dudley Wood,						
Dudley	1784	1,000	1786	1,000	434	(43%)
Wombourn and						
Swindon,						
Wombourn	1796	1,500	1807	1,500	451	(30%)
Rowley Regis	1799	200	1807	200	16	(8%)

Lord Dudley was lord of the manor in each case except Wombourne. In general, the awards affected a larger area than the estimate given in the Act and the area allocated to Lord Dudley is expressed as a percentage of the area included in the actual award. Lord Dudley received in each case considerably more than one-tenth of the waste, which was often the manorial allotment.[1]

An analysis of the various Acts and awards indicates that, with the exception of the Rowley Regis award, Lord Dudley received considerable areas of land, especially in the manor of Kingswinford. In 1774, out of a total of 7,315 acres in this manor, 3,028 acres were unenclosed waste and commons. Enclosure Bills were successfully introduced by John, Second Viscount Dudley and Ward, in 1776[2] and 1784.[3] It has been suggested that in bad periods, landlords initiated improvements to keep farms tenanted, and, in good ones, they promoted enclosures in order to push up rents. Lord Dudley's main motive in introducing enclosure Bills for Pensnett Chase, Dudley Wood, and Rowley Regis was probably to secure the most favourable conditions for mineral and industrial enterprise. In the case of the Ashwood Hay Enclosure Bill, Lord Dudley's motives were twofold: to exploit the area by agricultural leases; and to prevent the restoration of the status quo on the expiration in 1776 of an agreement made in 1685 whereby the area concerned had been arranged in consolidated holdings:

> Which . . . Agreement . . . about the year one thousand six hundred and eighty-five parcelled out among the Parties interested therein for a term of ninety-one Years . . . will expire on or about the fifth of April, one thousand seven hundred and seventy-six when the same, whether open and intermixed, or enclosed and

held in severalty, are to revert to their former State, and be enjoyed accordingly.[4]

The enclosure of Wombourne and Swindon was also primarily to facilitate agricultural development. For much of the eighteenth century it was more usual to enclose commons and wastes by agreement than by parliamentary Act; this procedure was also more frequent in areas where one or only a few landowners were dominant. The need for haste, in the case of Ashwood Hay, in order to give the force of law to the existing enclosures by agreement due to expire in 1776, and the desire to secure particular rights—especially in the mineral-bearing areas—probably explain why Lord Dudley resorted to enclosure by private Bill.

The rights of the lord of the manor were clearly stated in each case and various allotments were made for loss of such rights. In the case of Ashwood Hay, Lord Dudley was 'entitled to the soil of the said Commons, Waste Lands and Commonable Places, and to the Royalties within the said Manor and Parish [of Kingswinford] ... and ... also Right of Coney or Rabbit Warren ...' The award covered most of Kingswinford manor lying west of the Wolverhampton to Stourbridge turnpike as far as the manor boundaries on the Stour and Smestow streams. For loss or infringement of these rights he was to receive '... one full Sixteenth Part ... (Quantity and Quality considered), of the said Commons ... as ... Compensation for his Right to the Soil ...' Although the preamble to the Act stated that the area to be enclosed contained 1,400 acres, the award involved 1,594 acres. The commissioners made an 'award ... unto ... Lord Dudley ... one full Sixteenth Part ... (Quantity and Quality considered) ... containing 77 Acres 0 Roods and 23 Perches ...' for loss of soil. As this was far less than one sixteenth of the total area it suggests that it was land of a superior 'quality'. For loss of Coney Warren Lord Dudley was to be compensated by '... such Plots (Quantity and Quality and Situation considered) as shall ... amount to the ... yearly Value of one hundred and twenty Pounds'. Valuation was based on the average rent of the previous twenty years. This accounted for the largest of all the allotments made to him and contained '... 245 Acres 1 Rood and 6 Perches ... Quantity, Quality and Situation considered'. The allotment was divided into two large blocks of land. In addition, Lord Dudley was also compensated for loss of common rights as an owner of land in the area to be enclosed:

> ... which said four ... plots ... containing 72 Acres 0 Roods and 16 Perches ... are in full Satisfaction of all Right of Common belonging to ... Lord Dudley ... as Owner of lands ... in ... the said Commons ...

The last allotment for loss of rights, 33 acres 0 roods and 6 perches, was made in connection with an estate leased to John Keelinge at the time of the award.

Apart from land received in compensation for loss of lord's rights and right of common, the Dudley estate also benefited from a provision of the Act which entitled occupants of copyhold or customary lands, who were themselves receiving allotments for loss of common rights, to be enfranchised and become freeholders. This provision was not uncommon in parliamentary Bills of enclosure; Lord Dudley's permission was required and compensation had to be made to him as lord of the manor for loss of rights. Any costs arising out of enfranchisement had to be borne by those seeking the freehold of their allotments:

> ... all or any of the Copyhold or Customary Messuages, Lands, Tenements or Hereditaments ... and all or any of the Allotments of the said Commons ... shall with the Consent and Approbation of the said John, Lord Viscount Dudley and Ward ... be enfranchised and become Freehold; in consideration whereof the ... Commissioners ... shall assign ... unto the said ... Lord Dudley ... such Proportions, Shares or Parts of the said Allotments ... or ... Ancient Freehold or Copyhold ... Lands ... as shall ... be Equivalent ... to the respective Fines or Sums of Money agreed to be paid for such Enfranchisement, and a Compensation to the said ... Lord Dudley ... for all his Rights, Claims, Rents, Fines, Services and Customs ... [and] ... Costs

... attending such Enfranchisement and the making such Allotments to the Lord of the Manor ... shall be paid ... by ... the said Copyholders.[5]

No less than forty-five copyholders availed themselves of this right and each application is listed in a schedule attached to the award. The standard form of agreement reached between Lord Dudley and his copyholders is illustrated by the first item in the schedule:

... which said Copyhold Estate [of Richard Aynsworth] is subject to an Annual Chief Rent of Three Pence [the estate amounted to 3 acres 2 roods and 3 perches] ... is to become Freehold at and for the Fine of £12 13s. 9d. ... 3 Roods and 31 Perches, part of the Allotment ... in the said Commons ... in respect of the said Copyhold Estate is allotted ... to Lord Dudley as a full Equivalent to the said Fine.[6]

Although each copyholder seeking enfranchisement compensated Lord Dudley with a small unit of land, the total effect was the creation of two large composite areas rather than a pattern of small isolated plots. Large contiguous units would obviously have a greater value for the estate.

Copyhold land totalling 1,002 acres 1 rood and 6 perches was enfranchised for a total fine of £3,372 3s 8d; the loss of annual income to Lord Dudley from chief rents was £5 17s 3¼d. In addition he lost a heriot and a sum of £2 5s 0d on sixteen copyhold estates when the occupant held the office of beadle, reeve or forester. Against this loss of revenue must be set the fact that Lord Dudley was awarded 210 acres and 25 perches of land equivalent in value to the total fine of £3,372 3s 8d. The real financial value of copyhold estates was intermittent—when the manor court levied a substantial fine on the admission of the heir—plus the nominal annual chief rent. This income was far outweighed by the advantage to Lord Dudley of adding over 210 acres to his personal estate from which he could derive a regular rental of much greater value. As a result of the Ashwood Hay

Enclosure Award, his estate was increased by a total of 638 acres. The purpose of the Act was clearly stated in the preamble:

> ... the said Commons ... are capable of great Improvements, and the same would if divided and inclosed, so as to be converted into Tillage, be of great Advantage to the several persons interested therein, and of Public Utility.

In order to achieve this end more efficiently, Lord Dudley was entitled to let the land awarded to him on agricultural leases up to a period of twenty-one years. Lessees must develop the property in an efficient manner in order to increase its profitability and enable Lord Dudley to increase rents:

> ... lessees therein [shall] be obliged to spend and consume on the Premises in an Husband-like Manner ... so as the best and most improved yearly Rent ... be ... made payable thereon ...

In spite of this provision agricultural property on the estates was inadequately exploited for much of the period before 1833.[7]

The general structure, content, and features of the Ashwood Hay Enclosure Act and Award are typical of all the local enclosure measures introduced into Parliament by the Lords Dudley in the period 1774-1807. All were stated to have as their purpose the improvement of agriculture. In every case, Lord Dudley, as lord of the manor, received similar allotments for loss of manorial rights and right of common. His right to compensation when copyholders applied for the freehold of their property was granted in the case of the enclosure Acts for Ashwood Hay, Pensnett Chase, and Rowley Regis. With the possible exception of the Rowley Regis Act and award, every measure was particularly favourable to Lord Dudley in terms of the generous size of allotments made to him, their location, compensation by land in lieu of fines in the event of enfranchisement, and rights accorded to him which had a particular significance for mineral and industrial enterprise. Lord Dudley no doubt determined the content of each parliamentary Bill and his interests may have been sympathetically viewed by the commissioners who came from the Midlands area.[8] In every case, the secretary to the commissioners was either Richard Mee or Thomas Brettell of Summerhill in Kingswinford; both were agents of Lord Dudley and stewards of Kingswinford manor.

Allotments to the Dudley Estate in Kingswinford by the Ashwood Hay Enclosure Award, 1777

The Act of 1776 proposed to enclose 1,400 acres
The Award of 1777 included
   a total of ...   .   1,594 acres 0 roods 31 perches
Land allotted to road construction   74 acres 2 roods, 38 perches

Allotments to Lord Dudley	*acres*	*roods*	*perches*
(a) for loss of soil rights			
($\frac{1}{16}$ of total)	77	0	23
(b) for loss of coney warren			
(value £120 pa)	67	1	5
ditto	178	0	1
(c) for loss of common rights	72	0	16
ditto	33	0	6
ditto (Lady Dudley)	0	1	18
(d) for enfranchisement of			
copyhold land	210	0	25
Total allotted to the Dudley estate	638	0	14

Item (d) was in lieu of a total fine
of £3,372 3s 8d paid by copyholders
for enfranchisement.

Total copyhold land			
enfranchised	1,002	1	6
Allotments made in 1777			
included in this total	103	0	27
Total copyhold held of the			
lord of the manor before			
enclosure	899	0	19
Total annual chief rent paid by			
copyholders before enclosure	£5	17s	3¼d

The area covered by this award is west of the coalfield boundary and consisted of agricultural areas. It was bounded roughly by the Wolverhampton to Stourbridge turnpike and the Smestow and Stour streams.

Allotments to Lord Dudley by the Pensnett Chase Enclosure Award, 1786

The Act of 1784 proposed to enclose 1,300 acres

The Award of 1786 included
a total of ... ... 1,433 acres 3 roods 38 perches
of which ... ... 83 acres 0 roods 0 perches
were allotted to road construction.

Allotments to Lord Dudley	acres	roods	perches
(a) for loss of soil rights			
($\frac{1}{16}$ of total)	56	3	34
ditto	55	1	19
(b) for loss of free and coney			
warren	161	1	4
(c) for loss of common rights	174	0	23
(d) for enfranchisement of			
copyhold land	255	2	33
(minus the land restored to			
J. Foster)	23	3	17
Total allotted to the Dudley estate	679	2	16

Item (d) was in lieu of a total fine of £2,479 15s 8d paid by copyholders for enfranchisement.

The total of copyhold land enfranchised	1,205	1	5
Allotments made in 1786 included in this total	31	0	0
Total copyhold held of the lord of the manor before enclosure	1,174	1	5
Total annual chief rent paid by copyholders before enclosure	£5	1s	7d

The area covered by this award was approximately four miles south-west of Dudley and included the rich mineral-bearing land bounded by the Wolverhampton to Stourbridge turnpike, the Kingswinford to Dudley turnpike and the River Stour.

Allotments to Lord Dudley by the Dudley Enclosure Award, 1786

The Act of 1784 proposed to enclose 1,000 acres
The Award of 1786 included about   1,000 acres

Allotments to Lord Dudley	acres	roods	perches
(a) Manorial allotments (7)	52	0	17
(b) For loss of rabbit warren (4)	58	1	34
(c) As improprietor of tithes (4)	218	0	25
(d) As owner of certain 'Burgage Houses, Messuages' etc (8)	85	1	13
(e) To Lord Dudley in fee (2)	10	1	35
	424	2	4

There was no right of enfranchisement to copyholders. The area affected by this award lay approximately two miles south of Dudley between Netherton and Stourbridge where coal, clay, and ironstone measures outcropped or lay at shallow depths.

Allotments to Lord Dudley by the Wombourne and Swindon Enclosure Award, 1807 and the Rowley Regis Enclosure Award, 1807

Wombourne and Swindon
The Act of 1796 proposed to enclose 1,500 acres
The Award was made in 1807

Allotments to Lord Dudley	acres	roods	perches
(a) Manorial allotments (2)	138	1	34
(b) For loss of rabbit warren (2)	172	3	31
(c) As an owner of land	140		
	451	1	25

There was no right of enfranchisement to copyholders. The area covered by this award lay about six miles west of Dudley in the agricultural areas west of the coalfield boundary.

Rowley Regis
The Act of 1799 proposed to enclose 200 acres
The Award was made in 1807

Allotments to Lord Dudley	*acres*	*roods*	*perches*
(a) Manorial allotments for loss of soil (5)	10		
(b) As improprietor of tithes (9)	4		
(c) For cost of ring fencing the above (8)	2		
	16		

The right of enfranchisement was granted to copyholders and Lord Dudley received compensation. A total of twenty copyholders paid a total fine of £800 to Lord Dudley rather than give up land to him, probably because of mineral deposits. Average chief rents lost were about 3d per annum or a total of 5s. The area covered by this award lay about three miles south-east of Dudley and included mineral-bearing land.

It is evident that the local enclosures greatly increased the area of the Dudley estates and provided scope for a variety of economic enterprises. There is, however, little doubt that the awards concerning Pensnett Chase, Dudley, and Rowley Regis were intended to create conditions particularly advantageous to the Dudley estate in the development of mineral and industrial enterprise. It was not uncommon for enclosure Bills to have an industrial motive but those measures with which Lord Dudley was concerned were particularly explicit in detail and valuable to the lord of the manor. An analysis of the Pensnett Chase Act and Award—the most profitable for the estate in the long run—will serve to illustrate this feature.

The stated purpose of the Act was, nevertheless, similar to the other local measures:

> ... the said ... Lands ... afford very little profit or Advantage, but are capable of great Improvements and ... would, if divided and inclosed, so as to be converted into Tillage, be of great

Advantage to the several Persons interested therein, and of Public Utility . . .'[9]

But, the sections of the Act relating to mineral and industrial enterprise, together with the fact that many of the allotments made to Lord Dudley were located along the 'thick-coal' measure and on the line of the Stourbridge and Dudley canals, indicate another purpose. As already indicated, minerals had been exploited in Kingswinford Manor for many years and nothing in the Act was allowed to

> . . . prejudice . . . the Right of the Lord . . . of the Manor . . . or his . . . Lessees, in and to all Mines of Coal, Ironstone, Limestone, Glass House Pot Clay, Fire Brick Clay, and all other Mines whatsoever . . . in or under the said Commons . . . he and they . . . may . . . have, hold, enjoy, raise, get, take, and carry away all such Mines and Minerals . . . as fully . . . as before the passing of this Act . . . to use all Pits already sunk . . . and all Gins, Engines and Buildings thereon erected.

Lord Dudley was also entitled 'to get Clay for making and burning of Bricks, Tiles, Gutters . . . for the Use of any Colliery or Coal Work now open, or . . . to be opened'. Several brickworks and tile manufactories developed on estate property after 1784 and most of Lord Dudley's collieries had brick-kilns at the pit-head. The Act also reflects the spread of mineral smelting into the area as Lord Dudley was entitled to '. . . make, burn, and convert . . . Coal, as . . . the Lord of the said Manor . . . shall think proper, into Cokes, and also to burn and convert all such Limestone into Lime in and upon the said Lands . . .'

In particular, provision was made for more intensive mineral exploitation in the future by Lord Dudley who was given the right to work the minerals under the whole area of commons and waste covered by the award no matter who owned the surface. He could:

> . . . bore, dig and delve for . . . Mines . . . and build Fire Engines . . . for drawing . . . up the Water . . . and any Gins or other

> Engines for drawing or getting ... Minerals ... and to lay such
> Coal, Ironstone and other ... Minerals ... and the Rubbish,
> Earth and Spoil upon the said Lands.

The improvement and extension of transport facilities was also
provided for as Lord Dudley was entitled to:

> ... make and use all convenient Ways, Roads and Railways in,
> upon and over the said Lands ... for the use of any such Col-
> liery or Mines ... together with full and free Liberty, Power,
> and Authority to or for him to do all other reasonable ... Acts
> ... for the discovery, getting, working, converting, fetching,
> carrying away, selling and disposing of the said Mines and
> Minerals ... without Interruption ... and without paying or
> making Satisfaction to any Person ... for the Damage to be
> done ... in the said Lands ... doing as little Damage thereby as
> may be.

This right of access to minerals without the obligation of making
compensation for surface damage was to involve the Dudley
estate in periodic legal actions down to the twentieth century.[10] In
one other respect, the Act was beneficial to Lord Dudley as lord
of the manor. Much of the area was heavily wooded—timber
would be at a premium for fencing off allotments, building construction, mineral railways, and pit supports. Under the terms
of the Act, he was entitled '... within the Space of Twelve
Calendar Months next after ... the said Award, [to] fell and cut
down all Timber Trees or other Trees ... growing ... upon the
said Commons'. Profits from the sale of timber were considerable
after 1784 and Lord Dudley established a timber-yard at Round
Oak on the banks of the Dudley Canal. The New Level Iron
Works and Round Oak Steel Works were later developed on this
site. Lord Dudley took advantage of his right to all timber in
the area of the award as the Parish Survey of 1822 reveals that
all remaining woodland within the manor was on his property.

Of the 679 acres allotted to Lord Dudley in 1786, approximately 452 acres consisted of woodland. The overall pattern of
distribution and the large size of individual allotments resulted

in the allocation of a consolidated block of land to the Dudley estate. In addition to extensive woodlands, this block contained considerable deposits of coal, clay, and ironstone including the seam of thick coal at shallow depths. Moreover, the Dudley and Stourbridge canals passed through the property roughly following the line of the thick coal outcrop. The close correlation between the location of the allotments to Lord Dudley, their mineral wealth, and the existing canal system, suggests that he was well aware of the potential value of this area although in comparison with Ashwood Hay, the land was less valuable at the time of enclosure. By the Pensnett Chase Enclosure Award, 1,205 acres were enfranchised for a fine of £2,479 15s 8d in lieu of which Lord Dudley received land amounting to 255 acres 2 roods and 33 perches. This compares with 1,002 acres of Ashwood Hay enfranchised for a fine of £3,372 in 1777 in lieu of which Lord Dudley received 210 acres. The latter area was agricultural whereas Pensnett Chase was largely scrub-covered and relatively undeveloped as an agricultural area. M. E. Beresford has written that of fifty-three enclosures examined by him, half took more than four years to complete and eight of these took twice as long.[11] The fact that the Ashwood Hay, Pensnett Chase, and Dudley enclosure awards were completed within two years of the respective Acts suggests possible pressure from the second viscount to hasten the process in order that he might exploit the agricultural and mineral potential of the area without delay.

Legal Consequences

The potential value to Lord Dudley of the mineral rights allocated to him under the area enclosed by the Pensnett Chase Award is obvious. Similar rights were awarded by the Dudley Enclosure Award in 1786 and the Rowley Regis Award in 1807 which also contain clauses granting the same comprehensive mineral and industrial rights to Lord Dudley as lord of the manor. These rights were more extensive than those granted to other local lords of the manor in mineral-bearing areas. Professor A. J. Taylor has pointed out the variety of custom with regard to mineral rights in Staffordshire manors.[12] By the seventeenth century, custom had accorded to the copyholder rights which case law was subsequently to confirm for the generality of lease tenants in England—that if the property in coal belonged to the lord, the possession was in the copyholder. In effect, lord and tenant could impose a veto on working the coal beneath copyhold land. Nevertheless, there was no dispute over the lord's right to coal under commons and waste and virtually every eighteenth- or nineteenth-century enclosure merely underlined existing custom. There was, however, variation in provision of compensation for damage caused by mining.

The West Bromwich Enclosure Act of 1801 conceded the lord's right to mine—but not within 40 yards of any dwelling house existing at that time or erected in future on the commons and wastes covered by the Act. The lord was also required to restore land to its condition prior to mining operations. Similar obligations were imposed on the lord by the Cannock Enclosure Award in 1868: land must be restored to agricultural use and, in addition, pits had to be filled in and compensation paid to surface owners at the rate of £2 per acre plus compensation for damage to buildings and crops. Restrictions on the lord's right to minerals in the case of enclosures involving Lord Dudley were small by comparison—he was only required to do 'as little Damage' to land as possible. Where damage resulted to property, compensation was to be paid, not by Lord Dudley, but by a charge on all owners and occupiers of allotments, based upon the annual value of the property:

> ... great Damage may be done to some of the ... Allotments ... by reason of searching for and working the said Mines and Minerals ... by ... Lord Dudley ... the Proprietors of the several other Allotments to be made should ... pay a proportionable Part of such Damage ... when Lord Dudley ... or any other

Person . . . shall suffer any damage . . . to his . . . Allotment . . .
Damage shall be borne and paid by the Owners or Occupiers of
all the Allotments . . . according to the respective Yearly Rents
or Values.[13]

This freed the lord of the manor from paying costly bills and
provided a virtually unworkable arrangement for compensation.

Numerous legal actions resulted, however, down to the twentieth century as tenants of estate property and owners of surface
lands tried to secure adequate compensation from the Dudley
estate for damage caused by mining activities in the area of the
three enclosure awards for Pensnett Chase, Dudley, and Rowley
Regis. In the period 1894-1905, a major dispute occurred in the
Quarry Bank area of Brierley Hill when the Property Owners'
Association was formed by Albert Shaw, a local solicitor, to
secure compensation for damage. The Earl of Dudley's legal
position was clear and, although not liable, he offered to pay a
measure of compensation:

> Lord Dudley is so protected by the Pensnett Chase Enclosure
> Act that so far he has escaped the payment of compensation,
> though in a few cases he has doled out small gifts to the sufferers
> —£5 for example to widow Priest who sustained a loss of £200; a
> gift of £10 to Mr Tristram whose property was damaged to the
> extent of £700 and so on. At Amblecote [Brierley Hill] the
> position is still worse for the cottagers who are what is called
> 'tenants at will', and can be cleared out under an agreement, by
> which they have accepted whatever risks may be involved in the
> working of the mines.[14]

The Property Owners' Association attempted to raise money to
buy the coal beneath their properties and a number of plots and
the underlying minerals were purchased after the dispute had
produced an acrimonious debate in the national press. Such
publicity attracted the attention of the English Land Restoration
League which sent a representative, George Palmer, to Brierley
Hill in September 1897. In public meetings he proclaimed that
the league wanted to restore the land—their rightful inheritance

D

—to the English people. Palmer did not dispute the landowners' legal right to the use of the land but condemned such 'landlordism' as was then being practised by Lord Penrhyn in Wales and by the Earl of Dudley: 'A landlord's Parliament gave the Earl Dudley the powers he was using, and a working-man's Parliament must take them away.'[15]

Legal opinion was still being sought by the Dudley estate in 1915 when a full definition of copyhold and freehold rights was given.[16] In the case of base copyhold, the lord was entitled to two years' rent or the value of the property when it changed hands; on enfranchisement, a sum in excess of two fines was paid to the lord. Under base copyhold, the tenant was unable to work mines —except for his own consumption—without the lord's licence. With regard to free copyhold, the lord's rights were more restricted. He was entitled to a small annual chief rent which was compounded for at about twenty-five years purchase on enfranchisement but had no right to minerals. Counsel advised that the lord had no right to minerals in Kingswinford manor unless the copyhold property had been included in the Pensnett Chase Enclosure Award—in which case, the mineral rights of the Dudleys were clearly established. Minerals could be worked under all copyhold excluded from the award, without licence from the lord. The lack of base copyhold customs in Kingswinford may well explain why Lord Dudley was so keen to secure, by parliamentary legislation, the mineral rights and the right of access under the whole area enclosed by the award. Without this provision, minerals under their property could be worked by all existing free copyholders. In Sedgley and Rowley Regis manors, counsel established that the lord had a one-third interest in base copyholds there.

Apart from disputes over mineral rights, right of access, and compensation, legal proceedings also occurred over interpretation of the word 'minerals' as used in the Pensnett Chase Award. A typical case was in March 1876, when a landowner, Hale, attempted to work the marl under his property, claiming that the previous owner had done so—without payment of royalty to the Dudley estate—as the word 'marl' was not used in the Pensnett Chase Enclosure Act.[17] Local solicitors, consulted by the estate, advised that the bed of marl lying immediately under the surface clay at Commonside (between Dudley and Brierley Hill) belonged to the Earl of Dudley. Marl was defined as 'a superior kind of clay when ground up to Brick Clay'.[18] In the enclosure Act, all mines and minerals had been reserved to the lord except 'common Brick Clay, Common Free Stone and Rubble or Rotch Stone'. These were 'expressly excepted in favour of the Surface Owner. Marl is not mentioned.' Eventually, E. F. Smith decided to accept the advice to 'let the matter remain in its present form' and Hale was allowed to work the marl without payment of royalty.

There is no doubt that, despite intermittent legal disputes, the local enclosure Acts enabled the Dudley estates to derive great profits from mineral and industrial enterprise down to the twentieth century. This situation resulted from the great increase in the area of the estate, the natural mineral wealth of particular areas, and the inclusion in the Acts of conditions favourable to Lord Dudley. Initiated by the second viscount, the enclosure Acts and awards illustrate not only the significance of the enclosure movement for industrialisation during the Industrial Revolution but also the continuing link between land and privilege. For the Dudley Estate in particular, the enclosures constituted the cornerstone of the industrial empire which developed rapidly over the next half century, while the area in general also benefited from the revolution in land ownership.

Notes to Chapter 2 are on pages 246-7

CHAPTER THREE

Transport Developments

The Black Country region had always been relatively isolated by the absence of navigable waterways. This situation was made worse by the bad condition of local roads in the clay areas and the lack of any major road giving access to wider markets. The nearest, Watling Street, skirted the area to the east and north at a distance of about ten to fifteen miles. With the expansion of the local economy, improvements to internal and external communications became imperative and it is significant that the local enclosures did much in this respect also.

Roads

Some improvements had taken place in the half century before enclosure by the turnpiking of several roads linking the main towns and settlements within the area. The first such measure to affect the Black Country was a turnpike Act passed in May 1727 enabling tolls to be charged on the existing roads from Birmingham via West Bromwich to Wednesbury, from Wednesbury to Bilston, and from Wednesbury to Brettell Lane on the outskirts of Stourbridge via Great Bridge (Tipton) and Dudley. It is significant that this system linked the then main coal-producing

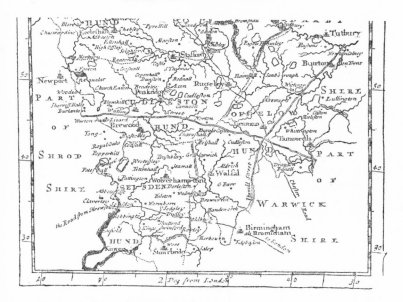

Figure 3 Staffordshire 1701, by R. Morden (in T. Cox, *History of Staffordshire,* published 1730)

areas to the east of the Sedgley-Northfield ridge with Birmingham and crossed the ridge at its lowest point at Dudley. West of the ridge, the turnpike ran across the sparsely populated Pensnett Chase to the glass-producing areas around Stourbridge. From here, a road connected with the river port of Bewdley on the Severn. The road from Dudley to Kingswinford was also included in the Turnpike Act of 1727. Additional roads were turnpiked in 1753 with Stourbridge as their focal point. These linked Stourbridge with Bromsgrove, Kidderminster (on the route to Bewdley) and Wordsley (on the route to Kingswinford and Wolverhampton). More local routes were turnpiked during the 1770s and 1780s and Lord Dudley provided a total of £6,200 at 5 per cent to help finance these improvements. Even after the construction of the local canal network, roads continued to carry a significant proportion of total goods traffic within the area—of which one seventh was conveyed by land (by teams) at a charge averaging 1s 3d per ton per mile in 1845.[1] The estate retained a financial interest in several of these roads which served areas lacking a canal link. Total turnpike securities amounted to £3,700 in 1833 at $4\frac{1}{2}$ per cent and the main roads concerned were:

Dudley and Rowley Regis road	£400
Dudley, Wolverhampton and Birmingham	£500 (5 per cent)
Stourport Bridge	£200 (5 per cent)
Kidderminster District of roads	£400
Dudley and New Inn road	£1,000
Dudley, Wolverhampton and Oldbury road	£500
Dudley, Halesowen and Bromsgrove road	£500
Sedgley and Wombourn road	£200

At the time of rapid expansion in the regional economy after the 1770s, turnpike improvements were supplemented by a series of roads laid down under the terms of the respective enclosure Acts. These provided the essential local network linking specific areas with the turnpikes and canals.

A considerable proportion of land affected by the enclosure awards was set aside for the purpose of providing public roads. In Kingswinford manor alone, 157 acres were excluded from the two enclosure awards for Ashwood Hay and Pensnett Chase and designated for roads of varying importance. Main roads, such as those linking Dudley and Stourbridge or Stourbridge with the Kidderminster and Wolverhampton turnpike at Wall Heath, were to be 60ft wide exclusive of ditches—rather wider than the present road. These main thoroughfares would provide ample space for wheeled vehicles to pass and lessen the likelihood of impassable rutted sections such as occurred on the existing narrow roads and tracks. Referring to the road between Wordsley and Kingswinford in 1781, the Court Leet rolls[2] record that it was wide enough for the passage of one vehicle only. This stretch of road was improved as part of the main road designated from Stourbridge to the Wolverhampton turnpike by the

Pensnett Chase Enclosure Award. A second category of roads
was laid down with a width of 40ft. Provision was also made for
bridle roads 20ft to 30ft wide, and public footpaths and cattle
paths varying in width from 6ft to 20ft. These improvements
may be seen as part of the co-ordinated approach of the second
viscount to facilitating economic development within the area
of his estate.

Canals

Nevertheless, the condition of most eighteenth-century roads
restricted the profitable movement of coal to a distance of
between ten and fifteen miles. It was the transport revolution of
the artificial cut which enabled the Black Country to thrive. It
provided it with lifelines suitable for the cheap transport of heavy
goods and materials within the area, and linked it to existing
river communications and developing markets. The process
began with the construction of the Birmingham Canal to the
Staffordshire & Worcestershire Canal, 1766-72, and ended with
the last major work—the Cannock Extension Canal—in 1863.
By then, the total length of canals constructed in Birmingham
and the Black Country was no less than 160 miles. The Industrial Revolution created no more extensive a canal network anywhere in the country. From their inception Lord Dudley linked
the fortunes of his estate to the canals and the link remained,
despite later developments in rail and road transport, until the
1940s.

At the time of the second viscount's accession in 1774, neither
of the two existing canals directly served estate interests. The
through canal from Stourport on the Severn to Great Haywood
on the Trent & Mersey Canal ran along the western fringe of
the Black Country between six and ten miles from the existing
coal-producing areas. The branch to Birmingham ran through
the mineral districts from Wolverhampton to Birmingham, but
it lay east of the Sedgley to Northfield ridge, whereas the bulk of

Lord Dudley's mineral rights and property lay to the west of the ridge. To remedy this situation, the second viscount introduced a Bill which petitioned Parliament for the right to cut a canal from the Staffordshire & Worcestershire Canal at Stourton (Stewponey) to Stourbridge, with two branches across Pensnett

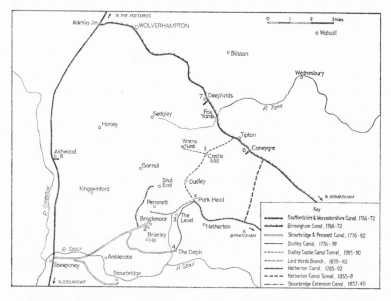

Figure 4 Transport development 1766-1850: canals and the Dudley Estate

1 1775 Castle Mill. Tunnel and private cut from Lord Dudley's limestone quarries to the Birmingham Canal
3 1784 The Level. Lord Dudley's storeyard—later
2 1784 Brockmoor. To serve Brockmoor Colliery Round Oak Ironworks
4 1784 The Delph. To serve the Old Level Ironworks
5 1790 Park Head. Mineral railway from Park Head Colliery to Dudley Canal
6 1797 Coneygre. Mineral railway from Coneygre Colliery to Birmingham Canal
7 1797 Deepfields. Mineral railway from Lord Dudley's limestone quarries at Sedgley to the Birmingham Canal
8 1827 Ashwood. Steam railway from Lord Dudley's collieries at Shut End to the Staffordshire & Worcestershire Canal

Chase. These together formed the Stourbridge Navigation.

Lord Dudley was the main proposer of the Bill and additional support came from glass manufacturers in the Stourbridge area. The potential value of the canal for Lord Dudley's mineral interests—especially the two cuts across Pensnett Chase—is indicated by one of the petitions submitted by coal-masters in opposition to the proposal. These petitioners worked minerals along the line of the Birmingham Canal in Bilston and Wolverhampton:

> ... the principal Coal Masters and Owners of Mines in the neighbourhood of Wolverhampton ... having been induced to pay heavy fines to the late Right Honourable Lord Viscount Dudley and Ward and other Lords of Manors for licence to get coal and other Mines under Copyhold Estates, and ... with large Sums of Money to Erect Fire Engines and Gins and to sink deep Pitts at the expence of Thirty-six thousand Pounds and upwards and have supplied with coal at a very easy and cheap Rate not only parts of ... Staffordshire but also the Counties of Worcester, Gloucester and Warwickshire ... find that ... Lord Dudley and others have presented a Petition ... for leave to bring in a Bill for making a Canal from ... Stourbridge to unite with the ... Staffordshire and Worcestershire Canal Navigation at ... Stourton ... and also two Collateral Cuts to places where Collieries now are or are intended to be Established as by the Execution of such places they will lose all prospect of reaping any fruit of their Labour ... do therefore ... Humbly Intreat this Honourable House ... not [to] suffer the said intended Cut.[3]

It was the development of minerals under Pensnett Chase where collieries 'are intended to be Established' which worried coal-masters along the Birmingham Canal. As coal mined west of Dudley along the Stourbridge Canal would be unable to compete in the Birmingham market, because of extra transport costs, it was the loss of markets in Worcestershire and Gloucestershire along the line of the Severn which the petitioners feared. The Stourbridge Canal joined the Staffordshire & Worcestershire

Canal 13 miles nearer to Stourport than the Birmingham Canal. Despite objections, the Bill was passed by 61 votes to 21 on 4 March 1776.

From the junction of the two canals at Stourton (Stewponey), the Stourbridge Canal was cut through agricultural areas along the banks of the Stour to the centre of Stourbridge. However, the two collateral cuts 'one from a place called the Fens upon Pensnett Chase ... and the other from the Black Delph, upon the said Chase, to join the first collateral cut at the Lays, in the Parish of Kingswinford',[4] were to prove far more profitable in the long run for the area and the Dudley estate than the cut to Stourbridge itself. Because of the topography and scarcity of water, many engineering problems had to be overcome. The cut across Pensnett Chase required twenty locks in $7\frac{1}{2}$ miles to raise it to the level of the Fens which provided a natural water supply, and it terminated at the point where the thick coal outcropped. This outcrop was followed by the second cut around the southern slopes of Brierley Hill to the Delph. Under the Pensnett Chase Enclosure Award, the second viscount was allotted extensive areas of land along the line of the two cuts and his position, in terms of potential mineral development, was further strengthened by the beneficial implications for the Dudley estate of certain clauses within the canal Act. The usual rates to be charged were:

> Sixpence for every Ton of Iron, Ironstone, Coal, Timber, Stone and other Goods ... which shall ... pass through any One or more of the Locks ... on the said Canal.

However, Lord Dudley's main colliery in the area at this time was at the Level—on the line of the proposed Dudley Canal. This canal would run from the Stourbridge Canal at the Delph to Park Head in Dudley. Accordingly, coal mined on the banks of the Dudley Canal was to be transported at reduced rates:

> ... Threepence upon each and every Ton of Coals which shall be ... carried ... upon the said Collateral Cuts, and which shall have passed through any of the locks ... upon the intended Dudley Canal.

Nine locks raised the Stourbridge Canal to the 442ft level of the Dudley Canal at the Delph—without preferential rates, coal transported along the former canal would be at a disadvantage when competing for markets along the Staffordshire & Worcestershire Canal. Lime and limestone were also to be conveyed at reduced rates on the Stourbridge Canal at 'not ... more than One-third Part of the Rates ... mentioned'. Lord Dudley virtually monopolised the supply of lime and limestone in the area from his quarries at Dudley Castle and the Wren's Nest. These were being extended to meet the increasing demand from agriculture and the blast furnaces. A further advantage afforded by the terms of the Act was that:

> Owners ... of Coal-Mines, Ironstone, Limestone, or other Mines, lying within the Distance of One Thousand Yards from the ... Canal ... [may] ... make ... Railways ... or ... Roads to convey ... their ... Minerals to the said Canal ... over the Land ... of other ... Persons.

In the period of rapid expansion between 1774 and 1833, the Dudley estate took full advantage of this provision—together with the clause in the Pensnett Chase Enclosure Act granting the right to construct railways—to establish wharves, cuts, and mineral railways throughout the estate so as to link collieries, timber yards, and ironworks with the main canal. The family connection with the canal was firmly established and the list of proprietors included the second viscount, his half-brother William (future Lord Ward) and the Lady Viscountess Dowager Dudley and Ward.

Concurrent with the Stourbridge Canal Bill was a second proposal, sponsored primarily by Lord Dudley and Thomas Talbot Foley, 'to make a navigable canal ... from the Great and Little Ox Leasow at Netherton in the Parish of Dudley, to the Black Delph'. This was the Dudley Canal Bill to link the end of the Stourbridge Canal at the Delph with mines in the Netherton area of Dudley. Where the Dudley Canal passed through

Kingswinford manor, it lay entirely across Lord Dudley's property, including the Level Colliery. There is little doubt that the line of this canal was determined by the outcrop of thick coal, shown on the plan,[5] and the intentions of Lord Dudley to develop this area of Dudley and Kingswinford manors. By the enclosure awards for Pensnett Chase and Dudley (1786), he was allotted extensive property on both banks of the Dudley Canal, including the line of the thick-coal outcrop, Archill Coppice, and Brierley Hill Coppice. Between the completion of the canal (1778) and 1833, a considerable proportion of the Dudley estate's industrial enterprise developed along the line of this canal.

The last of the local canals with which the second viscount was concerned was the Dudley Castle Canal Tunnel. On the occasion of the safe passage of this Bill through Parliament, the Dudley Canal Company recorded its thanks to Lord Dudley for his 'unremitted Attention to the Interests of this Company and for his very powerful and successful Exertion in Parliament in support of the Extension of this Canal'.[6] Considerable energy and influence must have been exerted to overcome the resistance of the Birmingham Canal Company to any link which would expose its monopoly of the Birmingham market to competition from pits west of the Sedgley-Northfield ridge. The Dudley Castle Canal Tunnel, constructed 1785-92, linked the Dudley Canal at Park Head, and thus the Stourbridge Canal also, with the Birmingham Canal at Tipton Green by a tunnel just over one and a half miles in length which passed through the ridge directly under the town of Dudley. This provided a much shorter connection, between the area west of Dudley and the older industrial Black Country region in Tipton, Bilston, and Wednesbury, than the longer route via the Stourbridge Canal to Stourton and the Staffordshire & Worcestershire Canal to its junction with the Birmingham Canal at Aldersley. It is possible that, in order to prevent such a link, the powerful Birmingham Canal Company had secured a clause in the Stourbridge Canal Act whereby:
... the Company of Proprietors ... or the said John, Lord

Viscount Dudley and Ward . . . are . . . restrained from extending, at any Time, the Canal hereby authorized to be made . . . to any Place . . . within the Distance of One Mile and an Half of the Birmingham Canal Navigation . . .

In the light of this restriction, the subsequent pattern of local canal construction was evidently part of a planned sequence of development, as in the case of the local enclosures, on the part of the second viscount. No such restriction exists in the Dudley Canal Act and the construction of this, together with the Dudley tunnel, in effect established a link between the Stourbridge and Birmingham canals. In fact, the tunnel was driven to Castle Mill to link with a private cut made by Lord Dudley, between 1775 and 1778, from the Birmingham Canal at Tipton Green to his underground limestone quarries on the Tipton side of Dudley Castle hill.[7] This private cut was sold to the Dudley Castle Canal Tunnel Company.

However, the cost of the operation had been underestimated. The original Act passed in 1785 empowered the company to raise £27,000. A further Act in 1790 allowed the company to raise an additional £10,000. Extensive loans were made by the Dudley estate to finance the tunnel and these reflect Lord Dudley's awareness of its potential value to his estate. A total of £4,500 was loaned on which annual interest of £202 10s was still being paid in 1833. The link with the Birmingham Canal not only connected the Black Country on both sides of the Dudley ridge with Birmingham, but also, via the Fazeley and Coventry canals completed in 1790, with the trunk canal routes from the Trent & Mersey Canal to London. Markets along these distant canals were exploited by Lord Dudley's collieries after 1798.

The Dudley estate played a significant part in the pattern of local canal development during the period which saw the emergence of the Black Country, both in terms of the sequence and timing of events and the route taken by many of the canals. Their benefit to the region is undoubted, but they also held a special significance for the Dudley estate in particular. Taken in conjunction, the developments in enclosures, canal construction and the granting of mineral and industrial leases must be seen as part of a coherent plan evolved by the foresight, initiative and capital of the second viscount in order to exploit the opportunities provided by national and regional economic trends.[8]

The commitment of the estate to the local canal network was maintained and extended during the latter part of the phase of rapid regional development, 1760-1860, as many projects were initiated by the trustees in the period 1833-45. This is not surprising considering the connection of the most active trustee, E. J. Littleton, with canals in general and the Staffordshire & Worcestershire Canal, of which he was chairman, in particular. In his first report to the trustees, the auditor, James Loch, offered his advice on the subject of canals in 1834:

> Some of the Canals pay regularly and will continue to do so . . .
> To dispose of any of this property now, would be a sacrifice and would be besides parting with that which gives an Influence on those concerns that are intimately connected with the property of the Mines and the Station of the owner of this Estate.[9]

Consequently, the trustees retained the estate's interests in canals. The total value of canal shares held in 1833 was £19,920 and the annual share income regularly reached £1,100. On its completion in 1835, additional shares were purchased in the Birmingham & Liverpool Grand Junction Canal.

In view of the regular income and influence resulting from the possession of these shares, it seems odd that the trustees should sell most of them in 1839, in spite of the opposition from Loch and the mineral agent, Richard Smith. The explanation is probably connected with the purchase of very extensive estates in that year from Lord Foley, which involved the trustees in considerable capital outlay.[10] As shares held in March 1833 were part of

the late earl's estate, an Act of Parliament was necessary to effect
their sale. The high capital value of some of the shares is indicated by Benbow's accounts recording their sale in the year ending June 1839.

Received of Mr. Downing for 64 shares	in the Dudley Canal	£5,440
	13 shares in the Stourbridge Canal	4,615
Received of Mr. Smith for 6 shares at £650 in the Staffs and Worcs Canal		3,900
Received of Lord Wrottesley by Mr. Downing for 3 of do.		1,950
Received of J. Benbow for 1 share of do.		650
Received of Messrs. Bourne and Co. by Mr. Downing for 15 shares in the Birmingham and Worcs Canal		1,095
Do. for 27 shares		1,971
Do. for 8 shares		584
Received of Messrs. Bourne and Co. by Mr. Downing for 3 shares in the Grand Junction Canal		585
Deduct Commission and Charges on Sale of these and other shares		8
		£20,782[11]

From these figures, it is evident that the most valuable shares
were those held in the Staffordshire & Worcestershire Canal—
£650 each; Stourbridge Canal shares were also valuable, while
Dudley Canal shares had perhaps the least market value because
of the high indebtedness incurred by the company when constructing the Dudley Tunnel.

This disposal of shares did not mark a reversal of the traditional estate policy of sponsoring canals: with Hatherton and
Smith involved in the conduct of affairs, such a change would
have been highly unlikely. In fact, many of the shares were pur-

chased by Smith, Benbow and Downing so that some degree of connection was maintained between the estate and the canals. Significantly, Smith purchased shares in the Staffordshire & Worcestershire while Downing, the least effective of the trustees, unwisely bought shares in the Dudley Canal. Considerable debate had preceded the decision to sell. Hatherton had informed Benbow in January 1839:

> You know my opinion ... that the owner of the Himley Estate ought to be proprietor in all the neighbouring Canals ... and my conviction is that to keep the Shares in your own and Smith's hands would not only be advantageous to yourselves but a prudent thing for the Estate.[12]

It is evident that the estate remained committed to canal transport, and that the sale of shares was occasioned by the need for liquid capital to meet as much of the outlay for the Witley estates as possible; for at the time of the sale of canal shares, Smith and Hatherton were supporting the plans which produced the Severn Navigation Improvements Act of 1842. This improved the river wharves at Stourport and at Diglis near Worcester, which obviously benefited the Staffordshire & Worcestershire Canal and the Black Country in general as movement of goods was facilitated. The estate subscribed £250 to the Severn Navigation Association in 1842, £50 to parliamentary costs incurred in the passage of the Bill, and £100 to the Severn Commission's opposition to the Dean Forest Railway Bill. Although regular dividends were paid on the thirty canal shares held in the Birmingham Canal down to 1845, the estate never again acquired shares to the same extent in local canals as the number held before 1839. However, this was no great misfortune as dividends began to suffer after the railway construction of the 1850s, and the estate was still able to avail itself of all the existing canal facilities. The Birmingham Canal shares were sold for £1,365 in 1848. Meanwhile, the estate continued to support the canals while benefiting materially throughout the trust by leasing more land for the construction of canal wharves in addition to existing estate wharves, and from the sale of mine drainage water to the various canal companies.

One canal, the Pensnett Canal or Lord Ward's Branch, was constructed during this period entirely on estate property, and the total capital cost was met out of estate income. This was cut in 1839-40, from Park Head locks at the western end of the Dudley Tunnel, across Pensnett Chase via Round Oak, to the Wallows area beside the Fens Pools in Brockmoor. About two miles in length, this private canal provided a canal link with the Birmingham Canal system not only for the collieries and iron-works in this area of Pensnett, but was also a more direct link between new developments at Shut End[13] and the Tipton side of the ridge. A significant factor which influenced industrial and transport developments after 1830 was the falling production of thick coal mined east of the Sedgley-Northfield ridge and the growing demand for thick coal mined in the new collieries west of Dudley. It was cut on a level along the whole of its length and there was no loss of time from passing through locks. This latter improvement resulted from an extension of Lord Dudley's Kings-winford Railway,[14] to be known as the Pensnett Railway, from Shut End to sidings at the Wallows where the canal terminated. In its obituary to Richard Smith in 1868, the *Dudley Herald* recorded that the Pensnett Canal had 'been of inestimable benefit to the trade of Brierley Hill and the district west of Dudley'.[15]

Because the canal carried estate and other traffic, profits from freight charges were considerable from the commencement of the undertaking. From 1840 to 1846, the canal made a profit of £4,888 7s. As the economic activity of the area grew, profits increased, reaching a total of £1,042 9s 8d in 1871. The Pens-nett Canal was a valuable addition to the pattern of local com-munications and, taken in conjunction with the Pensnett Rail-way, provided strong competition for the recently completed Stourbridge Extension Canal, as a faster link with Park Head and the older industrial areas where coal was in short supply east of the Dudley Tunnel.

E

Two other canal projects concerned the trustees—both of which had the keen support of Richard Smith—but the trustees were divided over policy in each case. The first was the Birmingham & Stourbridge Junction Canal which was subsequently built, in part, as the Stourbridge Extension Canal in 1837-40. This was first discussed in April 1836 as a proposal to link the Stourbridge Canal at Brockmoor via Corbyn's Hall, Shut End, and a second tunnel under the Sedgley-Northfield ridge at Sedgley to the Birmingham Canal at Tipton Green. A map[16] of the proposed route shows the canal commencing at Wallbrook Iron Works in Coseley, passing under the Sedgley ridge to Cotwallend, and joining the extension branch from the Stourbridge Canal at Oak Farm near Shut End. Although this project fell through, as the new canal began and terminated west of the ridge, hopes of completing the link remained. Hatherton, in his capacity as Chairman of the Staffordshire & Worcestershire Canal, had opposed it fearing that traffic would be lost to this new link between the eastern and western sectors of the Black Country. This was one of a number of occasions when a conflict of interests developed between the trustees and the estate.

Further attempts were made by Smith and Benbow to establish a direct link in 1840—after the Stourbridge Extension Canal was completed. Benbow informed Hatherton of his intention to introduce a Bill into Parliament to link the new canal with Tipton Green on the Birmingham Canal. The proposed route would traverse Lord Ward's property only and was so contrived as to pass numerous estate and leased enterprises. After an interchange of extremely caustic letters, in which Benbow accused Hatherton of encouraging opposition to the proposed link on the grounds that it would favour only Lord Ward, while the Bishop of Exeter asserted that it was Hatherton's duty to support the trust's interests, the proposal was dropped. A letter from William, Lord Ward, on whose behalf the trustees were acting, throws some interesting light on this project and on his own growing strength of character, which his usual pleasure-seeking activities belied.

He observed in a letter to Hatherton:

> I am glad that at last you have given leave to put an end to the unpleasant correspondence between Mr B. and yourself ... he says he cannot see that he has been guilty of any want of Courtesy towards you ... and that he has only spoken plainly to prevent the chance of misconception. Were I in full possession of my property, of course the case would be different, and I should laugh at the opposition of the Staffordshire and Worcestershire Canal Company.[17]

In all probability, Lord Ward suppressed his own good business sense on this matter, in the interests of preserving harmony amongst his trustees. It may be that Smith's subsequent activities in extending the estate railway from Shut End to the Wallows sidings, where it linked with the new Pensnett Canal, and thus the Dudley tunnel, were intended to effect the new link between the eastern and western sections—although in a less direct manner than the abortive canal proposal.

Smith's other scheme in 1839, to construct a canal branch from the Staffordshire & Worcestershire Canal at Hincksford to Pensnett Chase near Gornal, was also dropped. This may have been intended as a possible alternative to the link with Tipton which, as it would serve the Staffordshire & Worcestershire Canal, might be expected to meet with Hatherton's approval. However, it did not meet with Lord Ward's approval as it would pass 'through Himley Wood ... a part of my property that least of all others I should like to see cut up' although he did acknowledge that 'it would have been of great advantage to have had a communication opened between the mines on the Chase and the Staffordshire Canal'.[18] This reflects creditably on Lord Ward's priorities. In the long run, extensions to the Pensnett Railway and the construction of the Pensnett Canal secured the same end in terms of a quicker route to the east.

In general, the additional canals proposed by Smith during the trust period would have benefited not only the estate but also

the Black Country in general—as did the Pensnett Canal.
Although stock in the local canals was sold to raise capital in
1839, the estate remained closely interested in and dependent on
the canal system, and its contribution to the improvements of the
Severn Commissioners underlines the trustees' awareness of this
fact. However, towards the end of the trust, the Black Country
and, inevitably, the Dudley estate, became closely involved in the
expansion of main-line railways into the area. This introduced a
new factor into the question of local communications because, as
Smith asserted in 1845,[19] canals were still the basis of the estate's
communications, as private canals and narrow-gauge mineral railways linked with the main branches. Nevertheless, the need to
supply wider markets forced the trustees to support one of the
rival railway schemes for the area.

During the boom years of the 1850s immediately preceding
the long decline which began in 1860, several new canals were
constructed in the Black Country but these were mainly around
Walsall, to the east of the area. Only one undertaking concerned
the Dudley estate. This was the Netherton Canal Tunnel driven
under the ridge to link the Birmingham Canal on the east with
the Netherton and Dudley canals to the west. When proposals
were first made in the early 1850s, Richard Smith ordered an
independent survey by G. Taylor, one of the surveyors employed
by the estate. He recommended that the strongest possible support should be given to this venture and to the cut intended to
link the western end of the tunnel with the Dudley Canal near
Round Oak, where the main ironworks operated by the estate
was situated. This new link between the two sides of the ridge
was necessary because the Dudley Tunnel was even more congested than in 1844, as revealed at the time in evidence submitted to the inquiry on the proposed Oxford, Worcester &
Wolverhampton Railway. Canal barge traffic was increasing with
the continued expansion of the regional economy, and the exist-

ence of the new main-line railway tunnel did not provide any real attraction for the coal and iron trade between enterprises within the Black Country itself—it was far cheaper and less wasteful to transport materials directly to their destination by barge. The Netherton Canal Tunnel was opened in August 1858 and ran from Tividale (Tipton) to Oakham (Netherton). Its construction illustrates the advances in canal technology when compared with the narrow Dudley Tunnel constructed in the 1790s through which barges were legged. The new tunnel was 3,027yd in length, 17ft wide, had double towpaths and was lit by gas. This enabled an uninterrupted flow of traffic in both directions and provided a quicker route from the main estate mines in the Kingswinford area to Birmingham.

Canals were to remain the basis of internal goods communications within the Black Country long after competition from railways had produced a decline in traffic elsewhere. The probable reason for the continued widespread use of canals was the fact that most of the mines, ironworks, and factories were situated near enough to the canal system to construct their own wharf or cut which facilitated the movement of raw materials and goods. Moreover, there was a considerable interchange of iron between ironworks engaged in various manufacturing and finishing processes, and the main-line railways could not hope to compete effectively with the existing canal system within the area. Nor did any significant change occur when most of the local canals were taken over by the London & Birmingham Railway Company in 1846. Indeed, the company encouraged the continuation of existing arrangements within the area and was mainly concerned with capturing the long-distance canal trade. Cheap road transport in the twentieth century ousted the canals from their dominant position. Although the estate continued to use canals for the movement of local goods until 1947, the development of the estate's own railway system was increasingly used to the west of the ridge after the 1840s, while national and international markets for coal and iron goods were reached by the through rail links.

Railways

Under the impetus given by the respective canal and enclosure Acts, an extensive network of narrow-gauge horse-worked mineral railways had evolved throughout the area by the early 1790s, connecting individual collieries and ironworks to numerous distribution wharves on the canals. Several were on the Dudley estate and one line, constructed in 1797-8, probably introduced the iron edge-rail into the area. In spite of their tendency to fracture, the existing plate-railways provided a more convenient and economic means of transporting heavy goods and materials than extensions to the road system, which was also susceptible to adverse weather conditions.

Despite the increase in estate income as a result of the rapid expansion of the regional economy after 1766, the Dudley estate suffered from conservative managerial attitudes and inefficient administration of its mineral affairs after the death of the second viscount in 1788.[20] Charles Beaumont, a Newcastle mining engineer, was engaged by Lord Dudley in 1797 to overhaul his mineral enterprises and he it was who constructed the first edge-railway in the area. This connected the New Brockmoor Colliery, developed on the western slope of Brierley Hill after the Pensnett Chase Enclosure Act, with Lord Dudley's wharf at Brockmoor on the Stourbridge Canal. Writing to Thomas Jeans, Lord Dudley's London agent, Beaumont condemned the existing facilities:

> I shall . . . give you a just idea of the State of his Lordship's Coal Concerns at present—leading 1½ ton on a Coal Waggon with five horses downhill, no office at a Wharf for nine different Mines [at Brockmoor] and leting the Coals go from the Brockmoor Wharf without weighing or gauging.[21]

He had already directed Aston, an agent of Lord Dudley, 'to discover where cast metal railings [are] to be bought best and cheapest', in order to construct a 'waggon way' there as soon as plans 'which I have wrote for' arrived from Newcastle. Edge-rails were first introduced into the Tyne coalfield in the 1790s. A letter written in September 1797 throws some light on the capital costs of the proposed railway and the conservative attitude to change adopted by many of Lord Dudley's agents:

> I am told his Lordship is advised that the Waggon Way laying at Brockmoor is an act of Insanity and only throwing away £1,000. Mr. Honeybourne [an estate official] says if it had been done at the commencement of the Work (c.1785) it would have saved £20,000 by this Time . . . The way at Brockmoor [c.300yd] will not exceed £500 and will reduce the leading 4d. per Ton—breceage of Coals £3 at least weekly—keeping roads—leaving Engine Slack—with the great advantage in permiting a much greater quantity being led and Vended.

The railway was completed together with another of similar length at Coneygre in Tipton which linked Lord Dudley's collieries with his wharf on the Birmingham Canal. Two other railways were laid down shortly after 1798. One, at Park Head in Dudley, linked a complex of estate mines to the Dudley Canal near its junction with the Dudley Castle Canal tunnel. The other linked Lord Dudley's limestone quarries at Sedgley with the Birmingham Canal at Deepfields—a distance of nearly one mile. All of these railways ran downhill from the slopes of the Dudley ridge to the new canals. By 1833, numerous other railways were added as the scale of estate enterprise increased—most of them terminated at Lord Dudley's canal wharves at Brockmoor, the Level, the Delph, Park Head, Coneygre, Castle Mill or Deepfields.

The next significant improvement in the local transport system was the construction of main-line steam railways. These arrived relatively late in the Black Country and were laid down towards the end of the period of rapid expansion from 1766 to 1860. There were two lines by the 1850s, the Grand Junction Railway (1837) and the Oxford, Worcester & Wolverhampton Railway (1845-54). However, the first line was of only marginal value to the Black Country in general as it passed from Birmingham via Bescot to Stafford, and was too far to the north-east and by-passed

TRANSPORT DEVELOPMENTS

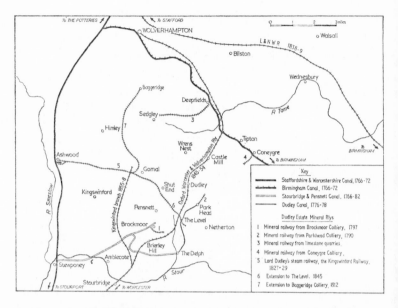

Figure 5   Transport development 1766-1850: railways and the
Dudley Estate

the main centres of iron and mineral production in Tipton,
Dudley and Wolverhampton. The second line[22] did pass through
the heart of the Black Country but terminated at Wolverhampton.
In contrast to the comparatively late penetration of the area by
the main-line railways, a steam railway had been operating on
the Dudley estate since 1829 as a link between the expanding
mineral district of Shut End, on Pensnett Chase to the west of
Dudley, and the Staffordshire & Worcestershire Canal at
Ashwood.

No canal existed at this time in the area—the nearest being
the Stourbridge Canal at Brockmoor. It is significant that a steam
railway was constructed rather than a canal extension—either to
Ashwood or Brockmoor. This not only speeded up the movement
of traffic to the Staffordshire & Worcestershire Canal but made

Lord Dudley independent of the slow and relatively expensive Stourbridge Canal. The potential value of this link and the Shut End area in general is indicated by the fact that the Staffordshire & Worcestershire Canal Company offered to build the link either as a canal or a railway. Lord Dudley declined this offer and also retarded the attempt by the Stourbridge Canal Company to cut an extension to Shut End until 1840.

However, the idea to construct a steam railway link was conceived as early as 1825, not by Lord Dudley or his agents, but by James Foster, the Stourbridge ironmaster, who was constructing blast furnaces and forges at Shut End to exploit leases of minerals which he had secured. As the line of the railway would cross considerable areas of Lord Dudley's land, Foster was in no position to contest Lord Dudley's decision to construct the line himself. In Foster's original proposal, he offered to

> make the Rail Road and maintain it in Repair at his own expence ... and allow his Lordship ... the free use and enjoyment of the same for the conveyance of any Mines and Minerals that may be raised at his Lordship's Collieries free of any charge.[23]

On the other hand, 'if Lord Dudley prefers making a Rail Road at his own expence', James Foster would pay him $1\frac{1}{2}$d per ton per mile. Foster estimated that the construction costs, excluding the value of land, would be £2,000 per mile taking account of 'Iron Rails, Stocks and Chains and Earthworks'. In addition to mines leased by Foster from Foley, extensive colliery operations were being undertaken by Mr Gibbons near Oak Farm and Shut End House. These, together with minerals carried from Lord Dudley's pits, would ensure a regular income for the rail road at $1\frac{1}{2}$d per ton per mile. Significantly he also raised the possibility of extending the rail road

> to Park Head [so that] the Mines of that extensive district would come down to the Stafford and Worcester Canal on cheaper and better terms for delivery at Stourport, than their present route of the Dudley and Stourbridge Canals.

Such an extension was to be made to the original line, but not until much later in the nineteenth century.

It was almost two years later that Foster and Lord Dudley concluded an agreement[24] to construct the rail road. Lord Dudley drove a hard bargain: not only did he construct the line from the canal to land at Shut End adjoining lands belonging to John Hodgetts Foley and leased to James Foster for the conveyance of coal, limestone, ironstone and other materials; but also, the rates charged were 3d per ton per mile for those commodities transported to and used on Foster's lease. For all materials conveyed and not used in Foster's works, the rate was 7d per ton. The final commitment was for Foster to make and maintain at his own expense a

> proper and commodious Canal or Basin in Flotheridge Meadow to communicate with the Staffordshire and Worcestershire Canal and Lord Dudley and his Lessees to pay ¾d. per ton on goods navigating the basin.

It was not until the 1880s that the whole line of the railway came under the sole ownership of Lord Dudley on the termination of Foster's leases.

The canal basin was 750 yards long

> parallel to which the railroad is continued on both sides, affording the means of loading 60 boats at the same time.[25]

The size of the wharf reflects the anticipated volume of traffic. Trucks were hauled up a gradient from canal level by a stationary winding-engine and a second stationary engine was required to haul the trucks up the slopes of Pensnett Chase to Shut End. On the level stretch in between, a steam locomotive, the *Agenoria*[26] (goddess of courage and industry), linked the two inclines. This was constructed by Foster's foundry in Stourbridge, Foster Rastrick and Co, and the line-engineer was John Rastrick. The contemporary description of the opening of the railway illustrates the wide public interest shown:

> This undertaking, the work of the Earl of Dudley and James

Foster, Esq. of Stourbridge, is . . . 3⅛ miles [long]. Commencing at the above-named coalfield, Shutt-end, with an inclined plane 1000 yards in length . . . a lofty embankment is carried—parallel to the village of Kingswinford, crossing the turnpike road from Stourbridge to Wolverhampton by a bridge . . . over the high road from Summer Hill to Swindon by another similar bridge . . . it arrives at the head of a second inclined plane. Passing this . . . a basin occurs . . . formed so as to meet the descended carriages . . . On 3rd June, 1829, this new and interesting branch of road was opened.[27]

The eventual capital cost was greater than the £2,000 per mile suggested by Foster in his original proposal. In 1833, a capital sum of £12,037 8s 9d remained to be met before the undertaking would show a clear profit over capital outlay. Following the example of the Tyne coalfield steam locomotives, a broader gauge, 4ft 8½in, was used than for the earlier mineral railways; this later became the standard gauge for steam locomotives. Each coal waggon carried between three and four tons and up to eight waggons were hauled at a time.

During the period of the Dudley trust, 1833-45, the estate extended the line from Shut End to the New Level furnaces at Round Oak in Brierley Hill. When completed in 1845, the total length of track from Ashwood was ten miles. As in the case of the original section from Ashwood to Shut End, numerous engineering and constructional problems had to be overcome. There is a considerable descent from the summit of Brierley Hill to Shut End. This was negotiated, in the early years, by means of a stationary winding engine at the top of the Barrow Hill incline —a 1 in 24 gradient—and an engine at the head of the Wallows Incline—a 1 in 48 gradient. In spite of its relatively short length —about 6¼ miles of track including sidings—capital costs were high and were assessed at £10,336 10s 3d in 1847.[28] Nevertheless, this scheme proved to be of immense value to the estate in the long run—especially after the construction of a main-line railway of the same gauge, 1845-54, which crossed the line of the Pensnett Railway at Round Oak. On Loch's advice, transport facilities were made available to iron and coalmasters in general and 11d per ton was charged for coal in 1839.

Over the next thirty years, the Kingswinford and Pensnett railways were extended in many directions until about eighty miles of track had been constructed. The network was so extensive and complete, that the Dudley estate and its lessees had a virtually independent transport system on the western side of Dudley. It connected with ironworks, 'landsale' wharves, and canal wharves throughout the area which gave access to wider markets. After the opening of the Oxford, Worcester & Wolverhampton Railway in 1854, the estate railway system connected with the through line at Round Oak and gained access to distant markets as well as to the eastern side of Dudley by rail. This predominant position resembled that established by Lord Durham when, in 1829, he broke from the 'Grand Alliance' of the Tyne and Wear coal-owners and exploited the Lambton estate of 17,000 acres by constructing a private railway network with its terminus in Sunderland. Because of the nature of the local and main canal system, one distribution point, such as the Lambton estate possessed, would have been uneconomic and totally inadequate. The estate railway alone had thirteen 'landsale' wharves by 1920 on both sides of the ridge. This expansion of the estate railway was all the more remarkable because of the general collapse of the traditional regional economy in the years 1860 to 1885.

The main additions carried the original Pensnett branch from its junction with the Oxford, Worcester & Wolverhampton line at Round Oak, via the tunnel under Dudley, to Lord Dudley's engineering workshops at Castle Mill and Coneygre Iron Works east of the ridge by 1856. A second major addition linked Shut End with new collieries being developed at Himley in the vicinity of Himley Hall itself in the 1850s. This was later extended to

Baggeridge Colliery in 1907-12. The last major addition carried the railway down the southern slopes of Brierley Hill into the Stour valley at Cradley Heath in the early 1890s. Including sidings, just over 100 miles of track existed by 1912 and the system linked with public railways at Round Oak, Castle Mill, Cradley Heath and Himley. The system contracted with the reduction in the level of mineral and industrial activity on the estate after 1918, but the last major section to close, as recently as March 1968, was the Baggeridge branch when the National Coal Board ceased operations at the colliery. The only section of track still in operation is that providing the internal transport system of Round Oak Steel Works and its link with the adjoining main-line system, first established in 1845-54.

By the mid-1840s, it was imperative that the Black Country should no longer be denied the benefits of a main railway link, though neither of the existing lines were satisfactory. The Grand Junction Railway by-passed the area to the east while the London & Birmingham Railway terminated at Birmingham. Even at this stage of development, some raw materials, especially limestone, were being imported into the Black Country and the existing canal links were proving costly in time, particularly in the case of the movement of finished iron goods from the area to the ports. Two rival schemes were projected in 1844. One, sponsored by the London & Birmingham Railway, proposed a link running north to south across the Black Country between Birmingham and Wolverhampton, with a branch to Dudley and Sedgley via a tunnel under the ridge at Dudley. This would be known as the London, Worcester & South Staffordshire Railway and would be built by Robert Stephenson. The alternative was a broad-gauge proposal sponsored by the Great Western Railway. Brunel was the engineer and the intended route would cross the area from Stourbridge in the south-west to Wolverhampton in the north-east, where it would terminate, passing under the ridge at Dudley. This was the Oxford, Worcester & Wolverhampton Railway. Both the proposed routes would speed up the movement of goods and materials to London—the latter to the South West also. The former route would also provide a link to the north from Birmingham via the Grand Junction Railway. At the ensuing commission of inquiry set up to examine the rival proposals in 1844-5, the clash between canal and railway interests and the battle of the gauges were central to the issue.

Generally, landowners did not invest in main-line railways but did support secondary lines where these were connected with mineral interests. In the case of the Dudley estate, Richard Smith, Lord Dudley's mineral agent, urged the trustees to offer strong support to the London, Worcester & South Staffordshire line, with which he was personally connected. For his part, Lord Hatherton also favoured the narrow-gauge line because it would serve areas to the north and south-east which would not present a serious threat to existing canal and river transport systems which he, as a Severn Commissioner and Chairman of the Staffordshire & Worcestershire Canal, represented. Hatherton wrote that

> my own individual Objection to any Railway linking together the towns in South Staffordshire, by expansion Works, Embankments and Cuttings throughout the Mining District remain unchanged. I conceive the mischief to the Mining Interests of the District would be very great, without any corresponding advantage.

While it remains true that a line would bring competing minerals into the area, the Dudley estate would be able to supply coal and, after 1839 when the estate began production on its own account, pig iron to a wider market. It may be that the extension of the Pensnett Railway to Round Oak, Smith's reconstruction of the New Level Furnaces[29] and his support for a main-line railway were all part of a long-term plan for the Dudley estate to market its own coal, pig iron and wrought iron on an unprecedented scale.

During the course of his long examination by the parliamentary commission of inquiry, Smith presented statistics[30] to show the movement of goods and materials in the region of the proposed narrow-gauge line. He calculated the total quantity per annum at 5,062,000 tons which, when broken down, indicated a daily figure of 16,224 tons or 1,333 tons in transit per hour. He was attempting to establish the point that such a volume of goods 'would be too great to be accommodated by any through [railway] line', and that the existing canal and private railway systems provided a more convenient service than a main-line railway. What he advocated was a branch line from the London, Worcester & South Staffordshire Railway—which would establish a major railway link between Birmingham and Wolverhampton, while the branch line would pass from the main line in Tipton, to Dudley, Brierley Hill (via a tunnel) and Sedgley. This would open up the Black Country by providing a link with a through line and also remedy the one serious defect in the internal system of local transport—the inadequacy of the Dudley Castle Canal Tunnel as an east-west link. When the second viscount had sponsored the Dudley Castle Canal Tunnel in the 1780s, it had been constructed without a towpath and was only wide enough to permit the passage of boats in one direction at a time. The practice had developed whereby boats passed through in one direction during the morning and in the opposite direction during the afternoon. Smith was not alone in wishing to effect a better communication between the two sides of the hill to meet the increased trade. An ironmaster, Mr B. Best, had earlier argued along the same lines:

Q. 6 ... are the canals adequate ... for the present wants of this
district?
They are not ... There is a scarcity of water ... and the inconvenience of passing the Dudley Tunnel ... causes a great delay in the transit of minerals, and ... a great many works and pits would be opened if there was a better communication ... there is abundance of ironstone on the eastern side, and a scarcity on the western while there is an abundance of coal on the western and a scarcity on the

> eastern . . . several furnaces are out of blast in consequence
> of the scarcity of minerals on the western side.

There was plenty of ironstone on the western side of the ridge
but it was not yet being worked in general. This was because it
lay beneath the main coal seams and was not worked until the
latter were exhausted; if the ironstone was worked first, subsidence would fracture the coal seams above and create dangers
and difficulties with consequent loss of production in working
the coal. East of the ridge, ironstone was being worked as the
upper and thick-coal seams had been exhausted.

Apart from asserting the greater convenience which a local
railway branch and through line would offer, Smith also argued
on the basis of transport costs and counter-attacked when representatives of the canals tried to establish points in their favour:

> Q. 470 . . . have you been connected with canals when they have
> been in competition?
>
> Yes.
>
> Q. 471 Has the general result been that the public have profited
> by that?
>
> I think, very little indeed; they commonly have come to
> an understanding . . . about terms.
>
> Q. 477 Do you extend that observation to canals and railways?
>
> I think it is very likely.
>
> Q. 478 Then you think it would be a better thing for the public
> either to have a canal or a railway?
>
> . . . considering the terms the railway propose to charge
> . . . it would be better to have a railway.

Another tack tried by the canal representatives was to assert that
the connection urged by Smith would supply 'the domestic district' where 'there is a great consumption of coal' and that this
export of coal would be to the detriment of the Black Country.
Smith disputed this as the Dudley estate had abundant supplies

of coal to the west of Dudley. What mattered to Smith was that
the Black Country iron trade in general should enjoy the best
possible marketing conditions because the vast majority of
estate profits came from the supply of raw materials to the local
iron trade. Not all of the 5,062,000 tons of goods and materials
in transit annually would use the proposed line and branch.
Smith estimated that 467,261 tons would be transported on the
through line—to the east of the ridge, and 235,063 tons on the
branch line from Sedgley, Brierley Hill and Dudley, producing
an income of £60,083 7s 9d and £16,098 2s 6d respectively.[31]
The remaining traffic, over four million tons within the area,
would continue to use existing transport systems—mainly the
canals.

Apart from the route of the proposed London, Worcester &
South Staffordshire Railway, Smith also favoured its gauge—
the narrow (standard) gauge of 4ft 8½in. Lord Ward's Kingswinford and Pensnett Railway had the same gauge and it was hoped
to connect it to the branch line so that wagons loaded at estate
collieries and ironworks could run on the metals of the branch
and main lines. The estate had recently purchased from the London & Birmingham Railway Company 'something like 300 carriage wheels and axles' in anticipation of the new facilities. For
this reason, Smith argued that if the rival Oxford, Worcester &
Wolverhampton line was built, the narrow gauge should be
extended outwards along the whole of its length as far as Bristol,
rather than introduce the broad gauge into the area. Smith fur-
their claimed that three or four tons was the maximum weight of
coal desirable in a railway wagon, 'that was the weight ... considered when Lord Ward's road was built'. The nature of Black
Country coal, especially thick coal, was

> very friable ... and the value of it depends entirely upon the
> size of the article we send to market ... The narrow gauge has a
> smaller carriage and ... there is less likely to be so much breakage
> by the weight.

The London, Worcester & South Staffordshire Railway was pre-

F

pared not only to allow Lord Ward's wagons to use their lines but also to construct 'two side lines ... for the special accommodation of the mines ... and ironworks'. At the time of the inquiry, the broad-gauge line of the Oxford, Worcester & Wolverhampton Railway had no such intention of establishing a double set of rails to accommodate local mineral railways. The canal companies tried to denigrate both the railway projects on the grounds of safety because of mining subsidence.

Q. 727 How many miles of railway ... have you? [the estate].

... about 10 miles.

Q. 729 ... is it ever in fact made?

Yes.

Q. 730 But do you not lose it in the morning sometimes?

No.

Besides the opposition of the local canals, especially the Stourbridge Canal, to any railway scheme, there was also opposition to the narrow-gauge line from other interested parties who supported the broad-gauge Oxford, Worcester & Wolverhampton line. At a public meeting held in Dudley on 13 September 1844, before the commission sat, the proposals of the Oxford, Worcester & Wolverhampton Railway were accepted by the majority, including Thorneycroft, Matthews and Gibbons, all of whom were leading iron and coalmasters in Wolverhampton, Brierley Hill and Kingswinford. Isaac Badger, a Dudley industrialist,

proposed that the Town should give its ... support to the Railroad in question notwithstanding what I said upon Lord Ward's determination to oppose it [and] ... that the Resolution ... be transmitted to Mr. Benbow, and that he be requested to give the Measure his best support in Parliament ...[32]

This was an embarrassing situation because Benbow, one of the Dudley trustees, had recently been returned to Parliament as the member for Dudley. Whatever course of action he determined

upon—and his support for a railway connection in the late
1830s was well known—he would antagonise either his fellow
trustees or powerful interests in Dudley. Apart from the personal
interests of Smith and Hatherton, it is not clear why the Dudley
estate and leading ironmasters in the district should be on oppos-
ing sides in this matter. However, their interests were really
bound together by the fact that the estate sold most of its
minerals to the local iron trade. The only real advantage of the
narrow-gauge line to the estate would be its ability to send
mineral wagons over a wide area, by the main line, without having to re-load them as happened at present where the estate
railways joined the canals. Re-loading would also be necessary if
the broad-gauge line was built without parallel narrow-gauge
lines over any real distance.

During the course of the inquiry, Mr Cockburn, representing
the Oxford, Worcester & Wolverhampton line, went to great
lengths to prove that Smith and the Dudley trustees had
attempted to use their influence against the wishes of majority
opinion in Dudley. Robert Stephenson was questioned in his
capacity as engineer to the rival narrow-gauge line:

Q. 6035 You say you have consulted the parties interested: who
do you consult?

Principally Mr. Smith.

Q. 6041 Has that line . . . been laid out with a view to Lord
Ward's interest?

It has not.

Q. 6044 Have you consulted the parties interested with the
exception of Lord Ward's agent?

I do not know that I have had much communication
with any.

This line of questioning was persisted with until a counter-attack
was mounted by Mr Serjeant Wrangham for the London, Worcester & South Staffordshire Railway:

Q. 6349 Are you in a situation to speak of the proportion of local
support which our plan receives from the ironmasters?
... the one in favour of the narrow is most numerously
signed.

Wrangham asserted that the Board of Trade report listed the
representatives of 46 ironworks, 57 furnaces and 98 collieries,
including the Dudley estate, as being in favour of the narrow-
gauge route.

However, the Kingswinford ironmaster, William Matthews,
stated that all the meetings of ironmasters held in Wolverhampton, Dudley and Stourbridge supported the broad-gauge line.[33]
He also ventured to disagree with Smith on his statement that
broad-gauge wagons would tend to break up the coal and claimed
that a comparison of the two memorials submitted to the Board
of Trade in support of the rival projects showed that the balance
of opinion was in favour of the Oxford, Worcester & Wolverhampton line. Moreover, he implied that the trustees had
brought pressure to bear on 'Mr Bramer' (Bramah) to change his
name from this list to the South Staffordshire line. Another
Kingswinford coalmaster, G. Bond, noted that the general opinion
amongst 'independent' coalmasters was in favour of the broad
gauge 'until recently, because the Board of Trade, I believe gave
their preference to the ... [other] line'.

Q. 8885 Do you know of any reason why that change of feeling
should have taken place?

There is a great deal of interest connected with Lord
Ward in our district.

There seems little doubt that the trustees and Smith would exert
considerable pressure at Westminster and on tenants such as
Bramah. In the final outcome, however, the decision of the commission of inquiry went in favour of the broad-gauge route. When
the decision was announced on 4 June 1845, neither the name of
Lord Ward nor his trustees appeared in the list of shareholders
while the railway company found that permission to go ahead

would cost them dearly as their proposed route lay, of necessity, through the extensive property of the Dudley estate especially west of the ridge.

Several clauses in the subsequent Act of Parliament did, however, take account of the claims made by the supporters of the rival line—especially the Dudley estate. Although the Oxford, Worcester & Wolverhampton Railway was to be a broad-gauge line, the company had to lay down additional rails (narrow gauge) between Abbotswood (near Worcester) and Wolverhampton 'for allowing the free and uninterrupted passage ... of carriages, waggons and trucks' and, between Wolverhampton and Stour-bridge, 'such side lines as may be necessary or convenient for the accommodation of the traffic in minerals ... and ... all owners ... or occupiers of mines ... [may] make branches therefrom'.[34] It was shortly after this, in 1846, that a royal commission advised that all future lines should be narrow gauge. Strict provisions were included concerning the exact line and level of the railway —presumably at the insistence of the trustees. Where the line curved from Stourbridge through Brierley Hill and climbed up towards the tunnel at Dudley, it passed through Round Oak beside the New Level Furnaces. The Pensnett Railway, still under construction, lay directly across the route. Smith refused to alter his levels by an inch and the Act stipulated that the main line must cross the level of Lord Ward's railway at right angles. Penalty clauses too were included:

> if the ... Pensnett Canal, or the towing path ... be obstructed ... or in case the space of any bridge be less in width or height than is ... prescribed ... the Company shall pay to ... Baron Ward ... the sum of five pounds for every half-hour during which the rail obstruction or construction shall continue ... and the further sum of ten pounds for every half-hour [above 72 consecutive hours].

Similar provisions operated where the line crossed Castle Mill wharf and the eastern entrance to the Dudley tunnel by a high viaduct. Even the freight charges appear to show extreme con-

sideration for the interests of the Dudley estate. Tolls levied for
every wagon not belonging to the company were not to exceed
5d per mile: Lord Ward's wagons would be the highest number
of private wagons on the line, as a junction was made with the
Pensnett Railway at Round Oak. Coal, ironstone and other articles
carried in private wagons could not be charged at more than
three farthings per ton per mile where the distance travelled was
more than 50 miles and not more than 1d per ton per mile for
less than that distance. Normal rates of charge for such materials
carried in company wagons was 1½d per ton per mile.

The company did not complete the link to Wolverhampton
until 1854. When the line reached Round Oak, an agreement was
made between Smith and the company's engineer, Vardon, that
the main line should 'alter its gradient so as to cross Lord Ward's
railway at a level'. It became tradition that main-line trains were
halted while engines on Lord Dudley's Pensnett Railway had the
right of way over the crossing! The estate sold a considerable
amount of land in Brierley Hill, Dudley and Tipton to enable
the line to be built. Under an agreement made in 1846, the estate
sold 23 acres of land in Dudley for £15,250, reserving all the
minerals. A further 16 acres were sold in Kingswinford and
Tipton in 1848 for £11,307 while compensation totalling
£7,803 15s was claimed by the estate in March 1848 for the
destruction of two lime kilns at the mouth of the Dudley Canal
tunnel. These figures are high and there seems little doubt that
the estate extracted every ounce of advantage from its position as
the dominant land and mineral owner in the district.

Even though the rival line, which had been supported by
Smith and the estate, had been rejected, the final outcome was
not very different. Estate wagons could run as far as Worcester
—and beyond after 1854 when the narrow (standard) gauge was
extended to Bristol. Its market in the 'domestic districts' of
Oxfordshire and London could be reached by this railway and

the bottleneck of the Dudley Canal tunnel could be by-passed by estate wagons using the narrow-gauge side lines from the junction with the Pensnett Railway at Round Oak, through the railway tunnel under Dudley to the Tipton side. It was from the opening of this link that the Castle Mill Engineering Works of Lord Ward became the main supply and maintenance centre for the Dudley estate when a branch was laid down from the main line into the works. Moreover, the narrow gauge connected at Wolverhampton with the routes to the north on the London & North Western Railway, which came into existence with the amalgamation of the London & Birmingham, Grand Junction and Manchester & Birmingham railways in 1846. A line was also built from the old Grand Junction into the centre of Wolverhampton. Not to be outdone by the commission of inquiry's decision to construct the rival line, Smith and his fellow-directors in the South Staffordshire Railway Company had in fact constructed a line as far as Dudley, from the eastern side, by May 1850. This did not pass under the ridge but ran eastwards through Wednesbury, Walsall and Alrewas where it joined the Midland Railway.

Two subsequent branches were built from the Oxford, Worcester & Wolverhampton line and, in each case, the interests of the estate were well-served. From Brettell Lane at the southwestern end of Brierley Hill, the Kingswinford branch was built across Pensnett Chase to Gornal and Himley in 1855-9. This served the latest mineral area, developed (during the 1850s) west of the ridge at Himley, and a junction was also made there with the estate railway. It was no mere coincidence that the last new addition to the local railway system linked the end of the Kingswinford branch at Himley with the main-line railway at Oxley, north of Wolverhampton. Commenced in 1913 and open for traffic by 1925, this line did not pass through mineral or industrial areas but served as a by-pass to the congested Black Country lines for traffic passing from the south-west to the north. Discussions on the proposed route commenced at the time when the sinking of the last new colliery to work the Black Country's thick-coal seam was nearing completion. This was the Earl of Dudley's Baggeridge Colliery[35] which went into production in 1912. The earl was a director of the GWR. It was connected to the Kingswinford branch by an extension of the estate railway from its junction with the main line to the colliery. This mineral line remained in operation until 2 March 1968 when the National Coal Board wrote 'finis' to the long history of coal-mining in the Black Country when Baggeridge Colliery ceased production.

Notes to Chapter 3 are on pages 247-9

CHAPTER FOUR

The Landed Estates

Agriculture

In keeping with general developments after 1774, the second
viscount pursued an enlightened and progressive policy with
regard to the exploitation of agricultural land. This outlook was
not maintained, and as the first phase of estate development drew
to a close in 1833 there was a deterioration in the condition of
farming property and in rent returns.

Unlike the majority of farm leases in England, which do not
appear to have contained improvement clauses at this time,[1] some
attempt was made to maintain and improve the quality of land
and property on the Dudley estate in the 1780s. Most leases were
granted for a period of twenty-one years with covenants for the
tenant to repair buildings, use manure, cover the land at regular
intervals, and not to sow flax, hemp, wood, potatoes or any other
seeds, crops or plants not producing manure.[2] The tenant also
had to clover down all lands sown with 'lent grain' in the last year
of the term—the lessor paying for seeds and sowing. In the case
of newly-enclosed land, a different set of conditions was established. Leases were 'for the term of one whole year and so on
from year to year as long as both parties shall please'[3] and were
terminable by six months' notice on either side. At their own

expense, lessees had to

> stock, make up hedges and fill in pits now on the land, level and convert and make the said Lands ploughable and as capable of bearing herbage and tillage as may be from the present impoverished state of the land.

Moreover, lessees were obliged to

> cultivate and employ the said lands in a regular course of husbandry [and] consume as much Hay, Straw, Fodder, dung, muck, manure soil and compost that shall arise or be made thereupon.

After three successive crops the lessee had to

> clover down the same with clover and grass seeds not less than ten Pounds of cover seeds to an acre and not plough or break up the same during the two next succeeding years.

Finally, he had to plant hedges and maintain ditches. Between 1789 and 1804, about forty-two such leases of newly-enclosed land were granted—in some cases two successive crops was the limit. This was a sound lease from the landowner's point of view; perhaps the only weakness was the absence of any reference to the maintenance of buildings on these new properties. Lack of this provision may explain the dilapidated condition of farm buildings by 1833. In respect of the annual lease—for recently enclosed land—the Dudley estate reflected new trends when short leases and even annual leases[4] were granted at the end of the eighteenth century to take advantage of increasing food prices. Corn mills were also leased with improving clauses. One such example concerned a water corn mill in Belbroughton leased in 1802 for a term of twenty-five years at £50 per annum for four years and £54 10s for the remainder. At least £300 had to be spent on rebuilding the mill within three years, £150 of which was to be allowed by Lord Dudley.[5] The tenant had to grind corn for the neighbourhood at 2d a bushel 'or such other fair and reasonable market price as shall be . . . paid in the Neighbourhood'.

In one final respect the Dudley estate pursued policies of a progressive nature similar to other landed estates of the period. An Act of Parliament in 1798 entitled landowners to purchase redemption of land tax and approximately one-third of all land was subsequently redeemed. The third viscount decided to 'exonerate' his property from land tax and, under a contract dated 30 April 1799,[6] purchased the land tax for most, but not all, of his properties in Kingswinford, Rowley Regis, Sedgley, and Tipton. The fact that such expense was incurred at this time, together with considerable capital expenditure on mineral enterprise between 1799 and 1802,[7] suggests that the Dudley estate was in a very liquid state at the turn of the century.

These enlightened policies were not maintained. A report[8] on the state of such properties in 1824 reveals a policy of neglect and inefficient management. Roberts, the land agent, observed that

> no consistent and convenient disposal of the Farms has ever been made, and that proper and judicious continuity of lands which is so necessary to enable a tenant to cultivate them efficiently, appears, except in a few cases, never to have been thought of.

He advised that every opportunity should be taken on the death or change of tenants to consolidate and re-distribute property. Inferior, unproductive land should be planted with trees. The arrangement of farm houses and buildings was generally inconvenient and most were in a dilapidated state:

> ... indeed the want of repair and improvement is so great that before anything be undertaken ... some persons should go over the whole and make a specification and estimate of what is necessary to be done ... that the expenditure for such purposes may be nearly ascertained. Plans of the Estate and a general Map thereof would be most convenient.

His final comment was to suggest a revaluation of rents so as to give to the landlord his full share of the produce of the soil, and to the tenant that remuneration which his labour, risk and capital employed, entitle him to.

This valuation relates only to agricultural property on the Dudley estate and excludes all cottage, mineral and industrial property. The overall decrease of approximately 3.3 per cent was marginal and it seems doubtful that the tenantry would adopt a more vigorous approach on the strength of this alone. Systematic planning and improvement could only be achieved by an enlightened policy pursued over a period of time by the chief land agent. This was not forthcoming and similar criticisms were to be levelled at the condition of agriculture on the estate by James Loch after the commencement of the trust in 1833.

The movement of agricultural rents throughout the period 1774-1833 does not closely correspond to the national pattern. The earliest available evidence of total rents is for the six months ending at Michaelmas 1797 when a sum of £3,082 11s 4d was received. Assuming that all available land was let by then and the number of properties remained constant, rents had gone up by just over half by Lady Day 1811 when receipts totalled £4,739 1s 1½d for the half-year. A considerable increase, probably from land enclosed in the 1770s and 1780s, occurred at this time as £8,045 16s 7½d was received for the half-year ending at Michaelmas 1811. This total gradually increased to £8,726 5s 7d for the half-year ending at Lady Day 1814, when the trend was reversed—receipts by Michaelmas 1814 were £8,408 19s 6d and £6,325 13s 4d at Lady Day 1816.[10] Roberts' survey indicates a slight recovery by 1824 when receipts for the whole year were £14,798 5s 9d. The last available rental for the period ending in 1833 shows the trend maintained as great rents for that year were £17,896 15s 11d.[11]

There is no evidence to suggest that the dramatic increase in total rents for 1811 resulted from an extension of estate property. It may be that marginal land was brought into use because of wartime conditions, as the increased rent coincides with a sharp

Survey of Lord Dudley's Agricultural Estates, 1824[9]

Parishes	Quantity			Present Annual Rent			Proposed Rent			Increase			Decrease		
	Acres	Rds	Perches	£	s	d	£	s	d	£	s	d	£	s	d
Himley	589	1	33	1,193	18	3	1,167	10	6	26	15	6	53	3	3
Wombourn	619	3	25	642	9	0	612	9	0		—		30	0	0
Kingswinford	1,373	3	34	3,242	18	6	3,136	0	2	43	0	0	149	18	4
Sedgley	2,233	2	14	4,402	14	10	4,201	2	6	13	0	0	214	12	4
Wolverhampton and Penn	140	0	7	193	1	10	186	13	0		—		6	8	10
Rowley	585	3	26	1,066	6	5	1,015	15	0	1	7	6	51	18	11
Tipton	182	0	27	362	7	11	363	0	0	7	0	0	6	7	11
Dudley	921	1	19	3,592	14	0	3,542	11	0	5	0	0	55	3	0
Belbroughton				101	15	0	101	15	0		—			—	
Total	6,646	1	25	14,798	5	9	14,326	16	2	96	3	0	567	12	7

Total Decrease £471 9s 7d

increase in expenditure on farm stock and grain by John Bradley
—land agent to Lord Dudley. There is also evidence of the
fattening of livestock at Himley Park and the purchase of meat
'for the poor'. Bradley's accounts suggest a more vigorous agricultural policy in the last years of the war accompanied by a
sharp increase in total rents for 1811—in that year his own
annual salary was raised from £250 to £315!

Roberts' survey demonstrates that this policy of improvement
had lapsed by 1824 and, according to trends in Bradley's
accounts, perhaps as early as 1814. The 1824 report also indicated the need to remove the inequality in rents and this makes
it difficult to calculate average rents per acre. The discrepancy
between rents for newly-enclosed land and established properties
is a further complication. In 1783, the average rent for established properties was between 22s and 27s per acre, and for
newly-enclosed land, approximately 12s to 16s. A valuation[12] of
certain farms in the latter category indicates an increase from
18s to 22s per acre in 1800—not a large increase in view of wartime conditions.

By 1824, the average rent was 41s per acre for all types of
property; this was too high and Roberts' survey considered a
revaluation. On the basis of these figures, Lord Dudley's estate
does not reflect typical movements of agricultural rents in this
period. Average rents[13] increased by approximately 100 per cent
between 1790 and 1816 while rents on newly enclosed[14] land
were increased, in extreme cases, by as much as 300-400 per
cent! The increase depended on the extent to which farming
efficiency was improved.

In the period immediately following the enclosure awards for
Ashwood Hay and Pensnett Chase, the second viscount made
extensive use of rights granted to him to remove all timber from
areas covered by the awards. A chancery case in 1788[15] indicates
that the second viscount had even sanctioned the removal of timber from the parkland surrounding Himley Hall and a restrain-
ing injunction was sought by his half-brother. Giving evidence,

Joseph Nicklin, employed on the estate at the time of the first viscount's death, stated that

> in 1774, there were great quantities of very fine and valuable Oak Timber growing in . . . the Estates and . . . since then Timber had been felled to the amount of Twelve Thousand Pounds and upwards . . . for Pale Timber . . . and working the Mines.

In April 1788, further quantities of timber were marked and valued for sale:

> Lord Dudley has lately marked trees in vistas, walks and rides at
> Himley Park—240 oaks at £1050 and upwards
> Baggarage Wood [Sedgley]—oaks and ash at £1350
> High Arcole Wood [Brierley Hill]—oaks and ash at £390
> Others—oaks and ash at £160.

William Ward was successful and an injunction was granted forbidding Lord Dudley to fell any timber in Himley Park necessary for its protection, or of ornamental value, on pain of a £10,000 fine. He was also restrained from felling immature trees anywhere on the estate. When he succeeded to the title and estate, William Ward was far less solicitous in preserving and protecting the interests of the estate.

Kingswinford was the most heavily wooded area of the Dudley estate at the time of the enclosures. Of the 679 acres allotted to Lord Dudley in 1786, no less than 452 acres consisted of mature woodland. The line of the Dudley Canal passed through these wooded allotments and Lord Dudley's timber-yard[16] established at Archall Coppice sold timber worth £12,000 between 1774 and 1788. Finished timber was sold for fencing at the rate of $3\frac{1}{2}$d per 'rail'—this price gives some indication of the vast quantity of timber which must have been sold by the second viscount. Bark was also sold at £5 per ton. Timber was purchased by pits owned and worked by the Dudley estate; the mineral agent, Edward Cockshutt, purchased timber worth £622 7s $1\frac{3}{4}$d between October 1788 and January 1790. The iron and timber-yard at Round Oak continued to flourish and became the most efficient of all estate enterprises by 1833.[17] This was the exception to the general state of affairs in the management of agricultural properties.

By the commencement of the trust period in 1833, agricultural rents had been supplanted as the main source of estate income by revenue from mineral and industrial enterprise. Nevertheless, agricultural properties remained extensive and continued to supply a considerable income. At the outset, the trustees were quick to appreciate that the emphasis on change, which was producing more efficient land use elsewhere, was not evident on the Dudley estate. Downing, as land and mineral agent, was the one trustee who was loath to accept this fact, as the deficiencies were the result of bad management rather than any shortage of landlord's capital.

Staffordshire did not escape the post-war trends in agriculture after 1815. High rents, resulting from the inflated prices of the war period, could no longer be paid and many 'liberal landowners'[18] reduced rents by 30 per cent, ignoring the discount system which enabled the official rent to remain high. The alternative was to convert the property to a tenancy-at-will.[19] In such conditions, the problems facing land agents on Lord Dudley's estate were intensified by the inefficient management revealed in Roberts' report of 1824. Loch repeatedly seized the opportunity to underline existing weaknesses and to urge remedies on the trustees:

although the farmers of this Estate cannot have been exempted from the operation of the same causes that have affected their brethren elsewhere, they ought, near the large Towns to have operated less severely where there are so many ways of turning their land to profit.[20]

The late earl's will had empowered the trustees to grant leases up to twenty-one years at rack rent, with obligations to 'keep and leave the buildings in repair'. Such powers to grant leases up to this term were usual on great settled estates, although not widely used. On the Sutherland estates, Loch had personally favoured long leases on the grounds that this produced efficiency in the interests of tenant and lessor.[21] He observed that the high expenditure on repairs to agricultural properties administered by the trust was not excessive in view of

the extreme state of dilapidation in which the buildings on these Estates were and the inefficient nature of those repairs which were done in the late Lord Dudley's time [though at great expense].[22]

In his first report he had stated that the dilapidated condition of farm properties on the Dudley estate 'generally exceed what in my experience in any other part of the country I ever met with'—a considerable indictment in view of his wide experience. Even so, with typical attention to detail, he criticised the fact that although the repairs to several buildings visited by him in 1835 were 'judiciously conceived and not too large', in some instances he was

less satisfied with the Character of the Brick Work which appeared to be not sufficiently Bonded . . . but Mr. Bateman was unluckily obliged to go from home the day after I got to Dudley, so I could not state my opinion to him.

Shortly after the commencement of the trust in 1833, Downing, who had held the positions of mineral and land agent since 1826, gave up the land agency and Bateman replaced him. Where farm buildings necessary for the occupation of the land were in a very poor condition, he urged the trustees to consider the desirability of letting the 'attached land for accommodation land'. This latter policy was not implemented although Bateman did engage an architect to survey and estimate the cost of repairs to farm properties. These continued at a high level, increasing from £1,420 0s 7d in 1836 to £2,958 19s 1d in 1837. Such an outlay was normal in times of distress so that tenants' capital would be released for farming operations and increased

G

output. This resulted in a theoretically clear distinction between landlord's and tenant's capital.[23]

The Dudley trustees intended to reduce expenditure on farm repairs as soon as all necessary work was done and to transfer the burden of maintenance to the tenants. This created friction which retarded the introduction of a new form of lease after 1838. Hatherton wrote to Lord Ward (William), that tenants would resist any attempt to bind them to maintain buildings in good repair 'never having been bound by strict agreements' and that

> the easy habits of the late Viscount having permitted it the Tenants have practically established a habit of procuring all repairs to be done by the Estate. An end must be put to this system.[24]

Lord Ward himself insisted that leases should be more clearly worded so as to obligate the tenant not only to keep but to leave the property in good and substantial repair. Ultimately, the farm tenants did accept the new form of lease which not only ran for a term of years—as envisaged by the late earl's will—but also contained clauses designed to procure efficient farming practices and administrative efficiency together with a clear statement of the tenant's and lessor's obligations. Typical of the new lease was one granted in 1854 to William Perry for a farm and premises at Sedgley.[25] The lease ran for nineteen years and covered an area of 58 acres at an annual rent of £86 16s 0d. The main conditions were:

1 Rent must be paid within thirty days when due.
2 Tenants must not 'suffer any spoil, destruction, decay or waste' but remedy it within one month's notice.
3 Growing crops must not be sold 'not being clover, vetches, potatoes or other green crops'.
4 A limit of two successive crops of grain or white straw corn.
5 Land not to be mowed more than once a year except for clover or lucerne.
6 After two successive mowings of grass land, no further mow-

ing allowed without first spreading '12 tons of good rotten dung, night soil or compost at least on each acre'.

7 Sheep must be fed with turnips on such ground.

8 Land must be cultivated in a good husbandlike manner 'according to the custom of the country thereabouts'.

9 Hedges must be neatly trimmed.

10 Trees could not be lopped without permission.

11 All game including hares and pheasants must be preserved for hunting by Lord Dudley.

12 Sub-letting was forbidden.

13 Within the last year of the lease, a new tenant could enter, plough and sow best grain.

14 Every year all hay, straw, fodder and clover produced must be used on the premises.

15 Tenant to pay all repairs to existing buildings or any erected —being allowed 'timber in the rough, bricks and tiles' by the landlord: the tenant also had to paint the outside and interior once in seven years 'in good and proper oil colours'.

16 Chimney pieces, grates and other features bought by the tenant could be removed by him at the end of the lease.

17 Mines and access were reserved to Lord Dudley.

18 Extra rents of £10 per acre were liable for every acre not farmed in a husbandlike way and £20 per acre for misuse of meadow and pasture.

This was a comprehensive lease which conformed to the standard form evolved by Loch and Hatherton after 1838. As a result, the condition and efficiency of agricultural estates administered by the trustees improved considerably, compared with that observed by Loch in 1833, along with the fortunes of Staffordshire farming in general. A contemporary writer observed that, in 1851,

the Rateable Annual Value of real property in the county is now £1,953,384 though in 1815 it was assessed to the property tax at only £1,150,285, and the rent of the land was much higher at that period than now.[26]

Soon after the commencement of the trust, Loch drew attention to the fact that

the Estates at one time were very unequally let and it was intended to have gone over the Estates for the purpose of equalising
the rents. If this has not been done it is, I am sure, essential that
it should be so.[27]

This policy was pursued, but with difficulty, after 1838. High
arrears of £6,297 7s 9d accumulated by 1833. Although these
were reduced to £3,831 1s 2d by 1835, the arrears accumulated
by the trustees after 1833 had reached £7,886 1s 10d by then.
Loch advised that Bateman should carefully examine both sets
of arrears and

> such as are hopeless should then be done away with as a person
> who once gets into arrear rarely ever pays in future with any
> regularity and may put off paying anything in the expectation of
> paying all and get quite reckless.

Furthermore, he proposed that the introduction of 'a small
allowance out of their arrear might induce such Tenants to make
an exertion to pay up the remainder'. Such a policy together with
the strict enforcement of 'payment from those who are able to
do so' would secure a 'considerable diminution in the amount
of arrears'. Arrears had been accumulated mainly by

> the Great Farm Tenants and by the Gentlemen Tenants . . . the
> farmers no doubt are affected by the price of Agricultural produce
> —the second class are not good payers.

On the Ellesmere estate of Lord Francis Egerton,[28] Loch
recommended the introduction of corn rents, but on the Dudley
estate he advised a firm line on arrears once the current debt had
either been settled or written off. His advice and concern went
unheeded so that by the end of the fourth year of the trust, in
December 1836, arrears were

> larger by a great deal than on any Estate with which I am
> acquainted—Exceeding one fourth of the Total Rental of the
> Estate.

By then, farm arrears amounted to £19,616 9s 6d and cottage
rents (which had been separated from the land agents' accounts

in 1836) totalled £5,252 15s 10d. During this period, it was principally the farms on clay which were severely affected by low prices and rent arrears; this was not the reason on the Dudley estate as the farms were on sandy soils. Such a situation could only be remedied, according to Loch, by strict adherence to the rule 'never to keep a tenant who gets into arrear for a second half years Rent'. The trustees were reluctant to enforce fully Loch's advice and operated it only on a modified scale.

It was only after the introduction of the new form of lease in 1838 that farming properties on the Dudley estate were more efficiently administered and the problems of high arrears, high cost of repairs and inefficient husbandry were gradually eradicated.

Most of Loch's recommendations were gradually put into effect after 1838. With very few exceptions, allowances of 10 per cent had been introduced for all farm rents on estates in the vicinity of Dudley by 1850. This allowance may have begun in 1844 as surviving accounts show that it was introduced for the first time on the Kidderminster and Witley[29] estates in that year and this would coincide with the general agricultural depression of the period.

In the light of the policy of improvement, particularly in terms of repairs to farm houses and buildings, it is not surprising that the Bishop of Exeter expressed the opinion in 1846 that: 'The receipts from the Landed Estates seem to be ... on the average about £14,000 per annum ... somewhat less than half the rental.' However, average figures for agricultural rents in Staffordshire were between £1 10s and £2 per acre in 1834. These had fallen to between £1 6s and £1 8s in 1851. Comparable figures for the Dudley estate show a fall from £2 1s per acre in 1824 to £1 19s in 1850. The proximity of large markets in the Black Country industrial area probably explains the higher rents enjoyed by the estate. Had all of Loch's recommendations been adopted sooner and consistently enforced by the trustees—including the bishop—the estates would probably have emerged

in a stronger position than was in fact the case. In spite of his
criticism, the point remains that, because of the work of the trust
period, the agricultural estates might expect increasing profits as
a result of capital outlay and administrative improvements. Great
landed estates were rarely farmed by the owner but were divided
up into tenanted holdings. The Dudley estate continued to conform to this pattern during the trust with the exception of direct
exploitation of timber and the sale of venison. 'Venison and
Tack' sold by the Witley estates was as high as £395 15s 6d in
1840.

Considerable timber reserves remained on the estates in the
vicinity of Dudley, and further plantations were included in the
Witley and Kidderminster estates purchased from Lord Foley.
As the timber was extensively exploited after 1833, a plantation
policy was also enforced to maintain this asset. On his early
tours of inspection, Loch examined the condition of local timber
around Dudley and, in 1835, reported that

> the extensive working of the Mines ... have ... affected the Oak
> Timber—nothing can save a considerable proportion of it. The
> moment that a Tree becomes stag headed (and many of them are
> so) it should be cut down.[30]

The effect of the smoke was to render the timber more brittle,
thus reducing its value, and 'by preventing the Bark from running the profit from that source (for tanning) is also lost'. In
the vicinity of Himley Hall where it was desirable to preserve
the wooded aspect, he recommended the planting of beeches
which were

> not affected by the Smoke nearly to the same extent—the smooth-
> ness of the Bark and Leaves prevents the soot resting upon them
> to any great extent and the first rain washes it off.

He observed that the new plantations 'near Wombourne ... are
remarkably well-executed'. By 1850, the estates around Himley
contained 1,147 acres of woodland of which approximately 220
acres had been planted after 1833. These woods supplied timber

for estate repairs amounting to £329 17s 11d in 1834 and £769 8s 9d in 1835.[31] An active policy of exploiting the timber was also pursued on the new estates at Witley and Kidderminster, and a timber yard was established at Clansmoor near Witley. Receipts for timber sales increased in the short term:

	Kidderminster			Witley		
1838	£48	10	9	—		
1839	356	18	9	—		
1840	241	15	0	£426	12	8
1841	126	13	6	693	19	8
1842	134	13	2	582	3	10
1845	6	0	0	260	9	0

This pattern reflects the rate of expenditure on general repairs and improvements and it may be that timber was largely consumed on the trust estates at Kidderminster and Witley. Timber was also supplied to the paper mill at Hurcott owned by the Kidderminster estate.

The Dudley estate had long held property in Jamaica and this remained under the direct management and control of the trustees and was not leased to tenants during the period of the trust. These substantial estates were as large as any in Jamaica and, in 1811, contained '640 Slaves and 572 Stock'[32] in the parish of Clarendon. Lord Ward received £13,186 12s 4d as compensation for loss of slaves after the Act of Emancipation in 1833. In that year, the profit from the Jamaica estate was £4,415 7s. During the trust period, the arrangements for the marketing of sugar and rum created a rift between the various trustees. This followed a proposal by Thomas Phillpotts, brother to the Bishop of Exeter, that the task of transporting and selling the sugar and rum should be removed from G. S. W. Hibbert & Co of London and granted to a company in Gloucester, with which he himself was connected, on the grounds that it would reduce costs and increase receipts by £500 per annum. This proposition was attacked by Messrs Hibbert & Co.

Gloucester wants that great Concentration of supply and demand

... for the general sale of sugar ... [and] is removed from direct intercourse with the Continent.[33]

Experimental consignments of colonial produce had recently been shipped to minor ports such as Newcastle, Newhaven, Leith, Plymouth and Limerick by Sir Simon H. Clarke, but these were now discontinued. If the trustees should decide to consign a proportion of Jamaica produce to another port, Hibbert & Co recommended Liverpool or Dublin as preferable to Gloucester.

The Bishop of Exeter was moved to write to Lord Hatherton enclosing 'a letter from my Brother on the subject of our West India concern' and stated that 'I have no personal wish on the subject'. This letter made out a strong case for consigning the produce of the Jamaica estates to Gloucester on the grounds that

the consumption of unrefined sugar in Gloucestershire, Worcestershire, part of Herefordshire and Warwickshire is about 4,000 Hogsheads annually ... The present importation to the Port is about 1,000 Hogsheads.

Phillpotts claimed that the large grocers 'who are now our customers' would rather purchase in Gloucester because of 'the injury which Sugar sustains by Water Carriage from a distant Port' and that sugar was 'worth 1/- to 2/- per cwt. more to them buying in Gloucester than it would be in Bristol, Liverpool or London'. In spite of this tempting offer, subsequent accounts refer only to Hibbert & Co. Profits remained fairly constant until the last years of the trust, reaching £4,376 19s 6d in 1836 and £3,518 15s in 1840, but thereafter yielding 'nothing for several years before the last audit [27 July 1849]'.

In general, the agricultural estate benefited from the administration of the trustees. In spite of the inherent conservatism of Downing and Benbow, a new form of lease was introduced, capital expenditure on improvements was increased, and the rationalisation of rents and farm units was also begun.

The income from agricultural leases after 1845 is not consistently shown by the surviving records. Between 1853 and 1878, the national trend was for agricultural rents to increase, but decline thereafter by as much as 50 per cent by 1898. In the case of the traditional Dudley estates in and around the southern and western fringes of the Black Country, total rents due amounted to £18,487 12s 4d in 1850 and £20,660 13s 6d in 1924. No records are available for the intervening period but these figures relate to estates which remained unchanged in area and were the last of the major agricultural properties to be sold by the family in 1947. By 1935, receipts had increased to £26,992 7s 11d and it may be that their increased value, as well as their proximity to the West Midlands conurbation, persuaded the family to retain these properties for so long. The total income from these estates in the 1930s consisted of:

	1930			1932			1935		
	£	s	d	£	s	d	£	s	d
Great Rents	25,795	10	1	25,540	18	0	26,877	9	11
Cottage Rents	1,992	2	3	1,807	16	3	1,075	10	1
Mines Office Sundries	1,141	19	5	1,221	10	4	1,190	13	2
Rents for Damaged Land	1,050	7	8	1,014	6	6	908	5	3
Sporting	525	0	0	500	0	0	500	0	0
Sundry	33	17	11	21	3	4	35	11	5
	30,538	17	4	30,105	14	5	30,587	9	10[34]

The decrease in cottage rents is explained by the continued sale of cottage properties which had been initiated by Lord Ward's Estate Act of 1847.[35] Rents for damaged land were received from mine tenants mainly in Himley, Kingswinford and Sedgley, where surface land was required for mining operations. Sporting rents were derived from the Blackhills Estate, developed for this purpose near Wombourn after 1918. Total income from the local landed estates had fallen to £27,820 7s 11d by 1942. Timber sales continued to provide a regular income after 1845 but ceased in 1935: receipts for 1930 were £2,971 16s 5d and £2,116 18s 2d in 1932. There are no records available for the other estates in Worcestershire, Scotland or Wales which show the rents received during the period 1852-1924 (when the last of these properties was sold). However, the national trend of a recovery and increase in total rents by 1853 is reflected in the Witley rents for 1838—£21,680—and 1852—£30,906 8s 4d. Net income from landed property, difficult to calculate because of the scarcity of records, amounted to £18,720 15s 3d in 1930 for the local estates. In the same year net income from mineral enterprise—based entirely on royalties since 1924—was £20,861; not since extensive exploitation of minerals on the Black Country estates was begun by the second viscount in the 1780s had the net income from these two sources been approximately equal.

There was no substantial reduction in the area of the local estates which consisted of 11,216 acres in 1883[36] and 10,623 acres in 1924. The decrease in area is accounted for by sales of small cottage plots and scattered mineral properties. Redmayne's[37] survey of 1924 described the Himley estate as:

> a large agricultural and mineral estate . . . including Himley Park.
> A considerable portion . . . has a value much beyond agricultural value and it is expected by judicious sales to considerably increase the revenue.

The various items in the rental consisted of:

		£	s	d
36 farms on yearly tenancies	5,101 acres	7,910	10	4
47 smallholdings under 50 acres on yearly tenancies	842 „	2,021	14	6
Accommodation land	1,608 „	4,008	7	1
18 houses on yearly tenancies		1,723	10	0
21 houses and warehouses on yearly tenancies		1,171	12	0
210 small houses and warehouses on half-yearly tenancies		1,727	13	0
36 houses on weekly tenancies		299	11	0
3 public houses on yearly tenancies		180	10	0

Wayleaves, window lights etc			115	0 0
Sporting tenancies (3)			650	0 0
Cottage rents: 1,358 cottages: tenancy at will or 6 months notice	465	„	2,339	6 6
Woodlands (gross rateable value)	961	„	335	8 0
Home Farm, Himley Hall and Park, Keepers' Houses (gross rateable value)	686	„	1,033	4 0
	9,663		23,516	6 7

Average repairs on all property over the last seven years was estimated at £3,164. After taking this figure into account, together with the expenses of management and income tax, the net rental was given as £15,000.

In spite of the near exhaustion of minerals under their property, the earls of Dudley retained possession of these traditional estates until 1947—probably because of their increased value as demand for building land in the area grew. Post-war developments in the area and changes in the position of the landowning aristocracy in general led to the disposal of the bulk of the local estates in 1947, although small plots were retained until recent years. By 1967, the Ward family ceased to own any land in the area from which the bulk of their fortune had been drawn.

Cottage Properties

The estate derived a regular income from cottage rents until the 1940s, but there was no consistent organised attempt to exploit the demand for accommodation created by migration into the Black Country as a result of the Industrial Revolution. Nevertheless, estate rentals reflect the expansion of the local economy, especially in the period 1774-1836, when total income from cottage rents increased by more than threefold. In 1768,[38] before the commencement of enclosure and intensive mineral exploitation, the total cottage rental was £240 14s 1d. Most of these properties, about 500 in all, were concentrated in the manors of

Dudley, Kingswinford and Sedgley. Average annual ground rent was 9s 10d but individual rents ranged from 1s 6d to £1 1s 8d. This low figure was supplemented by a large fine when the properties—all copyhold—changed hands.

The activities of the second viscount, and the subsequent influx of population during the 1780s and 1790s are reflected in numerous entries in the cottage rentals designated 'Cottage and New Enclosure'. Most were located on former commons and waste which were being enclosed after 1774. Because of the availability of land, average rents remained fairly static, rising to 11s 9d by 1817 although total income from this source had more than doubled to £572 18s 11d. A further and far greater influx of population took place during the 1820s but the Dudley cottage rental swelled only to £797 9s 3d by 1836. Most of the new plots were concentrated in the vicinity of estate mines and wharves at Wordsley, Brockmoor, the Level, Pensnett, Gornal and Deepfields.

The haphazard manner in which the estate had allowed cottage construction to flourish after 1774 had provided cheap accommodation for miners and iron workers, but produced a situation whereby a large potential source of revenue was lost to the estate while bad housing conditions and exploitation bred unrest. This was one of the problems which Loch, as auditor to the trust, brought to the early attention of the trustees after 1833:

> there are many Houses held by Cottage Tenure for the payment of a Nominal rent by Middlemen who live at a distance from the estate and who receive large rents from the actual Occupiers.

He advised that the occupants should immediately be made direct tenants of the estate and that the present economic rent paid to the middlemen should be reduced, 'to reconcile them to the change'. The latter paid only a nominal 'cottage rent' to the estate but enjoyed a much higher weekly rent from sub-tenants of cottages erected on the property.

The issue was again raised in 1841 when, having regard to his earlier advice, Loch proposed a change of policy which earned him the opposition of Hatherton and Lord Ward. He proposed that the estate should sell the land on which the cottages stood, giving the first option to the occupants. Lord Ward, always conscious of his responsibilities to his tenants and workpeople, objected that this would give the appearance 'of casting from under his care and protection a vast population which has been established on his property by the permission of his Ancestors'.[39] His reservations were overcome after Loch again drew attention to the exploitation of the cottage tenants by middlemen and the fact that the tenants did not enjoy his direct protection. The alternative, of Lord Ward asserting his control of the land and making cottage occupants his direct tenants, was now dismissed by Loch:

> no fortune, not even Lord Ward's, could afford to put them and keep them in repair—if they become the property of various landlords, this might and would be done.[40]

The only note of caution sounded by Loch was that his plan should not be put into effect 'when trade is at a low ebb' presumably because of the effect on the price of 'accommodation land' and the threat of popular unrest. Ultimately, Hatherton and the other trustees became convinced of the need to establish a clearer relationship between the estate and the cottage occupants, or to sell the land on which the properties stood.

Action was not taken until after the trust had officially terminated in March 1845. To enable William to dispose of a part of the estate, Lord Ward's Estate Bill was introduced into Parliament in 1847. In spite of some criticism from Lord Shaftesbury, Chairman of Committees of the House of Lords Committee on Private Bills—not on a matter of principle, but because of Hatherton's non-attendance through the illness of his daughter—the proposal became law on 22 July 1847. To justify the purposes of the Act,[41] the preamble asserted that tenants had no right to sell buildings erected by them and an increase in rent or a compulsory eviction 'might be ruinous to them' as the great majority were 'for the most Part of a Condition not superior to that of common Labourers'. The Act granted powers of sale to Lord Ward and schedules attached to the Act listed 1,056 properties, mainly in the manors of Sedgley and Kingswinford, but with a minority in Dudley, Belbroughton and Swindon. In area, the plots were very small: 99 per cent were under two roods, the remainder averaging one acre. Most of the ground rents were approximately 6s per annum, but individual rents ranged from 1s to £2 10s. After the power to sell was granted, the chief land agent, John Maughan, moved quickly and sent a circular to all cottage tenants on 30 October 1847. This informed the tenant of Lord Ward's intention to sell the property and that 'It is desired that you should have the first opportunity of purchasing'.[42]

The standard form asked for information concerning the tenant's name, address, valuer, area of the property, rent, names of undertenants if any, rents paid by them, when the house was built, and by whom. Typical of many forms returned to the office was one from Peter Turner, a boat builder, who owned a cottage in Can Lane, on an enclosed area of 106sq yd. His rent was 2s 6d per annum. An undertenant, Thomas Smith, paid him a rent of 1s 10d per week. Turner had built the cottage in 1832. Many, but not all of the estate's copyhold tenants, did opt to purchase their land. A total of 734 properties had been sold by 15 September 1854 and sales continued until 1926 when copyhold was abolished. Three record books were opened at the Priory Office after the Act.[43] One, begun in May 1848, recorded the sale of cottage properties until June 1946; a second recorded copyhold enfranchisements from May 1849 to January 1926; and the third listed the sale of property, other than cottages, from January 1850 to June 1948. As in the case of the local enclosure Acts, copyholders could enfranchise their land and become freeholders on payment of a fine to the lord of the manor—and, as Loch had forecast, many were prepared to do this. However, in

at least 40 per cent of such cases, Lord Ward reserved his rights
to minerals under the property. The extent to which he had
already worked minerals in the area would determine this.
Benbow, in his capacity as a solicitor, transacted much of the
business at a handsome profit. Exclusive of stamp duty, his scale
of charges was £1 where the purchase money was under £20,
£2 between £20 and £50, £3 between £50 and £100, and £4
above that figure. Typical sale prices of the land indicate that the
estate received a sum which would have taken many years to
equal from the existing nominal ground rents:

> No. 5. 29 May 1848, 38 square yards: James Eynon, tenant of
> Dwelling House at Gospel Oak, rent 3/- per annum, purchased
> for £12

> No. 10. 13 June 1848, 265 square yards: Richard Evans, tenant
> of Public House at Princes End, rent 2/- per annum, purchased
> for £55[44]

The fine for enfranchisement of copyhold land purchased was
even higher: for example,

> 25 February 1850, Messrs T. and I. Badger for lands in Lower
> Gornal, 16 acres 2 roods 18 perches, for £120

> 15 September 1850, B. Parkes for 4 cottages and 2 nailshops in
> Sedgley, 1 acre 1 rood, £50[45]

There is no evidence that the estate evicted tenants and undertenants by making a compulsory sale to third parties. This is
borne out by the fact that considerable numbers of cottage plots
remained on a copyhold basis down to 1926; the total had declined by that date as tenants applied to acquire the title to the
land.

There was a growing criticism in general of the condition of
many cottages on large estates at this time.[46] In many cases it
produced a programme of cottage rehabilitation but the scale of
the problem and Loch's desire for administrative efficiency led

to the disposal of the land. He had earlier been associated with a similar problem on the estates of Lord Stafford in 1812 where 'the cottages were all in the hands of middlemen'[47] who sub-let at a high rent. However, in this case, the cottage tenants were made direct tenants of the estate. In one sense, the Dudley estate —after 1847—took advantage of the growing demand for housing in the area by enabling speculators to purchase land and erect more cottages. But, apart from the sale of this land, no attempt was made to pursue a policy of urban property speculation on the part of the estate itself such as occurred on the Stanley estate in Bury and Liverpool.[48]

The available evidence makes it impossible to trace the subsequent pattern of income from cottage rents. However, despite the considerable sale of land after Lord Ward's Estate Act, the total rent for 1850 had risen to £1,227 11s 11d. This suggests an increase in the rent of individual properties. The peak was probably reached shortly before the decision to sell portions of the estate in the 1920s. A survey of 1924[49] shows an income of £2,339 6s 6d from 1,358 cottages. Thereafter, income declined to £1,992 2s 3d in 1930, £1,807 16s 3d in 1932 and £1,075 10s 1d in 1935. This would be on account of property sales rather than rent reductions.

Purchases and Sales of Property

One of the most significant achievements of the trust was the acquisition of extensive landed estates in Worcestershire, Scotland and Wales. This was particularly important in the long term because the value and income of the Black Country properties began to decline towards the end of the nineteenth century as production costs increased with the exhaustion of the more valuable mineral seams. Nevertheless, in comparison with other members of the landed aristocracy, Lord Dudley's estates remained relatively small. Roberts' survey shows that in 1824 Lord Dudley owned approximately 10,000 acres, of which 6,646 acres were agricultural and cottage property. This was situated in and around the Black Country. Subsequent purchases of isolated plots of mineral-bearing land increased this to 11,216 acres by 1873. Taking into account the landed property purchased by the trust, the second earl possessed no more than 25,554 acres at the time of his death in 1885. Even so, his net income of £123,176 was exceeded by only six other titled families, all of whom owned over 100,000 acres. These were the Buccleuch, Devonshire, Northumberland, Bute, Sunderland and Fitzwilliam estates.[50]

Following the increase in acreage produced by enclosure, the next real expansion occurred during the 1820s when John William, Fourth Viscount Dudley and Ward (created Earl of Dudley in 1827) purchased estates in Wales and Scotland. Over thirty estates were surveyed[51] between 1824 and 1827 in Scotland and Wales. Surplus capital was being generated by mines worked by the estate and also by leased pits and ironworks. There was no attempt to operate ironworks on behalf of the estate until the trust and it may be that Lord Dudley wished to broaden the basis of his income beyond the narrow geographical area of the Black Country, and invest in agricultural property to enhance the family's social and economic status. Many of the potential purchases yielded substantial incomes and valuations ranged as high as £170,000. Most of the surveys were carried out by such professional estate agents as George Robertson and I. W. Craig. Two major properties were purchased in Scotland—at Ednam in Roxburghshire and Glengarry in Inverness-shire. In Wales a large estate was purchased at Crogen in the Dee valley near Bala.

Under the terms of the earl's will, the trustees had a clear directive to pay the various charges set out in the will; the residue of the annual income was to be 'accumulated by investment in the Funds or on real Securities in Great Britain' or used to purchase 'freehold Estates situate in Great Britain or of Copyhold or Leasehold Estates conveniently to be held'.[52] At the time of the earl's death in 1833, his investments in government and overseas stock had produced a considerable income:

H

1833	March 27	Dividend on 25,300 French Rentes, 5 per cent	£	s	d
			486	16	2
	May 9	Dividend on 10,600 Dollars Pennsylvania Stock	541	0	0
	June 26	Dividend on 5,100 French 3 per cent Rentes	98	5	0
	Sept 25	Dividend on £24,000 Reduced Annuities	360	0	0
		Dividend on £14,000 Consols	210	0	0
			1,696	1	2[53]

This total represents only the half-yearly dividend. As stipulated by the will, the trust proceeded to purchase only those stocks issued in Britain, and, within the first year, sold not only the foreign but also the British stock. Capital realised by these transactions was £84,177 14s 8d. Purchases of new British government stock were made with part of the capital realised from these sales.

1833	Sept 26	Purchase of 1,050-16-11 Consols	£	s	d
			930	0	0
1834	April 1	Purchase of 22,160-13-4 Reduced 3 per cents	20,000	0	0
		Purchase of 21,947-17-6 Consols	20,000	0	0
		Purchase of 5,486-19-4 Reduced 3 per cents	5,000	0	0
		Purchase of 5,427-8-2 Consols	5,000	0	0
	May 19	Purchase of 329-4-4 Consols	305	15	3
			51,235	15	3

Further capital was invested in these funds until the total stood at £153,733 9s 2d in June 1836;[54] the total amount was then sold to purchase landed estates and produced a capital value of £137,485.

Throughout the trust period, such stocks were purchased and sold again whenever the need for liquid capital arose as more land was purchased. Apart from the income received from these investments, they also served the valuable purpose—for the trustees—of providing the greatest possible security for estate profits in the short run. Their unwillingness to entrust such large sums of money to the banks[55] was also a factor in this matter.

During the period of the trust, the volume of land transfers turned downward in the early 1830s, and from then until the end of the 1840s the land market was generally slack and dull, with one bright interval of revived business in 1838-41.[56] However, at the time of the largest purchase—the Witley estate—the purchase cost may have been increased in view of the temporary increased demand for land in 1838-41. Downing was, as in most matters, an obstacle in that he favoured the purchase of estates only within the vicinity of the traditional Black Country estate. One such property was the Oak Farm estate in Kingswinford belonging to Sir Stephen Glynne. This property of 97 acres was known to contain extensive minerals which were, as yet, only partially developed:

Farm malt house, flour mill and arable land	£6,550
Value of the mines including engine	14,500
	21,050[57]

Because of its proximity to Himley Hall, Downing wished to purchase to prevent the ironmaster, John Foster, from adding it to his adjacent mines and ironworks at Shut End. Although Downing subsequently made the highest bid in a public auction, £35,000, the property was not sold as Glynne was asking £50,000. The trustees' fears were realised in 1836 when Glynne formed the Oak Farm Iron Works Company, one of the subsequent shareholders being his brother-in-law, W. E. Gladstone, and constructed furnaces on the site. Hatherton noted that, as a result, 'Himley Hall is rendered uninhabitable', and hoped that something might be done if the price of 'iron should materially fall, which I incline to think it soon will'. It is possible that the inconvenience to Himley Hall caused by the furnaces, coke ovens, and engine houses at Oak Farm may have given some impetus to the search for another estate which might become the family residence. Certainly Lord Ward regarded Witley in this light when it came on the market in 1838. Local mineral-bearing land was purchased by the trustees at a cost of £25,000.

Additions were made to the Welsh estate at Crogen in the Dee valley near Bala, purchased by the late earl 'as a matter of fancy',[58] until the trustees owned land along a continuous stretch of the river almost from Corwen down to Bala, a distance of about thirteen miles. Benbow strongly favoured the purchase of the Hendwr estate lying between Crogen and Corwen, pointing out the fact that, apart from adding to the agricultural property of the Dudley estate in the area, 'of the existence of Mine there can be no doubt—and the price has been considered both by Mr Smith and Mr Downing'.[59] This referred to the limestone which might be quarried to supply the demands of the iron trade and agriculture in the area. A survey by H. C. Wright, a London valuer, provides a detailed picture of the estate which, comprising the manor of Hendwr, was 'about 30 miles round'.[60] The manor contained several townships and

> 10,000 Acres of fine Grousing Ground, ranging to the Summit of the Berwyn Mountains—over which ... the Lord ... has the exclusive Right of Sporting.

The estate itself consisted of 1,097 acres of arable, meadow, pasture and woodland which had a gross annual value, including the sheep walks, of £904 3s 10d. The annual value of the 'Rights of Sporting, Fishery, Estrays and Chief Rents' was £100. After deducting $7\frac{1}{2}$ per cent for repairs and expenses, the net income would be £930. Wright felt that purchase over a period of thirty years was justified at '£3 6s 8d per cent'; this, added to the value of the timber, £3,500, made a purchase price of £31,400. An additional £2,000 could be added for improvements from enclosure 'of the best Mountain Land, Planting and chance of Minerals'. As the land had sporting rights over the adjoining Dudley estate at Crogen, Wright assessed the total value at £35,000. Communications were good as the Dee valley turnpike road ran through the property and, if minerals were quarried, there was the 'prospect of selling lime in Corwen at £1 per waggon of 60 bushels'. Colonel Passingham, the owner of the estate, fixed the price at £40,000; ultimately, perhaps because of the particularly low demand for land in 1835-7, the property was purchased for £35,000. Additional small properties were purchased for a total of £11,861 11s 2d.

The second area where property was purchased in 1836-7, Kidderminster, was much more acceptable to the Bishop of Exeter, although still too distant for Downing's approval. These were Lord Foley's estates at Hurcot, for £135,000, and Oldington for £89,000. These transactions and the debt charges incurred by Lord Foley, which probably led to his decision to dispose of large sections of his estate, are set out in Benbow's account for 1836-7:

Payments		£	s	d
1836	Oct 3. Lord Foley deposit upon £133,000 for the Hurcot Estate	12,000	0	0
1837	June 2. The Rock Assurance Co. their Mortgage upon the Estate	70,000	0	0
	Mr Dawson's Representatives, their Mortgage	25,000	0	0
	Henry Talbot Esq, his Mortgage	7,000	0	0
	Lord Foley's Trustees	15,500	0	0
	Lord Foley	3,500	0	0
		133,000	0	0
	Interest on the above purchase money to the 12th	659	18	4
		133,659	18	4
	Feb 14. Lord Foley's Deposit upon £55,500 agreed for part of his Kidderminster Estate (Oldington)	5,500	0	0
	June 27. His Lordship's Deposit upon £33,500 agreed for a further part of his Kidderminster Estate	3,500	0	0
		9,000	0	0[61]

Both estates were again surveyed by Wright. Benbow had been

particularly keen to purchase these properties 'next to Kidderminster because of political interest in the Borough'.[62]

The largest single addition to trust property, the Witley estate,
lay to the west of the River Severn. When this estate was first
offered for sale in December 1837, it was valued by John
Hodgetts Foley at £680,000:

Witley Estate comprises 9,700 acres in the Parishes of Great Witley, Great Skelsey, Martley, Holt, Droitwich and Oldswinford	
Gross Rental about £13,000 per Annum	£425,000
Livings	20,000
Bewdley Forest	10,000
Witley Court, Park, Timber and Deer	150,000
Woodley Estate, about 1,000 acres	45,000
Timber except the Park	30,000
	680,000
Deduct Mortgage	130,000
	550,000[63]

One of the many problems created by the proposed purchase was
that an outlay of £680,000 would have to be spread beyond the
termination of the trust; this involved securing permission from
chancery and from Lord Ward who had to pledge his income
after 6 March 1845. Lord Ward was very anxious to secure the
property in spite of the 'personal sacrifice' he would make after
inheriting the full title to his estates as

it is an offer such as will never be in my power either to accept
or refuse again in Worcestershire and scarcely in any other...
I prefer it to the Duke of Norfolk's place at Worksop. At Witley
everything has been first rate and could be so again—neglect,
total neglect is the thing most observable there—and this only
in the grounds—the House tho' an ugly one being in perfect
repair.[64]

Several plans were drawn up to discover the best manner of
meeting regular payments and interest charges on the purchase.
One of the main problems was that, in view of Smith's current

reorganisation of the mines,[65] which involved leasing the pits, future revenue from this source was uncertain. In February 1838, Benbow[66] submitted the following forecast of income as a basis for discussion.

Mineral Income		£	s	d
Minimum Royalties of Leases Settled		9,677	0	0
Do. of Leases not completed		13,500	0	0
Do. for Mines in Treaty only		4,900	0	0
Average of Royalties for 1837 on Mines worked by Tenants at Will		7,623	12	6
Estimate of Profit on Mineral Concerns in Hand		14,400	0	0
Rents of Do.		3,000	0	0
Kingswinford Railroad		559	7	6
	[sic]	53,300	0	0
Maximum Royalties (suppose)		15,000	0	0
		68,300	0	0

Mines to be let extent of profit uncertain?

Estate Income Receipts	£	Charges	£
Himley	18,509		5,000
Witley	14,000		3,000
Crogen (all Welsh estate)	2,000		300
Hurcot	6,000		1,000
Broome (Kidderminster)	1,680		200
Mines (as above)	53,300	Lord Ward	8,000
Dudley House and Jamaica Estates	4,000	Lady Ward, Annuities	4,800
Interest on Canal Shares	1,350		
	100,839		22,300 0 0

Annual Surplus 78,539

Eventually, it was decided to purchase the property after Lord Ward agreed to pay off the outstanding balance in March 1845 and a survey of the Witley Court estate itself had been submitted to the trustees.

Quantity of land				Value
A	R	P		£
427	2	13	Timber, Woods, Plantations and Sheep Walks	72,810
11			The Mansion, Pleasure Grounds and Gardens	35,000
484	2	28	The Park and Timber thereon	66,464
25			The Pools	2,500
86	1	32	Ornamental Grounds and Plantations	22,428
			Fixtures	500
			The Deer	800
1,519	2	19	The Farms and Timber thereon	82,298
			The Advowsons	12,900
2,554	1	12	Total Quantity	Total Value £295,700[67]

This survey only covered the area around Witley Court itself and excluded those parts of the Witley estate scattered over the counties of Herefordshire, Worcestershire and Shropshire; the agreed purchase price for the whole estate was £667,939. Benbow was particularly anxious that Lord Ward should be quite clear about his commitment:

If he should unfortunately become embarassed, he would blame all parties for having deprived him for a time of a portion ... of his income.[68]

It was with this prospect in mind that Benbow reminded Lord Ward that his gambling debts stood at £16,000 and urged him not to renew his subscription to Crockfords.

The financial arrangement was that the trustees should pay £331,000 of the total cost of the Witley estate by March 1845; an initial payment of £55,000 was made in June 1839, and annual payments of £50,000 were made commencing in June 1841. In addition, interest was paid on the outstanding debt at 4 per cent. Lord Ward contracted to pay the balance of £336,939 within ten years by annual instalments of £40,000—commencing in March 1845; until then he was to pay 4 per cent annual interest on this debt which amounted to £13,477 11s 2d. The dangers of the situation soon became evident: estate revenue slumped with the decline in the iron trade in 1841-2, as debts owed to the Dudley estate for minerals purchased mounted, while Lord Ward further complicated the situation by borrowing £15,000 to pay his gambling debts and also contracted to purchase the Invergarry estate in Scotland for £95,000. He did this on the basis of an income of £9,000 from that portion of the Witley estate which he had contracted to purchase, £2,500 from the Ednam estate which he enjoyed in his own right as it had been excluded from the trust by the late earl's will, and £2,200 income from the Invergarry estate. In addition, he received an annual income of £8,000 under the terms of the will. Although he might claim the right to make this purchase out of his own income, the fact remains that his total net income was £21,700 while his commitments, in terms of interest payments, totalled £19,016 3s 10d. The trustees, especially Hatherton, felt obliged to assist him. Benbow, who always took a high moral line with the young Lord Ward, felt that he should sell Ednam to pay off his debts, but this was a vain hope. Fortunately, the boom conditions of 1847, together with the recovery of debts outstanding from local ironmasters, enabled the trustees to meet their commitment to Lord Foley while Lord Ward was able to maintain his payments until the purchase was completed.

During the course of the trust, the terms of the will, with regard to land purchase, had been faithfully carried out.

Local mineral property	1833-45	£16,109
Dudley glebe (mineral)	1836	9,000
Hendwr (agricultural, sporting and mineral)	1836	35,000
Properties in Llandrillo (agricultural)	1837	11,861
Hurcot (agricultural)	1836	133,000
Kidderminster (agricultural)	1836	89,000
Witley (agricultural)	1839 (by trustees)	331,000
Kidderminster and Dudley (agricultural)	1846	26,000
Purchased by the trustees		650,970

Witley	1839 (by Lord Ward)	336,939
Glengarry	1841 (by Lord Ward)	95,000
	Purchased by Lord Ward	431,939

This represents a total land value of £1,082,909 acquired out of the income of the Dudley estate, all of which became the property of Lord Ward when he assumed full possession of the estate in March 1845, although final payment on outstanding debts was not made until 1854.

After 1850, the land market in general was more active as confidence returned with the rise in agricultural rents—especially after 1853—and demand pushed up land prices to a peak in the early 1870s.[69] The Dudley estate did not participate in this trend and, despite the extensive purchases of the trust period, it remained relatively small in comparison with other landed aristocratic estates. Instead, the traditional policy of investment in estate mineral exploitation was intensified, to meet the demand created by the mid-century boom in the Black Country wrought-iron trade. Furthermore, as the local iron and mineral industries began their long decline after 1860, the Dudley estate invested heavily in the production of pig and wrought iron and, after 1890, in the manufacture of steel.[70] Then investments paid off handsomely until the nationalisation of these assets in the twentieth century. Nor did the estate at once reflect the general trend to sell agricultural property after 1878 as falling rents, mounting arrears, and accumulations of unlet farms convinced owners of the need to sell portions of their estates. The bulk of the agricultural properties owned by Lord Dudley were not sold until 1917-24. Such property as was sold before 1917 was mainly mineral property with diminishing returns.

On the old family estate around Dudley, Lord Ward's Estate Act of 1847 had led to the enfranchisement and sale of many cottage properties, but this, as in the case of the decision to sell mineral and industrial property after 1883, was in response to local factors rather than a turning point marking the initiation of policies intended to break up the estate. Local factors continued to influence policies with regard to the disposal of property—in addition to general developments in the mineral trade—and blocks of the local Black Country estates were sold periodically after 1930 as demand for building land grew. This last factor probably determined the retention of local property long after the landed estates in Worcestershire, Wales, and Scotland had been sold. The sale of these other properties was, no doubt, the result of national trends and developments which placed the landed classes under increased pressure[71] from the late 1870s onwards, although the Dudley estate in general remained relatively intact until a comparatively late date.

The first major sale of Dudley property was in July 1918 when the Broome and Hurcot estates, between Kidderminster and Stourbridge, were sold.[72] Prior to this, apart from sales of certain copyhold, mineral, and industrial properties, the only estates to be sold were those in Scotland and Wales. It is likely that they were sold as early as 1900, along with the Jamaica estates, because of their relatively limited value as a source of income. In contrast, the Broome and Hurcot estates did produce a reasonable income from agricultural rents. These estates were put up for sale on 30 July 1918 at a time when the land market had begun to pick up after four inactive years. This trend became an avalanche by the spring of 1919 when a 'revolution in landowning' was proclaimed and it was declared that 'England is changing hands'.[73] The particulars of sale indicate that the Broome estate was 560 acres in extent and consisted mainly of three farms of 98, 176 and 286 acres from which the estate derived an annual income of £960. The Hurcot estate of 2,682 acres consisted of 12 farms ranging from 42 to 460 acres and produced an annual income of £3,600. In particular, the sale catalogue stressed the potential value of the land for building development in the vicinity of Kidderminster, and the price would probably be higher than the average of £35 per acre, the price for agricultural land 'in the good years'.[74]

The most extensive and valuable estate sold was the Witley estate: this was offered for sale by auction on 27 September 1920.[75] However, the whole property had already been purchased by an unknown buyer, possibly a London 'syndicate', at an estimated price of £1 million.[76] The 8,500 acres of 'very rich freehold' were divided into 192 plots comprising:

> Pasture, fruit, hop and arable lands near Worcester, Stourport and Kidderminster . . . consisting of 41 High Class Farms (some of the most famous in the County), several Capital Small Holdings, residences, 3 Licensed Houses, valuable accommodation lands, about 100 well-built cottages and finely grown woodlands.

If the estimated cost to the syndicate was accurate, the earl received a price well above the average, which at £35 per acre, would amount to £297,500. However, although it was more usual for a landowner to retain his country seat while selling the land, the earl had included Witley Court in the sale and this, no doubt, would account for the abnormally high price for the estate as a whole. There were, in addition, several hundred acres of fine timber. Sale reports[77] of the Witley auction indicate that proceedings were lively, as tenants of the various lots made only low bids—giving the high bank rate as the cause. The auctioneer, reportedly, frequently dismissed bids as 'ridiculous' and a spokesman for the tenants claimed that the 'London men' were not giving them a fair chance: 'The country wanted food and these men on the Dudley estate know how to produce it.' The auctioneer protested that he had 'never been treated like this before. Let me make one point . . . Lord Dudley did not give my clients this estate—we had to buy it.' Unfortunately for many of the Witley tenants, demand was still high and they were forced to withdraw as the auctioneer was not prepared to accept their price. In view of this it seems likely that, whether or not the earl's selling-price was as high as £1 million, he had driven a good bargain as members of the syndicate were prepared to incur a good deal of adverse criticism in the press, and from the tenants, in order to recoup themselves.

After the disposal of Witley,[78] the only large estate remaining in the second earl's possession was the original family estate in north Worcestershire and south Staffordshire centred on Himley. Apart from the continuing sale of small mineral and copyhold properties which had reduced the size of the estate from 11,216 acres in 1883 to 10,600 acres in 1924, the first indication that a decision had been made to begin the disposal and break-up of this estate in general was in 1926. Records show that between July 1926 and February 1935, the value of sale of land negotiated by the Himley Estates Ltd[79] amounted to £462,237 8s; annual rent lost was £6,977 19s 9d, but interest on the sale money was £23,111 11s 1d at 5 per cent per annum. It is evident that Lord Ednam's re-structuring of the estate's economic activities after the settlement of 1923 also included the phased break-up of the landed estate itself, so as to realise the maximum market value and base the family income on investments alone. During the 1920s and 1930s, there was a considerable demand for land in the area for the provision of local authority and private housing; this was when the bulk of the local estates were sold. Typical of sales at this time was the purchase of 521 acres in the Priory and Castle Mill area of Dudley by Dudley Council —for £77,500: 'Dudley's land-locked condition will be greatly relieved by this purchase.'[80] Extensive council estates were constructed on this property after 1926.

Continuing demand for building land throughout the Black Country conurbation led to the auction of several blocks of estate property, in July 1935, valued at £80,000.[81] Most notable was the sale of 50 acres at Goldthorn Hill between Sedgley and Wolverhampton: this land was 'restricted to the erection of £400 houses'. In all cases, mines and all timber were included in the sale; generally, the mines at least had been reserved in all sales in the past. Prior to the sale, the area had already been divided

into 114 freehold lots which would constitute the Goldthorn
Park Estate. Presumably, because of the high demand for private
housing in the area, this division would increase the price of the
land. Other areas included in the 1935 sale were in Dudley,
Tipton, and Kingswinford. By June 1939, total sales since 1926
amounted to £712,911, in addition to an annual interest on the
sale money of £34,106 12s 10d; rent lost was £8,347 7s 1d.
Limited sales took place during the war and by 1944 the total
value of land disposed of amounted to £854,301. In general, the
boom in land values had passed by 1925 and the number of sales
dwindled. Local conditions ensured that the local Dudley estate
fetched such high prices in the period 1926-44; most of the land
sold was situated in the traditional mineral and industrial areas
of the Black Country in Dudley, Sedgley, Tipton, and Brierley
Hill.

The remainder of the Himley estate was sold after 1945—most
of it, including Himley Hall, in 1947. Pre-war trends which had
seen the emergence of dormitory areas in Sedgley and Kingswinford were now intensified as the post-war pattern of local
housing developed. This consisted of a movement of population
out of the old Black Country centres, such as Tipton, Bilston,
Wednesbury, Dudley, and Brierley Hill, to live in the rural
fringe areas of Sedgley, Wombourne, Himley, and Kingswinford
—while retaining employment within the traditional Black

Black Country Towns	Acres	1931	1951	1961
Tipton	2,167	35,814 pop.	39,382 pop.	38,100 pop.
Wednesbury	2,025	31,521	34,759	34,511
Dudley	4,064	59,583	62,526	62,965
Development Areas				
Sedgley	3,948	19,262	23,114	27,912
Kingswinford	4,246	22,224	27,757	34,300
Seisdon RDC (including Himley and Wombourne)	41,990	13,850	22,322	36,981

Country towns. Census returns indicate that, while there was only a marginal increase in the population of the older towns, 1931-61—or, even a decrease in some cases—there was a relatively sharp rise in the population of the fringe areas.

This was probably the main determining factor for the disposal of estate property in the fringe development areas in 1947. There was, however, another more urgent reason in that, given the political situation, landowners such as the third earl might lose the minerals while retaining the surface freehold. This would reduce the value of the land for housing development. Accordingly, the bulk of the remaining estate was sold in 1947 in two separate auctions—probably to secure the best price—in January and July.

In January a total of 2,711 acres was sold including Himley Hall, the Home Farm, eight farms in Himley and Kingswinford —ranging from 56 to 233 acres—and three large houses at Holbeche, Dawley and Ashwood. The land offered contained woodlands and was 'accommodation land suitable for development'.[82] Minerals, other than coal, were sold with the property 'except where the National Coal Board is acquiring under the Coal Industry Nationalisation Act of 1946'. This applied to the Baggeridge mineral area only; the remainder of the unworked coal lay at a great depth west of the boundary fault and the earl reserved his rights here. The coal lies at such a depth that the surface would be left undisturbed should it become expedient to work it at some future date. Therefore the sale price was not influenced by the earl's retention of his rights. Himley Hall and 200 acres of the park were purchased by the National Coal Board for £45,000; it was then converted into the regional office for the West Midlands area! Sir Ben Smith, chairman at the time, was criticised because of the cost of converting the property, but defended his action on the grounds that about 62 acres of thick coal—which would yield 2 million tons—lay under the property. This could be worked and, at that price, he claimed that he had obtained 'a bargain for the nation'.[83] Timber-bearing land fetched particularly high prices: £8,250 was paid for the Himley Plantation of 49 acres.[84] Including the hall, total sales amounted to £191,902.

A further sale occurred in July 1947 when parts of Himley Park, the agricultural and sporting Blackhill estate, fourteen capital farms, various cottages and residences, and the sand and gravel quarries at Blackhill and Hinksford—both going concerns —were sold.[85] In all cases minerals, except coal, were included. The sale, the largest yet, included 3,104 acres but the total price, £114,670, was less than the previous sale. This was probably because the schedule made no reference to accommodation land, and, with the exception of the sporting estate and quarries, it was sold as agricultural land. As the areas concerned are more distant from the Black Country, these properties remain largely agricultural today. The Blackhills Sand and Gravel Quarry was in fact withdrawn from the auction and was not included in the total sale price of £114,670. After the sale of Himley Hall, the earl lived at Ednam Lodge, Sunningdale; this too was sold in March 1949 when an estate was purchased at King's Langley in Buckinghamshire. The last auction of local property was in 1963 when 400 acres, containing land and buildings throughout the conurbation, were sold; the forty-two plots realised a total of £167,970—at £419 18s per acre, the highest value yet reached in the disposal of the estates.

Total sales of Dudley property during the period 1918-63 were:

		Acres	Price £	Price per Acre £ s d
July 1918.	Broome and Hurcot	3,200	200,000	62 10 0
Sept 1920.	Witley and Holt	8,600	1,000,000	117 0 0
1926-44.	Black Country in general	4,385 (estimate)	854,301	194 16 0
Jan 1947.	Himley Hall, Kingswinford, Sedgley	2,711	191,902	70 8 0

		Acres	Price £	Price per Acre £ s d
July 1947.	Himley Park, Worbourne, Swindon	3,104	114,670	36 18 0
Sept 1963.	Black Country in general	400	167,970	419 18 0
		22,400	2,528,843	

This excludes the value of the Jamaica, Scottish, and Welsh estates sold between 1888 and 1900. A comparison of the selling price per acre illustrates the fluctuations in the property market and the wisdom of the phased disposal of the local Dudley estate between 1918 and 1963. Within the area of the traditional family estates, all that remains is a number of small, historic areas closely connected with the Dudley family, such as the ruins of Dudley Priory and the Garden of Memories at Himley Hall.

Rents Due to the Dudley Estate, 1701-1942

Estates in the Black Country

	Cottage Rents £ s d	Great Rents £ s d	Total £ s d
1701	26 0 0	2,084 19 11	2,110 19 11
1768	240 14 1	—	—
1779	—	—	5,491 11 10
1783	—	—	6,238 17 8½
1797	—	6,164 2 8	—
1803	—	—	8,096 6 11½
1810	540 10 2	—	—
1811	—	9,478 2 3	—
1814	—	—	17,452 11 2
1817	572 18 11	13,520 1 8	14,093 0 7
1824	—	14,798 5 9	—
1833	—	17,896 15 11	—
1836	797 9 3	19,616 9 6	20,413 18 9
1838	1,039 18 10	—	—
1850	1,227 11 11	18,487 12 4	19,686 17 1
1924	2,339 6 6	21,177 0 1	23,516 6 7
1935	1,075 10 1	26,992 7 1	28,067 18 0
1942	—	—	27,820 7 11

J

The area of these estates was:

1824 — 6.646 acres	1873 — 11,216 acres
1883 — 11,216 „	1924 — 10,600 „
1944 — 5,815 „	1962 — 400 „

Other Estates

	Jamaica			Merioneth			Worcestershire			Scotland		
	£	s	d	£	s	d	£	s	d	£	s	d
1833	4,415	7	0	933	4	0	—			3,396	3	0
				(Crogen)						(Ednam)		
1836	4,376	19	6	940	1	0	—			6,601	3	3
										(all)		
1837	—			—			6,637	4	0	—		
							(Hurcot)					
1838	—			2,240	1	10	21,680	0	0	—		
				(Hendwr			(Plus					
				Crogen)			Witley)					
1845	—			2,032	19	0	—			—		
1852	—			—			30,906	8	4	—		

Notes to Chapter 4 are on pages 249-53

CHAPTER FIVE

Industrial Developments

The Clays

Extensive deposits of clay existed throughout the Black Country
estate and as these deposits were interspersed between the various
seams of coal and iron ore, all three materials were usually raised
from the same shaft—although shallow deposits of clay were
quarried. Fireclay seams were located in the south-western
sector of the estate between Brierley Hill and Stourbridge. Brick-
kilns, glass works, and pottery manufactories had all existed in
the area between Dudley and Stourbridge for many years before
1774 and glass manufacturing had been introduced into the
Stourbridge area by Huguenot immigrants at the beginning of
the seventeenth century.

Kilns were constructed at pits owned and worked by the
Dudley estate. The two main sources were Lord Dudley's New
Brockmoor Colliery and his store-yard at Round Oak. In 1833,
the wages bill for workmen employed in manufacturing bricks at
the store-yard was £620 3s 8d. The clay measures were directly
exploited by the Dudley estate for the manufacture of bricks only
—as a branch of mineral enterprise. Bricks, pottery and glass
were not manufactured by the estate for commercial sale although
numerous lessees produced such goods. A royalty of 1s per thous-

and bricks was charged by Lord Dudley and the sum paid by
one lessee, Isaac Badger, in 1788, gives some indication of the
extent of brick manufacture in this area to meet increased
demands from pits and house construction:

> 1788 November 5th. Received North and Homer, Royalty of 1/-
> per thousand on making 360,000 Bricks ... in the year 1788.
> £18 0s 0d.[1]

He also made 'plain tiles'[2] at 2s per thousand, 'ridge tiles' at 2s 6d
per thousand, and 'paving tiles' at 2s 6d per thousand in 1796.[3]
These rates of royalty remained constant throughout the period
1774-1833. Fireclay royalties were higher as this was a far more
valuable commodity than common brickclay. In 1801, Lord
Dudley was listed as one of the principal proprietors of fireclay
in Amblecote and Kingswinford: 'They gather about 4,000 tons
a year. ... This clay sells at Stourport for 34/- a ton.'[4] No
detailed evidence of Lord Dudley's profit from this source
survives.

Glass manufacturing developed on estate property in Amblecote and the Brettell Lane and Wordsley districts of Kingswinford
manor:

> Broad-glass [has been] ... manufactured here for several genera-
> tions ... Chrystal glass has long been made here but the art of
> cutting and engraving it was not long since brought from Ger-
> many to London and from London hither ...
> This manufactory is considerably increased of late years ...
> Persons ... employed in and about Stourbridge in the manufac-
> turing of glass are 520.[5]

Three glass works were in operation on the estate by 1790 but
two of them turned to the manufacture of pottery-ware after 1797
—reflecting the reduced demand for luxuries during the war.

The third was occupied by the Grazebrook family at Audenham Bank (Wordsley) under a lease granted for twenty-one years
in 1783.[6] By the terms of the lease, the glass house with furnaces,
millhouse, warehouses and buildings were rented at £53 per

annum and maintenance and repairs were undertaken by the lessee at her own cost. By 1825 the rent had increased to £148. The same family took out a lease[7] of Lord Dudley's land at the Delph in 1796 to supply clay to the Audenham Bank glass works. Under the terms of this lease, thirty acres were occupied at a rent of £32 per annum with the right to

> erect Engines etc to mine Glasshouse Clay at 9/- per ton Royalty, Pot Clay, 5/- per ton, Offal Clay, 2/6 per ton, Potters Clay, 2/-.

A ton was defined as 24cwt at 120lb. Further royalties were agreed at

> 1,000 of Quarries, Cress, and Gutters made from Common Surface Brick Clay, 2/6, and for each 1,000 Bricks or Tiles, 1/6.

In default, Lord Dudley could re-enter and sell the stock and machinery to recover the debt. His agents were entitled to enter weekly or from 'time to time' to 'weigh the quantities and inspect the books' and a minimum royalty of £500 per annum had to be paid. Potteries too were established throughout the southern parts of the estate, operating under terms similar to the Badger and Grazebrook enterprises. More numerous than glass works, these potteries were usually supplied by estate collieries.

During the period of the trust, all the forms of industrial enterprise which existed in 1823 were continued and brick, glass and pottery manufacture expanded in Brierley Hill and Wordsley as supplies of local clay and fireclay were exploited to meet growing demands. This produced greater diversification and specialisation of production on the one hand, and increased rates of royalty on the other. Certain areas of the estate in the old manor of Kingswinford—fast becoming the industrial town of Brierley Hill—became associated with particular products. Bricks and tiles were manufactured at Brierley Hill itself and the industrial villages of Bromley and Wordsley; earthenware manufacturers developed along Brettell Lane and glass works at Wordsley, Audenham and Brettell Lane. This distribution was probably determined by the nature of the clay and its accessibility in these particular areas. For example, fireclay lay at a relatively shallow depth along the line of the Wordsley to Stourbridge road where glass works were most numerous. In 1851 there were about fifteen manufacturers engaged in the production of brick, tile or earthenware products in Brierley Hill, and at least six of these were tenants of Lord Dudley. Many of the tenants leased not only land and buildings from the estate, but also clay and coal pits which they worked themselves, paying a surface rent, a royalty on minerals extracted, and a royalty on goods produced.

One of the larger manufacturers, Hughes and Eades, worked the clay mine at the Delph for the first part of the trust period; this was taken over by Webb, Harper and Moore, subsequently to become leading manufacturers in the area. Apart from paying a surface rent of £100 per annum in 1836, royalties were also paid which varied according to the value of the clay or product.

Best Clay	21/- per ton [fireclay]
Second Clay	7/6
Black Clay	7/6
Offal Clay	2/-
Red Bricks	2/- per 1,000
Tiles, Cress, etc	2/6 per 1,000[8]

Coal and clay were raised from another pit leased from the estate; coal royalties were 2s 6d per ton for best coal, 1s 6d for common coal, and 6d for slack. The lease reflects developments since the period of early expansion. Whereas the royalty for bricks had been 1s per 1,000 in 1790 and remained so until the 1830s, the increase to 2s per 1,000 indicates the growing demand for bricks in the Black Country towns. Increasing numbers of blue bricks were also being manufactured, for which south Staffordshire became famous, and great numbers of these were used in the construction of bridges and railway viaducts throughout the country. This explains the specific reference to 'red' bricks. Blue bricks were not manufactured from ordinary brick clay but from one of the inferior fireclays and the royalty on them would be higher. There was no change in the royalty charged for 'tiles' and 'cress' in 1836 from that charged in 1796. However, fireclay royalty had increased and a distinction was made between the various types. Whereas Messrs Grazebrook paid 9s per ton royalty for glasshouse clay in 1796, Hughes and Eades paid 7s 6d per ton for the two inferior fireclays and 21s per ton for best glasshouse clay. 'Offal' was the term used to designate the less valuable common brickclay.

Lord Dudley's income from these enterprises would be further increased by supplying coal and sand to the manufacturers. By 1845,[9] glass works in the area were manufacturing a total of 2,300 tons of flint glass per annum while Westwood and Moore alone manufactured 980 tons of bottles, pottery ware, and fire-bricks. This enterprise obtained 320 tons of clay, 450 tons of sand, and 3,500 tons of coal from the Kingswinford area—it is likely that much of it came from the Dudley estate. The trustees did not alter the earlier policy of estate enterprise: bricks only were manufactured, and no attempt was made to enter the glass or earthenware trades on an entrepreneurial basis.

The Iron Trade

With the introduction of the coke-smelting of iron, the steam blast engine, and Cort's puddling process, there was a phenomenal expansion in the output and scale of the iron industry in south Staffordshire from 4,500 tons of pig iron, produced by six blast furnaces in 1788, to 216,000 tons from 95 blast furnaces in 1827. Nevertheless, the fortunes of the iron trade varied considerably over the period. The price of pig iron remained steady to 1796 as output increased to meet the growing demand but, after 1800, new furnaces were erected when the Armed Neutrality of the North halted exports of Swedish iron to Britain. After the war, capacity exceeded demand and, apart from 1818, the iron trade remained depressed until 1822 when a more buoyant phase began. This was followed by a depression between 1825 and 1830. In general, the development of the iron trade on the Dudley estate reflects these trends. The average price of pig iron in south Staffordshire was £6 5s 0d per ton between 1801 and 1810, £5 4s 0d in the period 1810 to 1820, £4 9s 0d from 1820 to 1830, and £3 in 1832.[10] By 1833, increased demand produced a reversal of the trend and the price of iron rose to £5 10s 0d.

However, this recovery was not reflected in the fortunes of the Dudley estate at the commencement of the trust. Finished or bar iron used in the wrought-iron industry fetched £18 per ton in 1815 and £8 by 1833. Another factor which influenced the demand for Lord Dudley's minerals was technological advance —which reduced the quantity of coal needed to make one ton of pig iron from 10 tons in 1800 to 4 tons in 1840, and 58cwt by 1871.[11] So long as the Black Country iron trade continued to expand, the demand for coal would not necessarily decrease. Over the period 1774-1833, the productive capacity of local blast furnaces also increased—from about 750 tons per annum for each furnace in 1796 to approximately 2,275 tons per annum in 1827.[12] All of these factors need to be taken into account when assessing the state of the Black Country iron trade and the performance of the estate during this period.

One of the oldest ironworks on the Dudley estate was at Cradley on the banks of the Stour. This was leased[13] to Messrs Crofts on 1 February 1774 for a term of twenty years, at an annual rent of £210, under an agreement which did not place rigorous obligations on the lessees. The latter were free to take all the limestone they required from Lord Dudley's estate at Coneygre and the Old Park, and as the area was not yet enclosed, were allowed to take timber for maintenance free 'from the rough'. The works had to be maintained in good order and the lessee was entitled to 'purchase timber from Lord Dudley's woods for converting into Cole Wood . . . and to pay the Lessor 11s 6d a Cord'.[14] At this time there was no coke furnace on the Dudley estate and as Lord Dudley agreed not to sell 'cordwood' to any other furnace or forge, it is evident that charcoal, still the main source of fuel in local furnaces, was in short supply. By

1788, all the six blast furnaces at work in Staffordshire were using the new coke-smelting technique.

Wilkinson successfully introduced the new coke-smelting method into the area at his Bradley furnace in 1766. After this many of the new blast furnaces constructed in the Black Country were on the Dudley estate.

	No of furnaces in south Staffordshire	Furnaces leased from the Dudley estate	Total Output
1788	6	3	4,500 tons
1796	14	5	13,210 tons
1806	42	12	49,000 tons

There may have been additional furnace leases but no evidence survives. The first coke furnace on the estate was probably erected by Messrs Parker at Tipton Green, on the Birmingham Canal, in 1783.[15] They undertook to purchase all their ironstone, coal, and limestone from the lessor and to transport it at their own expense. A scale of prices was established for the different types and qualities of minerals.

Large ordinary coal	— 3/- a ton of 20 cwts at 120 lbs
Lumps	— 2/6
Slack	— 1/6
Limestone	— 4/-
Lime	— 3/- a quarter of 8 Winchester Bushels.

As defined here, both the ton and the quarter weights differed from those contained in the clay and limestone leases and the lack of standard weights in the local mineral trades makes it difficult to calculate production costs. Ironstone purchased from Lord Dudley's pits was to be measured in 'blooms of 35 cwts at 120 lbs per cwt. If the ironstone has lain on the [pit] bank for more than 1 month, the Bloom shall contain 33 cwts.' This use of the term 'bloom'—more usually applied to lumps of iron worked in the old bloomery process of iron-smelting—referred to the practice of piling ironstone into heaps on the surface 2ft high and covering an area of 12sq ft. These heaps were estimated to contain about two tons of ore.[16] Lones stated that this term, a crude form of measurement, was in use during the period 1776-1808. Oxidisation would account for loss of weight when the ironstone was exposed to the atmosphere over a period of weeks—this probably explains the variable definition if a ton of the ironstone had been 'on the bank' for longer than one month. Lord Dudley's income from the lease was drawn only from the sale of raw materials and a small ground rent of £3 per annum; there was no attempt yet to levy a minimum royalty or royalty on the amount of iron produced. This ironworks later became known as the Tipton Furnaces—two blast furnaces existed by 1784.

It was at the Level[17] on the banks of the Dudley Canal in Kingswinford that the largest concentration of ironworks developed on the Dudley estate before 1833. These works were known as the Old and the New Level Iron Works. A lease[18] of 1800 refers to the lease of land at the Old Level in 1784 to William and Richard Croft and it is likely that the Old Level furnace was constructed at that time by Messrs Crofts. It was a small stone furnace charged by hand—coke, limestone and ironstone were carried to the top in buckets. This was occupied by Messrs Gibbons in 1788 at a ground rent of £6, by which time a mill and a forge had been added to the ironworks. The latter also took over the Crofts' lease of Cradley forge on the River Stour at an annual rent of £210.[19]

In 1800, Messrs Gibbons extended their operations and took out another lease of estate property situated a short distance along the canal towards Dudley, and began to erect the New Level Iron Works. They undertook to construct 'a substantial furnace, foundry and ironworks with all necessary buildings for the manufacturing of ironstone into pig iron and castings'[20] within eighteen months. The new furnace, forge and mill were to be erected at a capital cost of at least £1,500 and the lessees were allowed to mine the coal and ironstone under their property on payment of royalty and a ground rent of £47 to Lord Dudley.

By 1806, two additional furnaces had been erected at the New Level Iron Works and a fourth one was added in 1815. Benjamin Gibbons occupied the works in 1825 when the three furnaces in blast each produced 40 tons of iron per week. The Gibbons family continued to occupy the Old Level mill and forge but Messrs Izons and Co worked the furnace after 1806.

The accounts for 1834[21] indicate the sources of estate income from the Old Level Iron Works:

Dr.	£	s	d	Old Level Iron Works	£	s	d	Cr.
Estate half a year's rent of land	50	13	0	Gibbons and Co interest on repairs	44	3	0	
Repairs at Mill and Forge	605	14	6	3 and ½ Years rent of Mill and Forge	506	5	0	
Store Yard	141	17	8	½ Years rent of Ditto	346	8	0	
Bal carried down	328	10	10	Izons and Co ½ Years rent of Iron Furnaces and Premises	230	0	0	
	1126	16	0		1126	16	0	
				Bal brought down	328	10	0	

The rent derived from Gibbons and Co for the mill and forge was probably a royalty based on production. The revival in the Black Country iron trade after 1833 is reflected in the higher rent for the last six months of 1834. A royalty on production was received from the New Level Iron Works—Izons and Co probably worked the Old Level furnace on a similar basis. Repairs had been carried out by the estate and materials had been purchased from Lord Dudley's store-yard at Round Oak—the credit item suggests that the tenant was called upon to offset the costs. The account for the New Level Iron Works (The Level Four

Furnaces) gives more detailed information concerning the basis on which royalties were calculated.

Dr.				*Level Four Furnaces*			Cr.
	£	s	d		£	s	d
Disbursements	232	10	0	Hemp, Leather, etc	22	16	6
Rates	8	12	6	Gibbons and Co rent at 6/- per ton on iron made at furnaces			
Bricklayers	70	19	4	1117 tons 19 c			
Store Yard	24	0	8	1 qtr	335	7	9
Park Head Colliery	302	15	6	Do. at furnace No 4, 657 tons 19 c 1 qtr	197	7	8
Bal carried down	299	16	7	For Blast from engine to refinery at 1/- per ton 738 tons 9 cwts	36	18	4
				On iron made at furnaces No 2 and 4 at 6/- per ton, 1132 tons 10 cwts	339	15	0
				Blast from engine to refinery at 1/- per ton, 129 tons 7 cwts 2 qtr	6	9	4
	938	14	7		938	14	7
				Bal brought down	299	16	7

In this case, Lord Dudley's income was increased by the construction of a steam blast engine owned and worked by the estate; a royalty calculated on the basis of iron worked at the finery (forge) was charged for this service.

Several other furnaces were constructed on the Dudley estate in the period 1774-1800. One was at Coneygre, Tipton where Zachariah Parkes was entitled to erect a blast furnace by a lease of 1794. Parkes was also involved in the construction of a blast furnace at Park Head near the southern entrance of the Dudley Canal Tunnel in 1795.[22] The lessees undertook to erect a furnace within three years and requested the 'priviledge of getting the Ribs and Pillars of Thick Coal found in Sinking for the Ironstone paying 1/1 a ton royalty'. They also requested that the 'time rent' should not be changed for three years. Thomas Brettell, the land agent, saw no objection to the proposed royalty but felt that with regard to the question of rent, 'His Lordship would not approve of so great a latitude being allowed'. This lease was inadequately drawn up and left too many loopholes for the lessees to avoid their obligations.

By 1800, no doubt influenced by Beaumont's[23] work in securing clear, specific and binding mineral leases, the conditions under which new blast furnaces could be erected were more clearly stated. A lease[24] granted to Messrs Attwood in 1800 reflects this trend. In some respects it resembles the early lease granted by the late viscount to Messrs Parker in 1783—in terms of the royalties charged for various minerals and the use of the term 'bloom' to define crude ironstone. However, the 1800 lease stated the royalty per bloom at 3s and defined it as '35 cwts in weight or 36 cubic feet'. Lones' definition suggested a measurement of 24cu ft. As in the case of the Level furnace, £1,500 was to be invested in construction costs, for a 'furnace . . . fire engine [blast] and other necessary buildings'. In addition to these points which were in common with earlier leases, there were conditions and clauses inserted to achieve greater efficiency and profitability. Quarterly accounts had to be presented in writing. No more than 5,000 tons of heathen coal per annum could be extracted under royalty by the lessees—additional supplies of coal had to be purchased from the lessor's adjacent Bumble Hole Colliery in Netherton. A minimum rent of £225 would be charged on ironstone used 'in case Messrs Attwood shall not get 1500 Blooms of ironstone per annum' for each of the two furnaces. All limestone, and any additional minerals used, had to be purchased from Lord Dudley: 'notwithstanding the above, lessees must purchase from Lord Dudley 6 tons of coal for every ton of pig iron they make'. The final condition obligated the lessees to purchase all tiles and bricks used in construction work from Messrs T. W. and M. Grazebrook. As the latter were lessees of Lord Dudley who paid him a royalty on production, this, together with the other conditions, ensured a variety of sources of revenue for Lord Dudley from this enterprise. The last surviving lease from this period refers to a furnace constructed in Dudley by Messrs Parker in 1800.

During the 1820s there was a 50 per cent increase in the number of blast furnaces erected in south Staffordshire. However, these were mainly in Tipton and Bilston. Because of deficient management, Lord Dudley's estate did not participate in this expansion and the main period of development in the iron trade on the estate was much earlier, between 1774 and 1800 in the formative phase of Black Country expansion.

By 1833, the organisation of the iron trade on the Dudley estate had become inefficient, as in the case of agriculture and the limestone quarries, and profits were declining. The Mines Report of 1836 observed that

> there are many Blast Furnaces, Forges, Rolling Mills, and one or two Foundries belonging to the Trust Estate, but . . . they are all under Lease to Tenants at Will . . . most of whom consume Coal, Ironstone, and in some cases even Limestone from Collieries and quarries not belonging to the Trustees.[25]

The loss of revenue to the Dudley estate is indicated by the fact that, to the south of Dudley alone, ironworks on the estate consumed '130,000 Tons of Coals of various descriptions per annum, 16,000 Tons of Limestone and 60,000 Tons of Ironstone' in 1834. It is evident that the carefully worded leases of the early 1800s had not been renewed when they lapsed. This is a further indictment of the slack management of Downing after 1826. Unlike mineral enterprise, the estate did not enter into production on its own account, with the exception of the mill and forge at the Round Oak Store Yard. The store-yard supplied not only timber and bricks to Lord Dudley's mines, but also manufactured all castings and steam engines used in the mines by 1822. However, it functioned as a branch of mineral enterprise rather than a commercial enterprise selling in the open market.

By 1830, the Black Country equalled South Wales and surpassed Shropshire as a centre of finished iron production. Wrought-iron production continued to increase until, by 1850, 600,000 tons per annum or one-third of the national output was made in the Black Country. Pig-iron production expanded by 300 per cent between 1830 and 1858, although Scottish production was expanding more rapidly by mid-century. The number of blast furnaces went up from 123 in 1830 to 175 in 1854 and production of pig iron from 213,000 tons to 743,000 tons over the same period. Associated trades inevitably expanded in the area and an increasing range of manufactured iron goods was produced such as cables, chains and tubes in addition to traditional products. In 1845, the 'principal export' of the district was stated as 'manufactured iron, pig iron and coal'.[26] By that time, there were 135 blast furnaces in the Black Country, of which 100 were in blast, producing 468,000 tons of pig iron. However, during the trust period there were temporary recessions in the general trend, especially in 1842-3 when the number of furnaces in blast fell to 75. There was heavy unemployment in the iron trade and, subsequently, a fall in mineral activity. Nevertheless, at the commencement of the trust, prospects for the trade were good and Downing wrote to Littleton:

> You will rejoice to hear of the returning prosperity of the Iron trade and to know that your old friends the Coal and Ironmasters are now in high spirits at the favourable prospect before them— that the prices and wages have been raised and that the working people have full employment.[27]

This trend was maintained and, in 1835, Smith noted that 'the Iron and Coal Trades are attended with unprecedented prosperity'. Loch acknowledged the situation but sounded a typical note of caution:

> Iron in Staffordshire has got to an extravagant price but I understood at Liverpool that it would be pulled down by a great importation of Scotch pigs.[28]

This general prosperity and temporary recessions were reflected in the price of Staffordshire iron:

1832 pig iron sold at	£3	per ton
1833	£5	10s
1841	£5	
1843	£2	10s
1844	£5	
1850	£2	15s

Bar iron rose more rapidly in price followed by a sharp collapse after 1846:

1833 bar iron sold at	£8	per ton
1845	£18	
1850	£6[29]	

White, writing in 1851, observed that Staffordshire supplied a large proportion of rails used in the period of widespread railway construction between 1835 and 1845 when the 'price of iron rose considerably, but has lately been much reduced'. This expansion in the demand for Staffordshire iron only partly explains the degree of prosperity attained by local ironmasters and, ultimately, by the Dudley estate. Another major factor was the introduction of technical improvements which increased productivity, reduced costs, and improved the quality of the iron.

Blast furnace efficiency was improved by increasing the number of tuyeres from one to three[30] and using a hot blast. This had been developed by Neilson in Glasgow and was introduced into the Black Country during the 1830s. In Scotland, use of a hot blast had produced an

> extraordinary saving in the production of pig-iron ... in 1833, a

ton of pig-iron was made with 2 tons $3\frac{1}{4}$ cwt of raw coal ... in 1829 in the same works, it required 8 tons $1\frac{1}{4}$ cwt of coal to make the same quantity with cold air and coke ... [also] a saving in the quantity of blast required and consequently in engine power as well as the expense of converting coal into coke.

However, in England and Wales, variations in the quality of the coal caused

the saving in English coal to be much less in proportion to the iron made ... it is often used in Staffordshire in the proportion of one third of hot to two of cold air.

The hot blast was first used in south Staffordshire by B. Gibbons at his Corbyn's Hall Iron Works, Kingswinford—although there is some possibility that he may have first used the technique as early as 1830 at the New Level Furnaces which he leased from the Dudley trustees.

Several other technical improvements were developed in the Black Country by local ironmasters. Gibbons re-designed the blast furnace and constructed a round one at Corbyn's Hall to replace the traditional square-based furnace; because of higher temperatures and a greater uniformity of heat, he was able to use puddling furnace cinder to charge his blast furnace—this, although rich in iron, was normally dumped as waste. Joseph Hall of Tipton pioneered the process known as wet puddling or pig boiling by using iron oxides as a bottom lining in the puddling furnace in the 1830s: this improved the quality of wrought iron produced. The mining commissioners inquiring into the economic depression and violence in the area remarked in 1843 that the current low price of iron had led to a search for economy which resulted in the introduction of new ideas for which patents had existed for many years. Among such improvements were the replacement of the traditional huge helve or forge hammer by more modern, efficient equipment and the practice of allowing molten iron to run direct from the blast furnace to the puddling furnace—thus saving the time and expense of casting and re-

K

heating pigs for use in the puddling furnace.[31] As a result of these technological improvements, production costs fell in south Staffordshire: in 1800, ten tons of coal were needed to produce one ton of pig iron and, in 1840, four tons of coal.[32] Productivity per furnace increased by one-third for each firing and overall production of pig and wrought iron expanded rapidly. These developments were reflected in the activities of the Dudley estate during the trust period in terms of technical innovation and increased production—both at ironworks leased from the trustees and managed by the estate, and in terms of an expansion of mineral activity by estate pits to supply the expanding local market for coal, iron ore and limestone.

However, at the outset of the trust, the upturn in fortunes enjoyed by the Black Country iron trade in general was lacking on the Dudley estate because of inefficient administration and short-sighted policies. This state of affairs was clearly revealed in the report on the mines and ironworks—commissioned by the trustees—submitted by Smith and Liddell in 1836.

Unlike the collieries, the blast furnaces, forges and rolling mills on estate property were not worked by the estate before 1836. They were leased 'to parties most of whom consume Coal, Iron-stone, and in cases even Limestone from Collieries and Quarries not belonging to the Trustees'.[33] This situation resulted from the practice of allowing ironworks and collieries to be worked by tenants-at-will or by lessees on terms which failed to secure the best interests of the estate. Whereas the estate had established a dominant position in the local iron trade during the 1790s, through judiciously worded leases, by 1836 it was failing to take advantage of its position even during boom conditions. To overcome this situation, Smith and Liddell suggested that leases should be

granted of a more permanent nature to lessees on condition that they either agree to consume certain quantities of mineral produce per annum or connect with the works certain tracts of Mine, at royalties to be agreed upon with Covenants binding the parties to raise a given number of tons of Coal, Ironstone and Limestone per annum, or pay for the same.

Of the ironworks leased by the estate in 1836, only one was leased on royalty based on the iron produced; the remainder merely paid a fixed rent which did not reflect the increased value of a particular concern. Another major defect of the existing organisation of the mineral and iron trades on the estate was the haphazard nature of mineral and ironworks leases. Although the technological advances of steam power and mineral smelting had enabled all the processes of iron manufacture to take place at one site (prior to this, the location of the forge and the furnace had been dependent on the availability of water power and charcoal fuel), such vertical integration had taken place elsewhere in the Black Country but not on the Dudley estate. This situation would be eradicated under the proposals made by the report.

In the same month that the mines report was submitted, Smith made detailed recommendations concerning the more important leased ironworks, most of which were subsequently carried out after his appointment as mineral agent later in that year. He made the observation that:

> In ordinary times, when the Iron and Coal Trades are not attended with such unprecedented prosperity as they now experience—the former is generally looked upon as an appendage of the latter for the purpose of consuming the Ironstone, Limestone and inferior Coal. The great difficulty of disposing of the refuse Coal which the Staffordshire and Worcestershire Mines produce has given birth to many Iron Works *which would not otherwise have been established*—and which serves to prove that the Capital expended in the erection of such Works, is done more with a view to making the best of the Mines, than for direct advantage to be derived from them independent of the Mines ...[34]

Smith's comment with regard to the establishment of many of the local ironworks is of particular interest in view of the multiplicity of small concerns which had developed in the area and their susceptibility to collapse during periods of recession. These policies were carried out by the trustees and, as Smith forecast, there was an increase in the number of ironworks leased and in the profit derived by the estate from the iron trade.

The Ironworks Leased from the Dudley Estate in 1836

Date	Type of Agreement and Parties	Property Let	Terms
1 Jan 1822	Grazebrook and Whitehouse (now H. B. Whitehouse) Lease	Land at Coseley to erect a furnace (Wallbrook?)	21 years at £37 5s
29 Sept 1825	Small, Shears and Taylor (formerly Attwood) Lease	Dudley Wood Iron Furnaces	Rent of £291 6s
ditto	ditto	Netherton Iron Furnaces, Engine Ware-house etc	Rent of £390
25 Mar 1832	Jones and Barker Lease	Deepfields Iron Furnaces etc	14 years at £150
17 Oct 1833	J. and B. Gibbons, written agreement	2 of the iron furnaces at the New Level	6/- a ton on iron made
31 Jan 1834	ditto	New Level Iron Furnaces	5/- a ton on iron made when more than 2 furnaces at work
25 Mar 1834	Evers and Martin, written agreement	Parkhead Iron Furnace	Rent of £260
25 Mar 1822	Izons and Co, Tenants at Will	Old Level Furnace	Rent of £460
29 Sept 1826	Samuel Evers, Tenant at Will	Cradley Iron Works	Rent of £300
25 Mar 1825	John Gibbons, Tenant at Will	Level Forge and Mill	Rent of £228
29 Dec 1826	Payton and Hopkins, Tenant at Will	Coneygre Iron Furnace	Rent of £250

By 1845, the furnaces at the New Level and the Coneygre Iron Works were being worked by the estate.

A comparison between the list of leased ironworks drawn up by Downing in October 1836[35] for the purpose of providing information to the trustees and the list of some of the major lessees in 1844[36] indicates that several of the established properties had been taken over by larger companies. Two new major projects undertaken by lessees were the Russell's Hall Iron Works, erected by Blackwell and Co, and the Woodside Iron Works, erected by Bramah and Cochrane. The latter works supplied iron for the construction of Crystal Palace.

Production Figures for Leased Ironworks on the Dudley Estates, in Brierley Hill and Dudley, 1844

	Lessee	Total Annual Production	Furnaces
Old Level Furnaces	Izons and Co	12,000 tons capacity (only 1 in blast) 6,000 tons of pig iron)	2
The Level Ironworks	Gibbons and Co	6,000 tons of manufactured iron	
Woodside Furnaces	Bramah and Cochrane	9,100 tons of pig iron	2
Park Head Furnaces	Evers and Martin	5,500 tons of pig iron	
Russell's Hall Furnaces	Blackwell and Co	11,500 tons of pig and castings	2
Holly Hall Foundry	Johnson and Co	1,000 tons of castings	
Dudley Wood Furnaces	British Iron Co	12,500 tons of pig iron	4
Netherton Furnaces	ditto		2
Deepfields Furnaces	E. Pemberton	10,000 tons of pig iron	3
New Level Furnaces	Gibbons and Co to 1843	15,000 tons capacity (not yet in blast)	4

This excludes the blast furnaces in Tipton and numerous small ironworks producing a variety of finished goods throughout the area of the estate.

The total annual income from leased ironworks in 1836, before the report's recommendations were implemented, was £3,184 14s 8d. This was made up of fixed annual rents from seven ironworks manufacturing iron and the two large forges at Cradley and the Old Level: a total rent of £2,366 11s 0d. The remaining income came from the New Level Iron Works and was based on a royalty per ton of iron produced: the amount received by the estate in 1835 was £818 3s 8d. In addition to annual rents after 1836, the trustees also received an income based on a royalty[37] per ton of iron made at the various ironworks and blast furnaces. This was augmented by a charge levied per ton for the supply of blast to the furnaces and forges.

A particularly important feature of the trust period was the increased number of steam engines owned and worked by the estate on leased properties—mines, ironworks and furnaces—from which the estate drew an income which varied according to the profitability of each enterprise. In 1839[38] there were thirteen steam engines owned and worked by the estate at the various ironworks—including Coneygre and the Level Store Yard, both of which were operated by the estate. Six of these were blast engines, three supplied power for rolling or boring mills, three drew materials up inclined planes serving blast furnaces, and one supplied power to a forge. By 1844, the number of blast engines alone had increased to nineteen[39]—no figures are available for other types of engine. These blast engines supplied air to nineteen hot-blast furnaces making a weekly total of 1,885 tons of pig iron; nineteen cold-blast furnaces were also supplied, making 1,319 tons of pig iron per week—a weekly total output of 3,204 tons or an approximate annual production of 166,608 tons. This would represent 35.4 per cent of the total annual Black Country production of 468,000 tons of pig iron in 1844[40]—from 135 furnaces of which 100 were in blast—and indicates the growing significance of the Dudley estate in the local iron trade as a result of the trustees' efforts.

The most significant feature of the period was, however, the involvement of the estate in the manufacturing of pig iron on its own account at Coneygre, after 1839, and at the New Level, after 1844. At the commencement of the trust period, the mines report submitted by Smith and Liddell had made no reference to the possibility of the estate producing pig iron for consumption in the local finished iron trades. Why then did Smith, as manager[41] of mineral and industrial enterprise after December 1836, initiate this development? Presumably the boom in the Black Country pig-iron and wrought-iron industry indicated the advantages of involving the estate in this lucrative development—especially with the trend to higher prices resulting from the railway construction of the 1840s. In 1838, Hawkes-Smith had commented on the boom in the south Staffordshire iron trade:

> there being upwards of 100 furnaces ... and their number is not likely to suffer diminution, as the immense demand for heavy castings for railways, main pipes for gas and waterworks, and other public purposes, promises still, to increase the quantity of iron annually consumed.[42]

This further impetus to the iron trade may have provided the main incentive for Smith to involve the estate in the production of pig iron for the first time since the days of Dud Dudley.[43] The ultimate and logical development, the production of wrought iron for sale to the finishing trades, was not taken until the 1850s when the Round Oak Iron Works were constructed. Circumstances, too, probably played their part because Messrs Payton and Hopkins relinquished the tenancy of Coneygre furnaces in 1839 and B. Gibbons removed his plant from the New Level to Corbyn's Hall Iron Works in 1842. In the case of Coneygre, alterations had already been effected by Messrs Payton and Hopkins after 1835 and the estate assumed control without great capital outlay. At the New Level, it is possible that Smith's attempts to re-negotiate the lease in the interests of the estate led to Gibbons' withdrawal. After the abortive attempt to lease the plant to Bramah and Cochrane, Smith decided to retain control in his own hands. One additional factor indicated the wisdom of the estate once more assuming an entrepreneurial role. This was the fact that by 1845, apart from Lord Dudley, there was only one other ironmaster with an independent supply of raw materials in south Staffordshire.[44] All other ironmasters were dependent on the Dudley estate or on limestone imported from Caldon Low in north Staffordshire or iron ore from Warwickshire.

At Coneygre the two blast furnaces were supplied by coal and iron ore from estate pits at the site and limestone was brought by canal from the mines at Dudley Castle and the Wren's Nest—a distance of about one and a half miles. Average weekly production was 50 tons of cold blast iron per furnace in 1843. Some of the pig iron was sold and the rest was worked in the finery and iron foundry at Coneygre. Customers included the Boulton & Watt ironworks near Birmingham. Improvements were continually being made and, by October 1844, the average total weekly production had increased to 170 tons.[45] Between 1839 and July 1846, total net profit from the Coneygre Works amounted to £15,439 10s 9d—the annual income before 1839 had been a fixed rent of £250. The net profit for 1847 alone was £8,185 11s 10d—this sum is all the more remarkable in view of the fact that by 1847 the railway boom was over and 62 per cent of Staffordshire furnaces were blown out.[46] Gross income for 1847 was derived from:

		£	s	d
Sale of coal		1,297	10	0
Sales of pig iron:	9,447 tons 10cwt	48,600	6	2
Sales of castings:	2,404 tons 15cwt	16,336	3	10

Thomas Holcroft was bailiff at the works until 1846, when he was replaced by Smith's grandson, Edward Fisher Smith, with the position of manager.

The major development in estate enterprise was, however, at the New Level Iron Works on the banks of the Dudley Canal at Brierley Hill. After Gibbons relinquished the lease, the furnaces were reconstructed in 1844-5 and the number reduced to three. However, the increased capacity of each furnace and the higher productivity achieved by use of a hot blast resulted in a total weekly production of 330 tons of pig iron.[47] In addition, a new blast-engine house was constructed, replacing Gibbons' plant, and the engine reservoir was extended. Communications were improved by extending the Kingswinford Railway[48] across Pensnett Chase and over the Dudley Canal. Taking advantage of the fall of land below the line of the canal, the railway was continued to the top of the furnaces and trucks were emptied directly into them, thus saving the expenses of constructing an inclined plane and raising raw materials to the furnace tops. As the line of the first public railway constructed in the area, the Oxford, Worcester & Wolverhampton Railway, also passed beside the ironworks, the New Level had excellent communications with estate mines for raw materials and could reach a much wider area for the marketing of pig iron.

Hot-blast iron was made at these furnaces and also cold-blast iron. There was a regular market for the latter because of its particular qualities for castings requiring great strength and easy machining. The next logical step in the process of integration was to erect a rolling mill and forge to convert the pig iron into wrought iron—this was done by Smith in the 1850s with the construction of the famous Round Oak Iron Works adjacent to the New Level Furnaces. It was unfortunate that the New Level Furnaces were blown in at a time when the Black Country iron trade suffered a temporary recession with the collapse of the railway boom in 1847. In that year, the quantity of pig iron sold was 2,731 tons for £14,468 10s. The manager of the plant was Frederick Smith, son of Richard, and net profit for the year was £990 8s 10d.

The closer integration of the estate as an economic unit and the integration of the estate with the region as a whole proved to be one of the most profitable investments undertaken by the trust. Local prosperity in the iron trade had not been fully reflected in the estate's revenue in 1833; by 1845 the record prosperity of the Black Country iron trade was closely linked to the Dudley estate and the estate itself participated in this boom to the full. In the long run, the role of the estate assumed an even greater significance as the local iron and mineral trades went into decline after 1860.

Peak prosperity was attained during the Crimean War and the Franco-Prussian War when pig-iron production reached 743,000 tons in 1854 and 726,000 tons in 1871—the last occasion when Black Country production passed 700,000 tons. After 1860, however, a fall in output was the general trend and after the brief recovery of the early 1870s, the traditional structure of the local iron trade contracted rapidly. There were many contributory factors to this 'collapse', and the fortunes and policies of the Dudley estate were caught up in the process. In the long run, the area remained a centre for the iron trade, but diversification and the import of finished iron were necessary before the transformation to engineering and finished iron goods could be accomplished.

The main cause of the decline in the traditional Black Country iron trade was the exhaustion of the more productive and the shallower seams of minerals, particularly ironstone. In 1860 it was calculated that local ores were sufficient for forty years but this was far too optimistic as the best seams ran out, or became flooded, long before 1900. Scrivenor noted the growing shortage of local ore to meet the expansion of the local iron trade as early as 1854: 'Is this as regards South Staffordshire, the beginning of the end?'[49] But for the advent of railways, the area would have declined sooner than it did—although the railways were also to hasten the downfall in some respects by the imposition of high freight charges. As early as 1866, the Black Country produced only 50 per cent of the ironstone consumed by the local iron trade, and 300,000 tons of pig iron were annually imported from Wales and Derbyshire in the early 1860s.[50] Later in the century, cheap, quarried iron ore was being imported from Northampton-shire and Oxfordshire. Even local limestone was in short supply and the area had to rely on imports from the Dee valley near Llangollen. As production costs increased, Black Country blast furnaces were blown out. However, the Dudley estate continued to enjoy a privileged position and by 1883 the Earl of Dudley's works were the only ones in the area still making pig iron from local ore. One special feature in this process of decline was that the pig-iron industry declined more rapidly than the wrought-iron sector: in 1856, the area produced 777,000 tons of pig iron—22 per cent of the national total—and in 1860, 470,000 tons—12 per cent of the total production. During the 1860s, the Black Country continued to supply 33 per cent of the national produc-tion of wrought iron because of the heavy concentration of skills in the area and the growing imports of pig iron.

However, the apparent continued prosperity of the wrought-iron industry was also doomed—apart from the fact that its prosperity was, to a large extent, geared to the fortunes of the local pig-iron industry. Technological developments were equally responsible because of the introduction of Bessemer's acid con-verter after 1856. This led to a rapid expansion in the use of cheap mild steel which was increasingly used by the iron industry in preference to wrought iron. The process was not taken up in the Black Country for two reasons: capital costs of converting the existing ironworks would have been prohibitive and local ore was unsuitable because of its high phosphoric content. A few Black Country firms did turn to the production of mild steel—including the Earl of Dudley in the 1890s—but this was after further advances in iron and steel technology following the application of the Gilchrist-Thomas process in 1879. This en-abled local ironstone to be used but came too late for the Black Country in general.

Other factors contributed to the difficulties of the area. One of the main traditional markets for Black Country iron was the United States: however, the financial crisis of 1857 led to the imposition of high import duties which drastically reduced the demand for Black Country iron. Perhaps because of the approaching exhaustion of local minerals, ironmasters were, too, reluctant to invest capital in new plant and machinery. The prevalence of old practices in south Staffordshire, except in a minority of enterprises such as Sir Alfred Hickman's at Bilston, Messrs Cochrane's at Woodside (a tenant of Lord Dudley) and the Dudley estate's works, was condemned in a paper entitled 'Hot Blast and Economy in the Blast Furnace', given to the Staffordshire Iron and Steel Institute in 1884:

> I am quite satisfied that if Staffordshire is to hold her own in the manufacture of pig iron, some further steps will have to be taken to improve her blast furnace practice.

A further disadvantage was the high cost of railway freight: the journals of the institute record the first discussion on the subject in 1885 when proposals were made to improve the Grand Junction Canal, 'One of the only canals that was not held in pawn as it were, by the railway companies', so that steamers of a reasonable size might travel from Birmingham to London. In the same year, the Wolverhampton Chamber of Commerce stated to the Royal Commission on Depression of Trade that:

> The most important circumstance affecting the trade of this district is the unfair, unequal, and excessive railway rates which are charged upon all its productions ... It is served by three ... railways ... and three canals; but instead of these producing the natural effect of competition, the railway companies have bound themselves not to reduce any rates without the consent of each other ... [and] Control of the principal canals has been acquired by the railway companies.[51]

This improvement scheme fell through and, as late as 1896, the journal of the institute observed that 'it cost more to send freight from South Staffordshire to London than from London to Amsterdam'.

In the light of these developments after 1860, the work of the

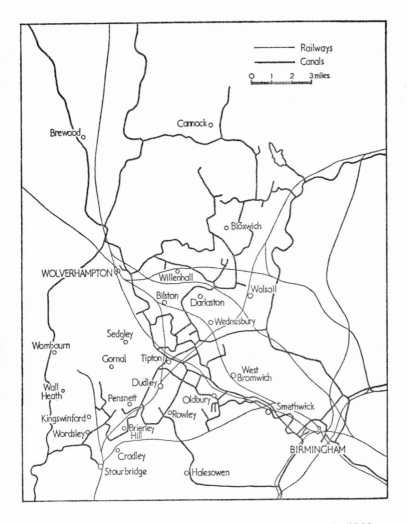

Figure 6   South Staffordshire and the Black Country in 1900

trustees assumes an even greater significance. It was fortunate that the policy of conservation of the minerals was replaced by one of maximum output in 1836 which enabled the estate to work the bulk of the minerals before the local iron trade collapsed. Involving the estate in the production of pig and wrought iron brought considerable profit during the years down to 1880, while the existence of integrated ironworks, able to use the estate's systems of transport, gave an advantage to estate tenants. This probably helped to maintain the level of employment in the area and may have slowed the pace of the decline of the Black Country iron trade. In the 1880s, most of the furnaces in blast were situated west of Dudley where minerals were still available from estate collieries. Many of the tenants were amongst the more progressive ironmasters in the area, but it was during the period of decline that the Earl of Dudley himself attained a leading reputation, both in national and international markets, as a manufacturer of good-quality iron and steel.

This expansion of estate production was carefully balanced by a policy of contraction in capital invested in leased ironworks. The general trend was clear and, as early as 1868, Frederick Smith[52] initiated a policy of selling ironworks with land and working mines attached, so as to enable purchasers to work the enterprise on an integrated basis. Most of the sales at this time were east of the Dudley ridge where the minerals had been worked for a longer period. Two of the more important ironworks sold were the Tipton Iron Works—the earliest mineral blast furnaces established on the Dudley estate as long ago as 1783 —and the Dudley Port Iron Works founded in the 1790s. Both were sold as going concerns with land and mines in November 1868. The rent account for 1871 and 1872[53] illustrates the extent of the contraction of leased pits and ironworks; this account recorded surface rents of leased pits and ironworks. Receipts for 1871 were £29,606 and, in 1872, £8,420; this sharp drop would also be accounted for by the closing of completely worked-out pits. Ironworks west of the ridge continued to flourish where the more productive estate seams remained. These too were eventually sold in the 1880s.

Throughout the period of decline, the Dudley estate increased its overall capital commitment to enterprises owned and managed by the estate, although income and capital in this sector were increasingly concentrated at the Level and Round Oak. Until the trust, integration of estate enterprise had proceeded only as far as the mining and distribution of minerals. The manufacture of pig iron was commenced by the trustees and during the 1850s the process was taken a stage further with the construction of the Round Oak Iron Works designed to convert estate pig iron into wrought iron. Further developments at this site included the construction of a chain works and the manufacture of steel in the 1890s, and, at Coneygre Foundry, the manufacture of castings for the motor trade after 1914.

The beginning of steel manufacturing at Round Oak necessitated additional sources of iron ore being found and, in 1899, the earl negotiated a lease of iron ore at Hook Norton near Chipping Norton where ore could be quarried cheaply and transported direct to the furnaces at the New Level. The lease[54] ran for twenty-one years from 29 September 1899 and the earl paid various royalties per ton of 2,352lb.

Raw ironstone	4d per ton
Calcine ironstone	6d per ton
Building stone and sand	3d per ton
Minimum royalty	£100 for the first year
	£300 for subsequent years
Wayleave	1d per ton of raw stone
	and raw iron ore

This lease was the beginning of a connection between the Dudley estates and the ore quarries of the area which led to the development of a large mining company, Edgehill Ltd, of which the Earl of Dudley was president. Estate quarries and mines were able to supply Round Oak with sufficient limestone and coal until after 1900, but production at the Wren's Nest limestone mines ceased altogether in 1924; limestone had been imported in increasing quantities since 1908. However, estate collieries continued to supply all coal used at the steelworks until nationalisation removed all connections with the Dudley estate.

The fall in demand for wrought iron led to the blowing out of all three furnaces at Coneygre for the first time in 1879. When this recurred in 1895, the estate decided to give up the works and, as there was no bid to lease the enterprise as a going concern, the plant was dismantled and sold in 1896. Minerals and iron had been worked on the Coneygre estate from late medieval times and it was here that the first steam engine had been erected by Newcomen in 1712 to drain Lord Dudley's pits. The foundry continued to produce castings for the earl's engineering works at Castle Mill. During the 1914-18 war, production increased as motor vehicle parts were manufactured for Austins. The foundry was closed down and sold by the earl in April 1925; however, it remained a going concern and is still in operation today.

The other estate enterprise, the Castle Mill Engineering Works, had been established on the Tipton side of the ridge by Richard Smith between 1845 and 1850 to replace the store-yard which had functioned at Round Oak since the 1780s. This took over the construction and repair of steam engines, rails, mining machinery, locomotives, and other equipment formerly carried out at the Level Store Yard and, with the rapid expansion of estate activities, increased the amount of machinery supplied to the estate. It had excellent communications with the whole of the area as the Dudley Canal Tunnel emerged within the property and, after 1854, it was connected by a siding to the Oxford, Worcester & Wolverhampton Railway which enabled estate trucks and engines from the Pensnett & Kingswinford Railway to reach the works. In 1871,[55] Castle Mill supplied machinery worth £24,573 12s 4d to the Dudley estate. Particulars collected by W. D. Curzon for the mines commissioners provide a detailed account of the Castle Mill Works at the peak of activity in 1882: they were

connected to the G.W.R. with a siding from Dudley Station and
... fully adapted to the requirements of His Lordship's Mining
Estate ... consisting of fitting, turning and erecting shops with
first class machines by Whitworth, Nasmyth, Glasgow, and
Hutton and Macdonald all driven by 15 H.P. horizontal engines.
There is a large smiths' shop—3 double and 2 single hearths,
cranes and 10 cwt steam hammer: extensive iron, oil, chain and
pattern stores: large carpentry and wheelwrights' shop: locomotive erecting and wagon building shed containing double sets
of rails with back and front entrances: oliver shops and boiler
sheds: shoeing shops: hinge, round and flat chain shops: with
convenient general and drawing offices. These works afford
employment for about 120 men. The whole of the plant on the
estate has been made and maintained at these works.[56]

This was a remarkable enterprise which established a reputation
for a high quality of workmanship in many fields. It was leased
to the Round Oak Works in 1924 and remained a property of the
Dudley estate until the break-up of the local estates in 1947. The
earl retained a financial connection with the property which now
operates as the British Federal Welding Company.

Increasingly after 1845, there was a policy of concentrating
the estate's interests in the iron trade at Round Oak where
eventually, by 1890, pig and wrought iron, heavy wrought-iron
manufactures, and steel were all made by the estate. This process
of integration had begun in the last years of the trust when
Richard Smith had reconstructed, enlarged and modernised the
blast furnaces at the New Level Iron Works. In 1855 the process
of integration was carried to its logical conclusion when the
Round Oak Iron Works was constructed beside the recently
completed Oxford, Worcester & Wolverhampton Railway, on the
opposite side of the canal from the New Level Furnaces. An
incline was built from the furnace hearths up to the level of the
canal and the trucks of pig iron were hauled up by a stationary
winding engine. From here, locomotives conveyed them across
the canal by another bridge to the new ironworks for the manufacture of high-grade finished bar iron. Compared with other

L

Black Country ironworks, the scale of this undertaking was enormous: it contained twenty-eight puddling furnaces, two hammers, two forge-trains, and five mills. The new Dudley enterprise was almost twice as large as the average ironworks and employed 600 men when it commenced operations in August 1857. Many local ironmasters regarded this development with anxiety as it was acknowledged that 'these works will be the best in the district both for design and construction, as well as in the character and quality of the apparatus employed'.[57]

Apart from the fact that Round Oak would directly promote estate interests by providing a market for estate minerals and pig iron in the production of finished iron at minimum cost, Richard Smith always asserted that he had the interests of the Black Country iron trade in general at heart when promoting the new works. This may well be true because the introduction of the hot blast in the 1830s, while reducing production costs, had enabled low-grade ore to be used which resulted in a poorer quality of iron. In its obituary on Smith, the *Dudley Herald* asserted that:

> Mr Smith has frequently stated at public meetings that these works were erected for the purpose not of competing with the other iron masters of the district but of maintaining the character of South Staffordshire for good iron ... Specimens of iron made at these works were exhibited ... at the International Exhibition at London [1862] for which he was awarded a gold medal.[58]

The paper also quoted a prominent metallurgist, Dr Percy, who had criticised the poor quality of iron made in Britain at the time:

> the Earl of Dudley's magnificent collection at the International Exhibition ... was the only one which worthily sustained—I may say vindicated—the reputation of this country in the estimation of the world.

Because of the scale of the enterprise—a fourth furnace was added in 1868—four grades of bar iron together with hot- and cold-blast pig iron were produced. The highest grade of bar iron was made from cold-blast pig and soon became acknowledged as a superior quality which commanded a premium price. Production had begun in 1857 at a difficult time because of the slump in trade following the Crimean War. However, as demand increased, Frederick Smith extended the Round Oak Works between 1865 and 1868. A fourth furnace, two forges and twenty-six puddling furnaces were added and productive capacity was increased to 550 tons of finished iron per week. Richard's grandson, Edward Fisher Smith, pursued a similar policy of expansion and added a fifth furnace at the New Level in 1877. The last additions, before the conversion of the ironworks to steel production after 1892, were made in 1889 when number one furnace was modernised, and a chain works was constructed. When operations began in 1891, it was capable of producing fifty tons of chain and cable per week and a three-year contract was received from the Admiralty. The probable reason for the expenditure on increased capacity was the desire to work as great a quantity of estate minerals as possible before the local and national markets for wrought iron disappeared altogether. In fact, after 1877, the productive capacity of the New Level Blast Furnaces outran the production of bar iron at the Round Oak Iron Works and increasing quantities of cold-blast pig iron were sold under the famous brand of 'DUD LN Fces' (Dudley New Level Furnaces).

However, it was on the basis of the wrought iron produced at Round Oak that the reputation of the Dudley estate as a manufacturer of high-grade finished iron was established—especially after the triumph at the London Exhibition in 1862. In the 1860s Round Oak supplied iron for the construction of early ironclads such as HMS *Achilles* and the Admiralty contract was retained throughout the century. Local and overseas markets in America, Japan, China and Russia were supplied with Round Oak iron in an increasing variety of forms including bars, angle-iron, rods, plates, girders, nuts and bolts. As the manufacture of local pig iron fell, the estate supplied increasing quantities of pig

iron to the larger wrought-iron manufacturers, the biggest of
which was the Bloomfield Iron Works of William Barrows &
Sons. Although this enterprise had no minerals or blast furnaces
of its own, its productive capacity was 1,000 tons of finished iron
per week—the highest in the area.[59] The reputation for high-
grade cold-blast pig iron was based upon the use of the best local
ore and sulphurless thick coal from estate pits. After being pro-
cessed at the Round Oak Iron Works, four grades of wrought-iron
bars were sold under the brand name of L 'Crown' WRO (Lord
Ward Round Oak): these were 'ordinary marked bars', 'best',
'best best' and 'triple best'. Because of superior quality, marked
bars from Round Oak were always sold at 12s 6d per ton over
the price of other Black Country producers.

Surviving records do not give a clear picture of the profitability
of the various enterprises at the Level and Round Oak. However,
there is some indication of receipts for the boom years of 1854
and 1871, and for 1889, the last full year in which the Round Oak
Iron Works operated under that name. Coneygre Iron Works—
consisting of a foundry and three blast furnaces—made a net
profit of £9,264 1s 0d in the year ending December 1854[60] and
the Level New Furnaces made a profit of £10,936 14s 10d. The
corresponding figures for 1871[61] were, for Coneygre, a net profit
of £78,743 14s 8d and for the New Level, £73,654 6s 5d. Total
net profit from all the ironworks operated by the estate, including
leased ironworks, was £315,825 3s 11d. Production figures for
estate enterprises reflect the boom of 1871 and the declining
demand for finished iron when this trend was resumed in 1872.
Falling figures for the production of estate finished iron, ironstone and limestone all indicate the trend which assumed the
proportions of a rapid 'collapse' in the local iron trade between
1875 and 1882.

During the 1880s,[62] production at the Dudley ironworks continued to decline but they did remain in operation at a time when
higher production costs were forcing many closures in the district. From a total of 37,642 tons of pig iron produced at

Dudley Estate, 1871

	Fitting Shops		Coneygre		New Level Furnaces		Round Oak Ironworks	
Production	*Tons*	*Cwts*	*Tons*	*Cwts*	*Tons*	*Cwts*	*Tons*	*Cwts*
Pig Iron	—	—	19,919	10	17,722	10	—	—
Finished Iron	—	—	—		—		22,347	—
Castings	—	—	2,561	12	452	3	—	—
	£ s d		*£ s d*		*£ s d*		*£ s d*	
Receipts	24,573 12	4	91,325 6	0	83,420 9	4	209,313 5	0
Stores sold	—	—	1,528 15	11	757 15	8	8,823 18	10
Total receipts	24,573 12	4	92,854 1	11	84,178 5	0	218,137 3	10
Payments								
Wages	8,209 1	0	8,984 16	7	7,613 3	11	37,806 10	4
Salaries	873 0	0	404 6	0	252 12	0	2,334 14	0
Tradesmen	8,135 10	0	4,721 4	8	2,658 2	8	21,924 18	0
	17,217 11	0	14,110 7	3	10,523 18	7	62,066 2	4
Net Income	7,356 1	4	78,743 14	8	73,654 6	5	156,071 1	6

Total Net Income: £315, 825 3s 11d (including leased ironworks)

Mineral Production in 1871: figures in brackets for 1872

	Dudley Estate	Black Country
Coal	1,189,980 tons (1,193,218)	(9,000,000)
Ironstone	101,832 (63,767)	(642,000)
Limestone	102,201 (71,986)	
Fireclay	14,868 (16,855)	
Iron Production		
Pig Iron	37,642 (37,927)	
Finished Iron	22,347 (16,936)	

Estate Mineral Income (Net)

	£	s	d
Estate Pits	141,680	14	1
Royalty	26,146	3	2
	167,826	17	3

Coneygre and the New Level in 1871, production fell to 30,718 tons in 1880 and 17,716 tons in 1886. Two other developments were associated with this decline as demand for wrought iron was replaced by demand for mild steel. Production of pig iron came to be concentrated at the New Level and increasing stocks of iron built up. This led to the closure and disposal of the Coneygre blast furnaces in 1895, the introduction of an experimental open-hearth steel furnace at Round Oak in 1888, and the foundation of a public company in 1890 to convert the bulk of production at Round Oak from wrought iron to steel, using pig iron which the earl continued to supply from the New Level Furnaces.

The time had come for a change of policy as net profit on the Round Oak Iron Works had declined to £15,489 6s 4d in 1889.[63] It is possible that the second earl decided to sell the works rather than attempt to construct a new enterprise under the management of the estate because of the risks involved. The iron and steel trades in general were depressed at this time and, apart from coal, raw materials would have to be imported to Round Oak in increasing quantities. However, a public company was prepared to undertake the risk and use the name, goodwill, and brands of the existing ironworks in an attempt to establish a similar reputation for high-grade steel. Ultimately, through force of circumstances, the new enterprise was to be repossessed as part of the Dudley estate and remained so until the nationalisation of steel in 1951.

The company was formed to take over the existing Round Oak Iron Works under the new name of the Earl of Dudley's Round Oak Iron and Steel Works on 15 September 1890. Details of the value and market of the existing ironworks were set out in the prospectus of the company issued in April 1890. The declared intention of the company was to continue to maintain the sale of iron under existing brands but to concentrate production on the manufacture of steel 'of which the higher grades are in great demand'. Because of the adverse conditions of the time, the company took the precaution of having the venture underwritten by the Lancashire Trust and Mortgage Insurance Corporation Ltd before inviting subscriptions for share capital worth £202,000. Because of the high reputation of the earl's brands of iron, valuable markets had been established:

> they are in favour with the British and Indian and Foreign Governments, as well as with the chief Engineering Firms and Railway Companies at Home and Abroad ... and command the highest price.

In addition, a three-year contract had been won in 1889 to supply the Admiralty with chain and cable from the recently erected chainworks at Round Oak. Although he was selling the Round Oak Iron Works, the earl would maintain a link by selling pig iron, produced by the estate blast furnaces at the New Level, 'on terms which the Directors regard as favourable'. He also undertook to supply fuel

> for a period of 30 years on the lowest terms upon which fuel of the like description may for the time being be sold by His Lordship for similar purposes in the neighbourhood and to deliver it into the works at a fixed rate of 6d a ton, which is to include truck, Line and other charges.

The value of the 'machinery, buildings, railways, sidings, brands, goodwill, the valuable concession made by His Lordship, freehold and favourable situation' was estimated at £190,000 by W. Blakemore, who was engaged by the Lancashire Insurance Corporation Ltd. It was in the earl's interest to offer reasonable trading terms for his pig iron and coal as he still possessed considerable quantities of minerals in the area and selling in an assured local market would produce the highest profit margin for the estate, which was geared to supply Round Oak by its private railway network. The purchase price was agreed at £160,000 of which the earl received £60,000 in cash, £50,000 remained on mortgage and £50,000 remained 'on mortgage or Mortgage

Debentures at his Lordship's option'. Both securities carried an annual interest of 5 per cent and the principal sum was to be reduced by yearly instalments of £5,000 commencing in January 1893. Blakemore estimated the cost of a new basic steel plant at £50,000 and that net profit in future would be £41,000. Estimated annual production would be 56,800 tons of steel at £5 per ton, 21,600 tons of finished iron, 2,400 tons of cables and 1,200 tons of steel strip.

The early optimism of the prospectus was undermined by the first report to the directors submitted on 14 September 1892.[64] Prominence was given to the growing demand for Round Oak chains and the negotiating of second contracts with the Admiralty and the Mersey Dock and Harbour Board. But the main object of the company, the manufacture and sale of steel bars and strip, was not progressing satisfactorily. The most remunerative sector remained the production of 'the celebrated brand of L. "Crown" WRO iron and Directors hope for an increase of this business in the future'. A new contract for this product had just been made with the India Office. In view of the depressed state of trade, the share capital subscribed amounted to only £135,000 and this explains the lack of progress, before September 1892, in erecting the new steelworks. This undertaking, when finally completed, consisted of three open hearth basic furnaces, one cogging mill, and one finishing mill. The first steel was tapped in August 1894; three months later, the company went into liquidation. As the mortgagee, the second earl once more assumed control of the ironworks and chainworks together with the newly constructed steelworks. Until 1897, these were all managed on the traditional basis from the Priory Office by the earl's cousin and general manager, Gilbert Claughton.

After considerable debate on the question of what should be done with the enlarged enterprise—whether to sell it or continue to operate the plant under the direct control of the estate—a compromise policy was decided upon. A new company was established in 1897, The Earl of Dudley's Round Oak Works Ltd, and all the share capital, £100,000, was held by members of the Dudley family. A new managing director, G. Hatton, who was experienced in the manufacture of steel, was appointed and the chairman was Gilbert Claughton. Under vigorous management, the new enterprise overcame the disastrous start of the late public company, and production increased as a reputation for the manufacture of steel, comparable to that for wrought iron, was established after 1900. The lease of iron ore at Hook Norton was negotiated in 1899 to maintain the supply of raw materials. Productive capacity was increased by the installation of larger and more modern open-hearth furnaces in 1907, and production costs were reduced by the construction of a railway to carry molten pig from the blast furnaces directly to the steel furnaces. A slag-grinding plant was installed in 1905 to utilise the basic slag.

Several experimental processes[65] were pioneered at the earl's works such as the manufacture of 4 per cent silicon steel in open-hearth furnaces; this was in great demand for electrical transformers and, after patenting it, the process was used by other steelworks who paid royalty to the Round Oak Works. Other innovations were the manufacture of Edrow Rust Resisting Steel, and modifications to gas producers. Of particular value was the licence obtained to operate the Bertrand-Thiel process: this was developed in Austria, and was used by only two works in Britain, Round Oak and the Brymbo Steel Works. Both companies purchased the right to operate this process which increased the weekly output of the furnaces by a third. Among the more valuable contracts awarded to Round Oak before 1914 was one to supply steel for the construction of the Victoria and Albert Museum and for the Calcutta Port Pier. A particularly specialised branch of the steel trade in the Midlands was dominated by Round Oak: this was the supply of rolls to manufacturers of steel. Round Oak chain was still supplied to the Admiralty and after the Trinity House contract was awarded to the company, the largest chains in the world were manufactured here, and there was a resident inspector until the demand for chain declined in the 1920s.

The works continued to flourish until the post-war slump which closed down all but four of the local furnaces. This reduced income to the point where there was insufficient capital to finance a policy of modernisation: it was this situation which, in 1923-4, produced a radical reorganisation[66] in the management of estate affairs and the influx of outside capital to finance the improvements. Share capital was increased from £100,000 to £600,000 and an immediate loan of £252,000 was negotiated. Under the chairmanship of Viscount Ednam (the late earl), the works were modernised and extended and continued to flourish. Ownership of the property by the Dudley estate ceased when the works were

Production of Pig Iron and the Total of Blast Furnaces
in the Black Country, 1740-1939

	Total	In Blast	Pig Iron Produced	Puddling Furnaces in Operation
1740	2	—	2,000 tons (1717)	
1788	6	—	4,500	
1796	14	—	13,210	
1806	42	—	49,000	
1823	84	—	—	
1827	95	—	216,000	
1830	123	—	213,000	
1840	135	116	364,000	(1839)
1844	135	100	468,000	
1852	159	127	743,000	(1854)
1860	181	108	396,000	(1861)
1865	—	—	693,000	2,155
1867	—	—	516,000	
1870	171	114	726,000	(1871)
1880	137	46	326,000	(1879)
1886	107	28	293,000	(1887)
1894c.	58	20	250,000	683
1905c.	40	—	190,000	
1913	30	20	467,000	661
1922	29	4	—	
1939	—	13	300,000	
1952	5	5	—	

nationalised in 1951; after denationalisation in 1953 they were valued at almost £6 million and were taken over by Tube Investments Ltd. This finally severed the link between the estate and the manufacture of iron which had flourished at the Level since the 1770s.

Mineral Output of the Black Country, 1800-1950

	Coal	Ironstone
1800	840,000 tons	60,000 tons
1850	5,000,000	—
1855	7,323,000	—
1859	4,450,000	785,000 (1860)
1865	9,000,000	660,000
1872	9,000,000	642,000
1887	6,000,000	110,000
1900	4,500,000	51,000
1913	3,000,000	32,000
1950	900,000	Nil

Notes to Chapter 5 are on pages 253-7

CHAPTER SIX

Mineral Exploitation

Limestone

As the regional economy developed, the deposits of limestone[1] at Dudley Castle Hill, Wren's Nest and Sedgley were more intensively exploited as a source of lime for agricultural purposes and for limestone as a flux in the blast furnaces; the right of ownership gave the Dudley estate a virtual monopoly in the local supply of these commodities. Particular geological features of the limestone outcrops determined the mining techniques resorted to. The two vertical beds of upper and lower Wenlock Limestone were quarried along the eastern line of the hill. On the western slopes, the upper bed was quarried and the lower bed was mined by a pillar and stall method whereby the limestone was followed downwards into the ground leaving pillars of stone to support the inclined roof. This bed was worked downwards until the working reached the level of the canal tunnels driven into the limestone from the Castle Mill Basin on the Dudley Castle Canal Tunnel. Ironmasters preferred the upper bed as its qualities provided a more satisfactory flux; both beds of limestone could, however, be used for agricultural or industrial purposes.

The estate worked all the limestone mines and quarries before 1795 but, because of falling profits and technical difficulties,

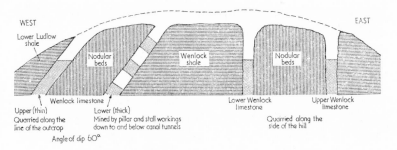

WEST | EAST

Lower Ludlow shale

Nodular beds

Wenlock shale

Nodular beds

Wenlock limestone

Lower Wenlock limestone

Upper Wenlock limestone

Upper (thin)
Quarried along the line of the outcrop

Lower (thick)
Mined by pillar and stall workings down to and below canal tunnels

Quarried along the side of the hill

Angle of dip 60°

Figure 7   A section through Wren's Nest Hill

Lord Dudley decided to lease some of the workings to Charles Norton and other local limestone merchants:

> I am sorry to see that the net profits gradually decline and that his Lordship will be disappointed in his expectation of their produce of £3,000 a quarter. There is a very great devaluation indeed in the Lime Account but this Mr Norton's Contract will in future remedy.[2]

Norton circularised the local market in a bid to increase the sale of limestone:

> Wren's Nest Hill Limeworks. Chas Norton begs leave to acquaint the public that there will be a regular supply of Lime at 3/6 per Quarter of nine Winchester Bushells and to prevent Impositions, each Quarter shall weigh 800 weight at six score to the hundred to be weighed at the Machine erected at the Works and to be paid for on delivery or at the end of every 3 Months.[3]

Other limestone leases were concluded between 1796 and 1800 in addition to the arrangement with Norton. All of them were sound[4] and designed to produce a considerable income for Lord Dudley and efficient exploitation of the mines and quarries.

One lease granted at this time was a new arrangement[5] with Norton, Fereday and Turton in 1800 to work all the quarries and mines worked at that time by Norton. These were the workings originally developed by Lord Dudley after 1775 from Castle Mill and extended after 1786 by canal tunnels into the eastern side of Castle Hill and along the line of the lower limestone measure towards the southern end of Wren's Nest Hill. The 1800 lease was the most extensive granted by the Dudley estate and covered all quarries at Shirt's Mill Tunnel (Castle Mill), Mons Hill Tunnel (at the southern end of Wren's Nest) and the two northern strata at Wren's Nest Hill. It was a particularly difficult undertaking because 'using all existing railways, wharfs, canals, cuts, aqueducts, levels, kilns etc', the lessees had to extend the canal tunnels already cut from the Dudley Canal Tunnel at Castle Mill into the eastern side of Castle Hill and towards the Wren's Nest Hill, and work the limestone deposits along the northern slopes of the hill. This involved working the lower deposit by pillar and stall down to the canal level (about 300ft), extending the canal, and quarrying the upper deposit at the same time. Safeguards were included in the lease to ensure the efficiency of the operations:

> Levels and Cuts must be made in a workmanlike manner so as to convey Boats and other Vessells from the face of the Work with full lading . . . [and] at the end of the Lease to yield up all Cuts or Canals in . . . a perfect navigable state and brought up to within 30 yards of the face of the Work.

It is significant that these particular lessees were allowed to 'dispose of all the Limestone . . . by Water Sale only'. Other lessees were obliged to sell limestone 'land sale' and it is evident that Lord Dudley used his monopoly to prevent a free market in the distribution of limestone to local markets. A minimum of 45,000 tons was to be sold yearly at a royalty of 2s per ton: this would produce an income of at least £4,500 for Lord Dudley. The price of limestone was not to exceed 4s 3d a ton 'into the boats' and the lessees had to raise amounts over 45,000 tons to supply iron furnaces on Lord Dudley's estate at Kingswinford, Dudley, and Sedgley which Lord Dudley was 'under contract to supply at the present price of 4s 6d into the Boats or Waggons'.

Lime was to be sold at 9s 4d per ton. The lease was to run for two years only, probably to allow Lord Dudley to amend it, if necessary, in response to market conditions and prices.

Some of the limestone workings remained under the direct management of the estate. The leases alone would produce a minimum of £7,500 per annum in royalties on 85,000 tons of limestone. Over the years, the scale and complexity of the workings increased. The canal tunnel to Wren's Nest cut the hill in an east-west direction and, eventually, an underground basin 210ft long and 25ft wide was constructed 300ft below the surface. Limestone was brought to this basin along railways running to the northern and southern sides of the canal, and following the line of the upper and the lower seams, both above and below the level of the canal itself.

However, limestone enterprise, as in the case of agriculture and collieries, became less profitable and was inefficiently managed by 1833. In their report on Lord Dudley's mines presented in 1836, Smith and Liddell provided a detailed account of the state of the limestone workings after fifty years of intensive exploitation. In general, the quarries and mines 'fully manned, would supply almost unlimited demand'. Many lay idle in 1836. Parts of the Wren's Nest workings had been carelessly engineered so that the roof had fallen in blocking the access between various stalls (areas worked between the supporting pillars or ribs) and the canal tunnel so 'cutting off the supply of stone and destroying the communication for ever between the wall of Stone and the place of export'.[6] By 1836, workings extended several hundred yards from the line where the canal cut the southern end of Wren's Nest Hill—but at varying levels: some workings were above canal level, others along the same level, and there were deeper workings at three levels below the canal. All water above canal level was fed into the canal tunnels by a series of adits, while steam engines pumped water from the lower workings into the canal. This arrangement served the dual purpose of draining the mines and maintaining the water level in the Dudley Tunnel where it cut through the watershed of the Sedgley–Dudley ridge. A total of sixteen stalls was being worked at the Wren's Nest and a further four at Hurst Hill, Sedgley—the latter were connected by a railway to the Birmingham Canal at Deepfields.

It is evident that although the scale of existing operations was considerable, the limestone mines were not working to full capacity and were inefficiently managed:

> We observed in our survey much inconvenience and some loss by a perseverance in the old System of Rail Roads [probably plates] still practised throughout the Limestone Quarries where the gradual introduction of rails of more modern construction, and Wagons of better gear would enable the Workmen to convey the Stone from the respective forefields [working faces] to the pit Shafts or Canal Boats ... with greater facility, and render unnecessary the present loss of level in working the Stalls which we presume has been done by the Workmen to relieve themselves in propelling the loaded Waggons over these defective roads by manual labour.[7]

In defence of his management of affairs, Francis Downing, the chief mineral agent, submitted his own observations on the mines report to the trustees:

> the Railways now in use are proved by experience to be best suited to the purposes they are used for and much less expensive than the modern construction here referred to.[8]

This was typical of his casual and conservative approach to the problems of mineral enterprise. Further evidence of this attitude is provided by the report's criticism of marketing arrangements in 1836 which were considered inadequate to meet growing competition from more distant limestone sources:

> The present depression ... is principally occasioned by great competition ... from the introduction into this district of the Mountain Limestone from Caldor-low in the Northern part of Staffordshire, the Walsall Quarries now very extensive, the

Sedgley Beacon Stone Pits, and from the recent discovery of
Limestone at Dudley Port [Tipton] ... on the banks of the Birmingham Canal, where the Upper bed of Stone only is worked
which is generally considered by Iron Masters preferable to the
Lower Bed, as a flux in smelting Iron Ore.[9]

Both beds of stone were worked at Lord Dudley's undertaking
'and each Customer is required to take such Stone as may fall to
his Lot, whether the quality is suitable to his purposes or not'.
Two-thirds of the limestone sold by the Dudley estates in 1836
was from the lower seams and some ironmasters working furnaces
on the estate west of Dudley were even purchasing limestone
'conveyed from Dudley Port, past a part of the Limestone Works
of the Trustees [at Castle Mill]'. The report recommended an
increase in working the upper beds of limestone and a guarantee
that ironmasters would receive only the best quality of stone.
This would increase the market for Lord Dudley's limestone
and allow him to increase the price of his limestone from 4s 6d
per ton to 5s per ton—the price charged for upper limestone at
the Dudley Port quarries.

It is not clear at what point the estate had begun to work the
limestone quarries and mines again, but it may have been as early
as 1808, when all the leases negotiated before 1800 had expired.
Nevertheless, in spite of managerial deficiencies, the limestone
workings sold lime and limestone worth £13,509 9s in 1834; but
as working costs amounted to £11,356 the net profit would be
far less than that enjoyed by the third viscount in the 1790s. It
was the efforts of the trustees which revived and expanded the
enterprise and profitability of the limestone workings after 1833.

After Downing was replaced by Smith as mineral agent in
December 1836, the trustees implemented all the policies recommended by the report. Internal transport within the limestone
workings was improved by the purchase of wrought-iron rails,
costing £412 11s 8d from John Bradley and Co at Shut End.
This would represent a considerable length of track and the rails
were used to replace the old plate-ways in the limestone work-

M

ings. The demand for lime in the agricultural and building markets was met by an increase in the number of lime works leased by the estate. In 1836, four were listed in Downing's record of mineral and ironwork leases.[10] By 1846,[11] three more had been added. Of these, the largest was the Ashwood Lime Works lease, leased to John Simpson in 1839 for fourteen years, at a rent of £45 per annum. This concern supplied lime for agricultural purposes in the farming areas west of the Black Country along the line of the Staffordshire & Worcestershire Canal. Another increased source of income came from the supply of limestone bricks (blocks) and quarries to the building trade. Such lessees paid a royalty on production in addition to a ground rent. Typical royalties were those paid by Daniel Hughes in 1847:

Hurst Hill: Bricks,	156,400 at 2/- (per 1,000)	£15 12s 10d
Wrens Nest: „	157,000 at 2/- (per 1,000)	£15 14s
Wrens Nest: Quarries	51,301 at 2/6 (per 1,000)	£6 8s 5d

The main recommendation of the report—that the productivity of the thin or upper limestone workings should be increased and that this commodity should be sold separately to the ironmasters—was also implemented. Sections of the limestone workings were leased to chartermasters who cut and brought out the stone, for distribution by the estate from its wharves at Castle Mill and Deepfields, in return for a charter or payment by the estate per ton of stone mined. In the case of the collieries, Smith introduced royalties which were paid to the estate per ton of minerals worked by ironmasters who mined coal and ironstone which they either marketed or used in their own furnaces and forges.[12] The charter per ton was reduced in 1843 as demand for limestone fell because of the depression in the Black Country iron trade which began in 1842. For some time before the end of 1842, the charter paid to the twelve chartermasters engaged in working sections of the thin beds had been fixed at between 2s 2d and 2s 5d per ton depending on the nature of the stall or section being worked. Because of the depression, these payments were reduced to between 1s 9½d and 1s 11d per ton by April 1843. Seven chartermasters were engaged in working the thick limestone in 1842 and the charter paid varied from 1s 10d to 2s 0d. This fell to its lowest point in April 1843, ranging from 1s 6½d to 1s 8d. Offices and weighing machines were erected by the estate to supervise and check the activities of the various lessees and chartermasters. No fewer than seven weighing machines were built at the Wren's Nest and Castle Mill lime works and two more at Hurst Hill. Additional steam engines were constructed and, by 1839,[13] eleven were in operation at the various limestone workings.

Throughout the period of the trust, the bulk of the production came from the Wren's Nest and Castle Hill workings; the quarries at Hurst Hill supplied only about 13 per cent of the total output in 1834 and had virtually ceased operations by 1845, except for building material, because the accessible seams were exhausted. Downing's accounts for the year ending in December 1834 indicate an improvement: total receipts were £13,956 17s 5d and total costs, £10,419 15s 4d.[14] The limestone produced was 74,267 tons 16cwt and, in addition, 2,951 tons of lime were sold. Smith's figures supplied to the commission of inquiry for the proposed Oxford, Worcester & Wolverhampton Railway demonstrate the consumption of limestone by blast furnaces in the Black Country in 1844[15]: out of a total of 110,914 tons no less than 92,164 tons came from the Dudley estate's mines and quarries at the Wren's Nest and Castle Hill. The latter figure would largely represent the upper, thin limestone mined for use in the iron trade and would not take account of production by estate mines to supply blast furnaces not adjacent to the proposed line. It also excludes limestone mined from the lower, thick beds to supply the building trade and agriculture. Dudley Castle and Mons Hill limestone came from mines and quarries owned and worked by the Dudley Estate. The list below includes most of the leading ironworks in the Tipton, Dudley, and Brierley Hill area.

Sources of Limestone Supplied to Ironworks Within the Black Country, 1844

Ironworks	Source:	Dudley Castle	Dudley Port	Froghall	Walsall
Oak Farm		3,500 tons pa		2,500	
James Foster's		1,550	7,450		
Corbyn's Hall		6,000		2,000	
Corbyn's Hall New Furnaces		14,500			
Ketley's		6,500			
The Lays		c 8,000			
Brettell Lane		3,000			
Old Level		2,800			
New Level		Not in blast			
Woodside		6,000			
Ashwood Basin Limeworks		3,148			
Parkfields		4,500		2,500	2,000
Prior Field		8,500			
Ettingshall		1,200		2,300	
Bovereaux		2,525			
Tipton	(Mons Hill)	4,500			
Park Head		4,252			
Russell's Hall		6,320			
Blower's Green		5,329			
Stourport		40			
		92,164	7,450	9,300	2,000
	Gross Total	110,914			

The estate had evidently reasserted control of the iron trade's supply of limestone in much of the Black Country and defeated the challenge from Walsall, Dudley Port, Caldon Low and elsewhere for the time being. The supply of lime is also excluded from Smith's list—with the exception of limestone sold to Ashwood Lime Works.

Surviving accounts[16] for 1847 provide an accurate indication of the improved state of the limestone workings:

	Tons	Cwts	£	s	d
To Sales on Credit: Limestone	182,976	18	42,331	2	1
„ „ „ „ Lime	2,383	8½	1,307	18	8
			43,639	0	9

		Tons	Cwts	£	s	d
To Sales for Cash:	Limestone	1,063	9	185	17	1
„ „ „ „	Lime	1,090	18	593	12	4
				44,418	10	2
			Net profit	£14,349	1	7

The actual selling price of limestone had fallen to 3s 5d per ton cash or 4s 0d per ton on credit, probably the result of the 1847 depression in the iron trade. Lime sold at 10s 9d and 11s 0d per ton respectively: the lower rate for cash sales was to induce iron-masters and other customers to pay their debts promptly. The reduction in prices suggests that the Dudley estates recovered their predominance of the limestone market in the local iron trade not only by greater efficiency, guaranteed quality and increased productivity but also by more competitive prices. Moreover, a comparison between the gross income and net profit for 1834 and 1847 shows that real profitability of the limestone workings in terms of net income and gross income had also increased from 25.3 per cent in 1834 to 32.3 per cent in 1847. The total net profit for the period from 1 January 1837 (when Smith's accounts commenced) to 27 July 1846 was £75,092 4s 8d—an average of £9,344 per annum as compared with the net profit of £3,537 for 1834.

There is no doubt that the trustees amply fulfilled their task of reinvigorating the limestone interests of the Dudley estate during the period 1833-45 and that their success was closely linked to their general policies with regard to the iron and mineral trades both on the estate and in the locality as a whole. The fame of the Dudley limestone workings was considerable. In December 1843 they were visited by the Duke of Bordeaux and, in September 1849, by the British Association for the Advancement of Science; while in the following year sections of the finished workings were opened to the public after the installation of gas lighting.

After the trust period, output remained at a high level until

the last boom in the Black Country iron trade in 1871, when the
Dudley limestone workings produced 102,201 tons. Thereafter
local demand declined with the fall in pig-iron production
because of the collapse of the wrought-iron industry. Limestone
sold by estate pits and quarries fell from 62,784 tons in 1893 to
37,661 tons in 1905. Production ceased in 1924 except for a
short-lived attempt from 1935 to 1944 to operate quarries at
Wren's Nest as a source of roadstone.

Coal and Ironstone

If the wrought-iron trade was the main regulator of economic
development in the Black Country, the ownership of vast reserves
of coal was the greatest single source of estate income from the
late eighteenth century until the 1920s. Estate mineral enterprise
did not conform to the usual pattern in two important respects.
The scale of each enterprise and the manner of working the pits
differed from other Black Country enterprises. Secondly,
although it was more usual for landowners not to run the risks
of industrial undertakings, especially in the coal trade, preferring
to act as rentiers rather than entrepreneurs, mineral enterprise
on the Dudley estate remained largely entrepreneurial until the
early 1900s.

After 1774, mineral enterprise had been rapidly expanded to
take advantage of the situation created by the second viscount's
work in enclosures, transport improvements, and the development of the iron trade. However, rapid expansion was achieved
at the expense of efficiency and an attempt was made after 1797
to remedy the weaknesses.

Collieries were worked directly under estate management
rather than leased to coal-masters. In some cases, coal was leased
but usually for the use of the lessee only, as in the case of the
ironmasters who erected furnaces on the estate. Lord Dundonald
leased land and coal at the Level on which he erected 'tar kilns
and buildings necessary for extracting tar from pit coal'.[17] After
the dismissal of Cockshutt the mineral agent, for incompetence,

Charles Beaumont was engaged in March 1797 to reorganise the pits. In common with most Black Country mines, Lord Dudley's collieries, although much larger, were inefficient.[18] Elsewhere in the Black Country, the prevailing system of landownership led to a proliferation of small enterprises.

Beaumont, a distinguished mining engineer from Newcastle-upon-Tyne,[19] was engaged to secure

the best which can with Equity be done for his Lordship's Concerns . . . saving all the Coal possible . . . raising the greatest quantity and on the lowest terms . . . and Simplifying a Work of such Vast Extension so as to prevent imposition.[20]

His correspondence on mineral matters was all addressed to the Reverend Thomas Jeans of Paddington. Jeans, a personal friend of the third viscount and tutor to his son, had been invited by Lord Dudley to 'superintend my concerns' early in 1797 and acted as his London agent. In addition to the usual fixed salary and allowances—in this case, 'Two hundred pounds . . . home, Coal, horse and Journeying'—Beaumont negotiated a further payment based on results.

Particular emphasis was to be placed upon 'an extension of the Water sale *to the utmost extent*',[21] in order to take advantage of the developing canal network. Within a month of his appointment, Beaumont made proposals to secure wider markets for Lord Dudley's coal 'at Birmingham—and on the line of the different Canals to near London . . .'. The main competition on the canals beyond Birmingham would come from the Warwickshire coalfield especially at Coventry 'which is the first place of note where the Competition takes place'. Comparative costs were set out by Beaumont.

The Staffordshire Coal pr. ton of 21 cwt			
is sold to the Dealer at	£0	6	0
Tonnage 62 Miles at 1½ pr. mile		7	9
Haulage on 20 tons at 1/- pr. mile		3	1
		16	10

		s	d
Common (Warwickshire) Coal pr. ton of 26 cwt		10	0
Tonnage 6 Miles			9
Haulage			2¾
		10	11¾

In favour of the Common and the difference
in weight   5   10¼

He proposed to counter this difference by 'price-savings and extra demand'. According to Beaumont, the

> Colliers at present give 21 Cwt to the ton, but have not more than half the work they could turn out—and a great part of the lumps (or Cobbles) lost to the Owner and Colliers by want of a demand for this Article.[22]

By increasing the demand for Lord Dudley's coal and paying for the cobbles, Beaumont increased the productivity of the pits and provided the colliers with full-time employment in return for which they had to accept payment on a ton of 26cwt. As the coal owner, Lord Dudley paid the butties a lump sum per ton of coal raised to the surface. This was the charter price. The butty or chartermaster then paid the gangs of miners engaged by him and Lord Dudley's agents sold the coal. To make his proposals attractive to the dealers on the Fazeley, Grand Junction and Oxford canals, he suggested that their boats should be loaded at Birmingham rather than at the estate collieries, 'so admitting the Dealer to make a greater Vend with the same boats, Men and horses', and guaranteed the quality of the coal. Under further proposals outlined by him, dealers at Coventry would be able to sell Lord Dudley's coal at 8¼d per ton cheaper than Warwickshire coal, while beyond Coventry transport costs would be the same for both sources of supply:

	s	d
To the Dealer at Birmingham [price per ton]	6	0
Tonnage and hauling [tolls and working costs from pits to Birmingham]	1	11
For saving in time and additional weight [5 days on average and an extra 5 cwt per ton]	1	1
	9	0

Further the Dealer has to pay at Coventry 50 Miles
    tonnage at 1½d per mile [Canal tolls paid on
    return journey to Birmingham]   6   3
Haulage do. on 16 tons [working costs of one barge]   3   1½

Total cost to dealer at Coventry   18   4½
Common Coal [Warwickshire]   10   0
Tonnage and Haulage   11¾   10   11¾

Difference between Staffordshire and Warwickshire
    coal at Coventry   7   4¾
The difference in price [retail?] on these coals at
    Coventry at 2d per cwts on 26 cwts is   4   4
5 cwt increase at 9d   3   9   8   1

                  per cwt [ton?]   8¾
in favour of Staffordshire—above Coventry the
    tonnage and haulage is the same on both.

All of these calculations were based on the London chaldron of
26cwt 'which is the same weight as the Warwickshire ton and
causes it . . . necessary to fix the Staffordshire that Weight'.
Beyond Coventry, Lord Dudley's coal would meet increasing
competition from Newcastle coal transhipped via London.
Nevertheless, Beaumont calculated that, by his arrangements,
the long-standing monopoly of Newcastle coal would be challenged even in the Thames valley. At Oxford, Staffordshire coal
would be 19s 10½d per ton cheaper than Newcastle coal, and,
at Reading 12s 9½d per ton cheaper.

On the Newcastle Coal
This Coal on the average to London cannot be
    calculated under the price stated in my plan on
    that Subject which is into the Barges to take
    up the Country—say   £2   0   0
To Oxford for expences and Dealers profits   12   0

                                 2   12   0
Staffordshire Coal to Coventry   18   4½
76 Miles tonnage to Oxford   9   6
Hauling on 16 tons   4   3   1   12   1½

(Difference in favour of Staffordshire coal at Oxford)					19	10½
Say the Newcastle Coal to Reading				£2	8	0
Staffordshire to Oxford	1	12	1			
Hauling to Reading 50 Miles	3	1½		1	15	2½

(Difference in favour of Staffordshire coal at Reading)	12	9½

If there is tonnage it will be paid on both.[23]

By these arrangements he hoped to 'dispose of 3 or 400,000 Tons anny. to the best advantage'.

Beaumont's proposals were attractive to dealers 'of the first Consequence . . . on the different Canals'.[24] It was agreed that the price per ton was to rise and fall in accordance with prices charged by neighbouring Black Country pits, but the key to increased sales, the 26cwt ton, was to remain constant. He also extracted a promise from the dealers 'most beneficial for his Lordship's Interest, to land no other Dealers' Boats on the Oxford and Grand Junction Canals'[25] which would enable Lord Dudley and the company to 'lead the Vend'.

Having secured a dominant share of the market beyond Coventry, Beaumont entered into negotiations for the Birmingham market:

> reached Birmingham and . . . had the Subject in full over with the Compy. there. They are agreeable to the same terms and Contract for a term of years . . . and will take . . . not less than 50,000 tons—the first year and soon increase the quantity.[26]

This would be approximately 25 per cent of the existing market in Birmingham.[27] The new marketing arrangements were put into effect by June 1797 and the activity of the Dudley pits increased. However, to avoid hostility in the area, should details of his plans leak out, Beaumont arranged for the companies' boats to be 'charged and cleaned out as hitherto—they deducting the 5 cwt and remitting payment on account . . . The colliers to give the same weight as formerly, 21 cwt.'[28] Inevitably, rumours and speculation occurred and one local coal-master, F. Dumaresq, informed Jeans that Beaumont was giving 26cwt to the ton: 'this will ... considerably lower the price and ... other works must follow'.[29] He asserted that, in spite of falling profits, owners would be unable to reduce wages, because of the 'scarcity of miners'. Jeans added a footnote that 'the answer to this will be merely evasive'.

Dumaresq's observation indicates that the demand for Black Country coal had expanded so rapidly that there was a shortage of miners; the influx of miners from South Wales and Shropshire solved this labour shortage in the 1820s. This labour shortage, together with the dangers of working the thick-coal seams, was probably responsible for the payment of relatively high wages to the Black Country miner which resulted in high absenteeism from drunkenness at the commencement of the week. Beaumont attempted, in vain, to induce the miners 'to work on Monday— giving up their Holydays—But ... I gave up Monday and shall attempt to save Tuesday and Wednesday'.[30] He was also anxious to replace weekly pay by a settlement of wages every fortnight —this would reduce absenteeism and increase output. The incidence of absenteeism indicates a relatively high standard of living amongst the local miners. This phenomenon persisted into the nineteenth century and provoked comment from the parliamentary commissioners in 1842, although wages were paid every second Saturday by that time.[31] Drinking and gambling were prevalent in the area and the fact that miners could afford these pleasures while working only a three- or four-day week, even in times when demand for coal was high, is an illuminating commentary on the 'exploitation' of the working classes under laissez-faire management.

Having secured a regular and expanding market of over 400,000 tons per annum for Lord Dudley's coal, Beaumont turned his attention to increasing the efficiency of the pits and reducing production costs. His first concern was to establish a new charter or contract for the butties who worked the Dudley pits. This was first introduced in September 1797[32] and is of particular interest, not only because it introduced new sub-contracting arrangements into south Staffordshire, but also because it was printed in a standard form with details added as appropriate to each particular case.

First of all, the relationship between butty and coal-owner was defined to ensure that all work would be done under the direction of Lord Dudley's agents and that all working costs would be met by the butty. A minimum amount of coal had to be raised to the surface every fortnight in 'a proper and workmanlike manner' and so prevent damage to the pit by safeguarding the owner from the worst effects of the butty system.[33] The charter, or payment for coal raised to the surface, was then laid down in the standard contract. Lumps and slack remained fixed at 1s 6d and 6d per ton respectively, while the price of best and second-grade coal was to rise and fall in proportion to the movement of the selling price above or below 6s 0d or 5s 6d respectively. In this particular contract, the butty, Cartwright, was to receive 2s 11½d per ton for best coals and 2s 0d per ton for second-grade coal, leaving a profit for Lord Dudley of 3s 0½d and 2s 6d per ton. Significantly, the butty had 'to allow as many Hundred Weight . . . to the Ton, as his Lordship allows to the Buyer'. The last section of the contract laid down conditions to apply in particular circumstances. If Lord Dudley erected a steam engine at the pit, his capital expenditure and working costs were offset by a reduction in the charter paid—4d a ton in Cartwright's case. To discourage butties from leaving slack in the pit, because it was less profitable, all slack 'which is not wanted below in the Pit', was to be brought to the surface. This would also encourage the butties to cut the coal with care so as to reduce the amount of small broken coal produced.

Many of the features in this contract were new to the Black Country coal trade at this time. It was more usual for the owner, both here and in other coalfields, to lease his pits on royalty rather than exploit them as part of estate enterprise.[34] Payment of charter according to selling price, removal of slack to the surface, and a ton of 26cwt were all new to the area. Moreover, the standard printed contract, probably unique in the district, would 'simplify the Books and prevent all imposition', a reference to the abuse of power in the past by Lord Dudley's agents and the butties when the form of contract was less explicit—probably a verbal agreement—as in other local pits. The major costs remaining to be met by Lord Dudley were 'heading and . . . sinking' which Beaumont levelled at the existing organisation inherited and a profit of over £20,000 would be secured. Under the new contract and marketing arrangements, the butties' men and equipment would be more fully occupied and contracts were quickly made with butties throughout the Dudley estate.

However, there was some opposition at this time from Lord Dudley's agents who resented the criticism, real and implied, which Beaumont levelled at the existing organisation inherited from Cockshutt. Criticism of his expenditure on railways[35] and wharves was constant—in spite of the resulting reduction in transport costs from the pit-head to the canal wharves, and the elimination of haphazard methods of recording sales by erecting weigh-beams and offices. Alternative marketing arrangements were proposed in July 1797, by Charles Norton, the limestone lessee, who also offered to take over the working of the pits from Lord Dudley on the west and south of Dudley. Beaumont criticised these proposals on the grounds that Norton's intention of 'Stacking on Wharfs and *Compelling* Traders to come in thro' fear of Opposition'[36] would lead to 'hostilities which will prove as ruinous to his Lordship's Concerns as the present War to England'. However, an arrangement to market Lord Dudley's coal was made with Fereday and Turton[37]—two other limestone lessees. They undertook to

> purchase and take all the Coals and Cokes to be raised and made at the Parkhead and Level Collieries now worked and carried on by the said Viscount.

A minimum of 80,000 tons of coal were to be purchased and sold either 'land sale' at Park Head or along the line of Dudley Canal from Netherton to Selly Oak on the outskirts of Birmingham. Lord Dudley reserved the right to sell coal on his own account in this area and limited the lessees to supplying no more than 10,000 tons per annum in the 'Stourport Market'. These provisions for regulating the distribution of minerals were similar to clauses in the limestone leases which ensured that particular lessees would be restricted to supplying given areas.

It was not until early in 1798[38] that Beaumont submitted proposals for a comprehensive reorganisation of the pits. Methods of sinking pits were condemned as expensive and inefficient as estate pits had followed 'The Provincial method of sinking . . . by two Shafts of 6 feet diameter . . . for a free communication of air'.[39] This limited the distance which could be worked between the shafts to 100 yards—new shafts then had to be sunk. Beaumont proposed to sink only one shaft, twelve feet in diameter, with a 'Wood bratige [brattice] down the center . . . which would carry the air much stronger down'. The construction of trap-doors would improve ventilation and enable galleries to be driven 300 yards from the shaft and one pit would 'answer for four' of the existing pits. This more efficient system of ventilation, sinking shafts, and driving galleries had been in operation at Newcastle for many years.

Methods of cutting and extracting the coal were next considered under a plan whereby '$\frac{2}{3}$ if not $\frac{3}{4}$ will be saved' and by the same number of men 'as at present'—about 200. Instead of bringing down a pillar of coal 30ft high, Beaumont proposed to work the thick coal from the bottom to a height of 6ft only and extend the work up to 300 yards from the shaft. Then a second layer would be removed and so on until the whole height of the seam had been cut; this would drastically reduce the proportion of small broken coal produced by existing methods. To speed up and facilitate the handling of coal both above and below ground, he proposed to introduce tubs 'containing 24 pecks, or 3 bolls Winchester Measure', thus standardising measurement, and each miner was to be paid

> 3s 6d per score of tubs making 60 bolls of $2\frac{1}{2}$ cwt to the boll which gives $7\frac{1}{2}$ tons for 3/6—to the Collier say per ton £0. 0. $5\frac{3}{4}$d.[40]

The total expense per ton was estimated thus:

Drawing from the Collier to the Surface	5d
Overman, deputy, controller, Banksman, horse with all remaining expenses	$1\frac{1}{4}$
Total expense per Ton (to the surface)	£0 1s 0

As the existing charter paid to the butties was 'from 2/2 to 2/10 per ton, the saving on 300,000 tons would amount at 1/6 per ton including extras to £22,000'.

This proposal for the coal-owner to employ labour directly was revolutionary in the Black Country and would necessitate the abandonment of the butty or chartermaster system. Direct employment already existed in the Newcastle coalfield by the end of the eighteenth century, but in the Black Country, where units of land tended to be small, the butty system was predominant and was valuable to the small landowner because working capital was supplied by the butty who took all of the risks. Various arrangements had evolved in the coal trade whereby a coal-owner could exploit his property. In some cases he employed butties to work a pit or sections of a larger colliery and paid the butty so much charter per ton of coal raised to the surface. The butty engaged and paid his own men and the mineral owner sold the coal on his own account. This was the practice on the Dudley estate between 1774 and 1798. Occasionally—as in the Newcastle area —the owner might employ miners directly to work the pits for him; both of these arrangements ensured that pits would be directly managed by the owner's bailiffs. The latter arrangement was the form proposed by Beaumont in January 1798. Under a third arrangement, illustrated by Norton's proposals, the owner might lease the pit to a coal-master who would either work the pit by labour directly employed by himself or engage butties to exploit the lease on his behalf. The lessee would sell the coal on his own account and pay a royalty per ton to the coal-owner. This was an arrangement adopted by the trustees after 1836. Because of the extensive nature of his property, Lord Dudley was able to develop large collieries, and, as he did not depend upon the butties for working capital, he could dispose of them if it could be shown to be in his interest to do so.[41] Beaumont's proposals, to cut out the middleman's profit by abolishing the butties, were accepted and the butties were dismissed from the Dudley pits— a decision which was to produce a considerable impact in the area.

Unfortunately for Beaumont and the future prosperity of Lord Dudley's mineral interests, his extensive reorganisation had earned him the enmity of many butties and agents while neighbouring coal-owners were jealous of the active state of the Dudley pits. He informed Jeans that he had received information

> That the Coal Masters found themselves so hurt that an outburst would soon take place and that from our discharging the Butties and bringing up 300 Men from the North, an insurrection would take place the day of their arrival.[42]

The butties undoubtedly resented the loss of the opportunity to work the Dudley pits by the new contracts introduced in September 1797. However, the miners were evidently satisfied with the new arrangements made in January 1798 whereby they were freed from the exploitation of the butties and employed directly by Lord Dudley's agents at a fixed, regular daily wage for a given stint of work. Beaumont observed:

> went to every pit—and find the Wagemen [miners] to my wishes willing to defend me on any occasion and no objections to the Mens coming as they themselves are assured of Constant employ.

Riots and general unrest did occur and Lord Dudley's residence at Himley and his pits were threatened with destruction. The arrival of 'foreign' miners provided the butties and rival coal-owners with an opportunity to create unrest and champion the cause of the local miners in the interests of full employment, by alleging that Beaumont's association with Newcastle, and his preference for methods in operation there, would result in the replacement of local miners by men brought from the Tyne. This indicates the influence of the butties who traditionally exercised great power in the area as the hirers of labour and to whom the men were further bound by the indebtedness produced by the truck system. Beaumont defended his actions in a printed pamphlet[43] and asserted that the Newcastle men would only sink new shafts and not be engaged in mining the coal. However, faced with these disturbances, Lord Dudley dismissed Jeans[44] and Beaumont.

Beaumont achieved a great deal during his brief period in office and the pits continued to work at reduced costs and higher profitability, although the incentive to the dealers of a 26cwt ton and the new method of sinking shafts did not survive his dismissal. His capital expenditure on weighing machines, railways and the re-siting of steam engines remained valuable assets. However, deprived of his personal influence, it seems unlikely that Beaumont's arrangements to dominate the 'vend' in Birmingham and beyond Coventry on the line of the Grand Junction and Oxford canals would prevail for long, although Lord Dudley's coal no doubt competed on equal terms with other Black Country coal in these markets. But, the extent to which his methods of cutting the coal and direct employment of miners at a fixed daily wage persisted is not clear. Coal was sorted to meet the particular demands of dealers and 'wagemen' were employed in the Dudley pits in 1833—but there may have been some lapse in these practices after 1798 before their obvious advantages persuaded later agents to reintroduce them.

The continued prosperity of Lord Dudley's mines after 1798 is further illustrated by his policy of erecting steam engines. At least four steam engines existed on the Dudley estate by the mid-eighteenth century; between 1797 and 1801, twelve more were constructed.[45] Accounts for 1804 show that, although the estimated annual profit of £22,000 per annum forecast by

N

Beaumont in 1797 was not being reached, there was an average net profit of £17,684 7s 1d over the preceding five years.

Parish	£	s	d	Poundage		
Sedgley	8,227	4	0	411	7	2
Kingswinford	5,624	8	0	281	4	2
Tipton	277	9	0	13	17	6
Dudley	3,555	11	1	177	15	7
[sic] £17,684		7	1	844	4	5

£844 4s 5d pr. ann. poundage.[46]

This document indicates a parochial basis for mines accounts and shows that Roberts, the mineral agent, was receiving 'poundage' or commission calculated at 1s per pound profit—as in the case of the agreement on salary negotiated by Beaumont. Towards the end of the first phase of expansion, in 1833, the profitability and efficiency of estate mineral enterprise declined —especially after the appointment of Downing as mineral agent in 1826.

This state of affairs was revealed by the report on the mines submitted to the trustees by Smith and Liddell in 1836. Liddell was a professional mining engineer from Northumberland and Richard Smith, a local man and an acquaintance of Littleton, one of the trustees, had distinguished himself as the mining engineer in charge of the General Mining Association's concerns in Nova Scotia. He was subsequently appointed mineral agent to the Dudley estate in December 1836. The trustees were determined to have a thorough survey made and issued a detailed list of instructions and inquiries to be pursued.[47] Their report, concluded by March 1836, provided the blueprint for reorganisation and further expansion after 1836.

Beaumont's policy of exploiting all the mines for immediate profit and maintaining productivity at a maximum level, had been allowed to lapse and many pits were conserved as assets. Only three pits were 'prepared to get Coal out of the Mines ... and we consider those were not in a very active state', a situation all the more serious because 'both Coal and Ironstone of every quality being now in great demand and at high prices'.[48] The report criticised the fact that some shafts

> are in bad repair ... highly important to the future ... working
> ... of the thin Coals and Ironstone measures as well as in clearing
> out all the old ribs and pillars left in the broken Mines of thick
> Coal.

After sixty years of intensive working, there were many old shafts and galleries which presented a danger to existing works, but, as the report pointed out: 'The Trustees' Office does not afford any plans of the underground workings except in one or two instances and these of an imperfect nature.'[49] Smith and Liddell were forced to consult the mine bailiffs but 'found difficulty in procuring information that could be relied on regarding the extent of former workings'.

Francis Downing, the mine agent since 1826, presented his own observations[50] on the report and, in seeking to defend and justify his administration of affairs, succeeded merely in providing further evidence of his own incompetence. He asserted that, since the bailiffs were able to supply information to Smith and Liddell, 'this tends to prove that they are possessed of the knowledge qualifying them for their duties' and that 'the Catchings [quantity mined] have been marked on the surface'. This was the traditional and crude method of recording the amount of coal worked in the Black Country. In this and other respects, the Select Committee on the Mining Districts, reporting in 1850, indicated that Downing was no more incompetent and conservative than other local mine agents: 'Fourteen years ago [1836] there were scarcely any regular plans made of the workings in this district.'[51] The professional efficiency of Beaumont, unsurpassed in 1797, was still confined to few besides Smith and Liddell in 1836:

> Besides butties there is a superior class of persons ... the mine

agents, of whom there are about 60 in the district. They have the
supervision of the coal and ironstone pits ... about 15 cannot
write or read ... there may be 25 who are educated men: the
rest, say about 20, are in a sort of intermediate state as regards
intelligence.

It is a serious loss to all the iron and coal works of the district,
and to the capital employed in them, that the whole of the mine
agents are not equal in point of education ... [52]

Nevertheless, the extent and complexity of Lord Dudley's enterprises magnified the errors of management on his estate before
1836, and the report by Smith and Liddell asserted that the only
way to secure efficient control was 'to place the responsibility of
this Department on a professional Mine Engineer'. Because of
the absence of accurate plans, the report warned that there were
'instances where the Coal has been got by Lord Dudley beyond
his Lordship's boundary line'. Moreover, the safety of the Dudley
Canal Tunnel was endangered by the mining of coal within the
limits laid down by the parliamentary Act.

On the matter of the basis on which the mines were operated,
the report concluded that

we recommend their being let on royalty: indeed the Trustees
... have let some of the broken Mines of thick Coal ... at various
rates per ton and by the Superficial Yard.

In fact most of the coal mined in 1833-4 was from 'broken mines'
leased to contractors employing their own butties. However, these
arrangements were unsatisfactory because

the parties to whom the Mines are let are only Tenants at Will
and therefore ... will [not] spend Capital ... or push works with
the same energy as they would do if they received possession by
leases granted for a proper term of years.

Having described the existing state of the collieries and
analysed the deficiencies of management and control, Smith and
Liddell made a number of recommendations to the trustees. In
order to take advantage of the current demand for minerals, they

advised that the mines should be exploited for immediate profit rather than conserved as an asset—as had been the case under the first earl. All the collieries should be worked to capacity and the old shafts sunk down to the deeper seams in order to work the thin coal and ironstone which lay under worked-out sections of thick coal. The subsequent problems of establishing a co-operative mines drainage scheme which were to bedevil similar attempts[53] later in the century, were already apparent as several engines drained estate and neighbouring mines. It appeared that 'the best time for getting the Lordship Mines is whilst other persons fill an interest in subscribing towards the expense of drawing the Water'.[54]

Perhaps the most significant recommendation of all was their proposal that the basic policy, whereby the estate worked the pits directly until the main thick-coal seam had been exhausted, should be replaced by a system of leasing the mines on royalty. Smith had prepared the ground for this radical innovation in a letter to Hatherton before the report was submitted:

> It is very difficult for Trustees to steer a clear course through a trading will. It most commonly happens that they end in unpleasant and perplexing Chancery suits, frequently with great loss to the most cautious Trustees, and in some instances, in total ruin. A strict adherence to the Royalty system will avoid such consequences, taking care that the Mines are judiciously let, and worked in a proper and workmanlike manner.[55]

Fortunately for the estate, and the trustees, the late earl's will empowered them to grant mineral leases, an unusual feature[56] in an early nineteenth-century will, and the trustees could implement this recommendation without delay. The current practice in Staffordshire with regard to letting mines was

> to take a ... proportion of the Sale price; in some instances $\frac{1}{8}$ in others $\frac{1}{7}$ and as high as $\frac{1}{5}$ even for Maiden Mines, where the Lessees have to incur all the expences of plant etc ... the Lessor finding no Capital whatever.[57]

The report advised that all the mines on the Dudley estate should be let at the high royalty of 20 per cent on sales. Coalmasters and ironmasters leasing the estate pits would work and sell (or consume) the minerals themselves, meet all working costs, the capital costs of opening new seams or extending existing workings and pay a proportion of the total income (based on sales) to the Dudley estate. The lessees could either work the pits themselves or resort to the traditional chartermaster or butty system whereby the lessee paid charter to the butty calculated on production. After 1836, none of the Dudley lessees were allowed to employ butties who trucked their miners. As well as working costs and other expenses capital outlay and its depreciation in value should be borne by the lessee. A clear distinction would be made between landlord's and tenant's capital. Existing capital costs already incurred by the estate, together with book debts, amounted to £100,000 by 31 December 1834 and the report proposed a charge on the lessees of such properties to recover these costs:

> It is generally accepted that money in trade will pay at least 10 per cent ... it will be right to charge trading Interest upon the floating Capital always more or less at risk ... which ... is equal to £10,000.

Working costs were £54,156 5s 4½d.

These recommendations constituted a plan for the radical reorganisation of mineral enterprise on the Dudley estate. By the 1830s, landowners leased their minerals on royalty in most of the coalfields—except in Durham and Northumberland.[58] A proportion of Yorkshire coal was worked directly by landowners throughout the nineteenth century and, as late as 1890, probably one-eighth of the total output came from this sector.[59] In the Staffordshire coalfields, most of the minerals were worked by lessees on charter or on royalty from the outset—except in such cases as the Lords Dudley and Stafford. After 1821, Lord Stafford's mines were leased on royalty. The tendency for landowners to avoid the risk of industrial undertakings—particularly in the case of the coal industry—resulted in a situation whereby only 5 per cent of all collieries in England were owned and worked by landowners in 1869.[60]

Loch proved a powerful advocate in support of the proposals made by Smith and Liddell:

I have read the Report upon the Mines . . . and I concur generally in the recommendations it contains . . . A too extended Management never can be carried on as economically as one which is more concentrated—least of all in the hands of a Landlord. I say this from my experience of two similar Concerns of vast magnitude with which I am connected.[61]

Smith and Liddell concluded with a recommendation concerning the management of affairs:

The only way to effect this object [efficient control] is to place the responsibility of this Department on a professional Mine Engineer . . .[62]

and expressed the hope that the

very respectable Gentleman who has so long been at the head of these important Concerns . . . will not attribute to us any intention to disparage the merit so justly due to him.

Downing was bitterly resentful. After maintaining a stubborn silence for a month, he attacked the report:

It is with extreme reluctance that I enter upon the subject of the 'Mine Report' considering it to be characterized by a disposition to find fault founded in some cases on mere speculative opinions and in others evincing a deficiency of knowledge.[63]

Nevertheless, the remaining trustees approved the report, and Hatherton noted that Downing had been informed that 'though a Trustee, he was also our Agent, and that the majority must appoint another person'.[64] The post of mine agent was offered to Richard Smith in November 1836 and he took up his responsibilities at the beginning of December. Downing was allowed to retain his salary of £1,250 per annum and his residence at the Priory,[65] and was given the title of General Superintendent of the Mineral and Landed Estates. He continued as a trustee and assumed responsibility for the collection of mineral royalties derived from the new policy of leasing the pits. However, his new title was merely a sop to injured pride and effective executive authority was wielded by Smith, as mine agent, and Maughan the land agent. Downing resigned in 1840, after adopting obstructionist tactics to the exasperation of all his colleagues, and became a mineral entrepreneur on his own account which ended in his financial ruin by 1843.

Smith's salary was fixed in accordance with his services—and recalls the commission calculated on profit paid to Charles Beaumont. In addition to a basic salary of £1,200 per annum he received a payment of $2\frac{1}{2}$ per cent on net profit above £35,000. Net profit for 1836 from all mineral and iron sources was £25,005 8s 4d; but the minimum figure beyond which commission would be paid was fixed at £35,000, both as an incentive and in anticipation of an increase in income from the new policy of leasing the pits on royalty introduced in December 1836. Between 1 January 1837 and 6 March 1845, total net income amounted to £509,202 16s 3d; Smith was paid commission on £222,969 18s 9d—a total of £5,574. His income per annum from commission increased after the termination of the trust as the long-term benefits of his policies took effect. Net income between 6 March 1845 and 31 December 1859 amounted to £1,542,391 1s 9d and Smith's total commission was £22,618 1s 4d.[66]

When Downing was replaced by Smith as mineral agent in December 1836, there were several agreements in operation to work sections of the mines but these were mostly broken mines.[67] Royalties paid varied in amount and type from 2s 6d per ton on best thick coal to 1s 6d for common coal and 6d for slack (thick coal); heathen coal slack produced a royalty of 3d per ton. Ironstone royalties ranged from 2s 6d per ton of best black ironstone to 1s per ton for inferior stone. The form of royalty[68] also varied including a fixed price per ton, a charge levied per acre of minerals worked and by the superficial yard. Only two tenants paid royalties based on the selling price of the minerals.

Smith had to evolve new forms of accounts to record the income and expenditure for each colliery: parts of a particular colliery might remain under estate exploitation while other sections and shafts within the same colliery might be let to various tenants on royalty. A comparison of the accounts for Park Head Colliery in 1834 and 1837 illustrates the more complex organisation evolved to meet this situation. During 1837, the monthly disbursements paid out by the bailiff to miners employed by the estate decreased from £1,325 10s 10d in January 1837 to £392 4s 6d as the estate worked fewer sections of the colliery which were then leased to entrepreneurs. The various lessees are indicated by the valuation put upon the sections leased to them—for the purpose of calculating the 10 per cent charge on capital costs; in the case of this colliery, all the lessees were ironmasters who leased ironworks from the estate such as Gibbons, Evers and Martin, and Izons & Co. The new account for 1837 records the income from cash and credit sales of minerals worked and sold by the estate; the income from rents and royalties was recorded in other accounts opened by Richard Smith in January 1837. Although many parts of a colliery might be let, the overall management was closely controlled by the estate's bailiff. His responsibility was to ensure that the lessees worked their sections according to the practices and standards laid down in the leases, and that all minerals sold by the lessees were carefully recorded by weighing machines owned and controlled by the estate. The former practice of recording transactions of the Mines Department on a manorial basis was replaced by a system based on a few large colliery units—such as Park Head, Kingswinford or Coneygre collieries—which incorporated all activity in that particular area, whether by the estate or by lessees. This enabled the colliery manager and his section bailiffs to organise that particular mineral unit in the most efficient manner. See accounts on pp202-5.

Account for Park Head Colliery from 31 March to 31 December 1834

Dr

	£	s	d
Disbursmts	7,741	18	10
Castings	119	4	5
Chains	42	4	9
Ropes	86	6	6
Rates	270	9	5
Rent of Land	17	0	0
Damaged land	42	2	0
Brick Maker	122	13	0
Bailiffs Salary	90	0	0
Timber Yard	313	4	9
Castings	146	19	7
Balance carried down	6,595	3	2
	£15,587	6	5

Cr

	Tons	Cwts		£	s	d
Sales by estate						
Coal—						
ready money	7,668	11		3,328	12	2
,, credit	22,063	6		7,273	2	3
Fire coal	253	14				
	[sic] 29,985	17		[sic] 10,565	14	5
Slack—						
ready money	4,503	5		956	2	7
,, credit	18,033	—		2,558	17	10
Engine slack	545	—				
Fire slack	20	5				
	23,101	10		3,515	0	5
Cokes—						
ready money	5,950 (sacks)			223	2	10
,, credit	24,589 (sacks)			855	15	7
	30,539 (sacks)			1,078	18	5
Royalties						
Coal—credit	11	10		11	6	
Slack— ,,	599	7		14	19	7
Ironstone ,,	395	1		42	15	11
Sundry sales of bricks, ropes etc				284	11	3
Water ease				82	13	5
Use of whimsey				2	1	6
				[sic] £15,587	6	5

Dr   Cr

	Tons Cwts	£ s d		Tons Cwts	£ s d
Disbursements for		1,766 17 1	Bal. brought down	5,468 14	6,595 3 2
ironstone			Ironstone—credit		3,111 18 1
Bal. carried down		8,068 1 8	Dudley Canal Water		118 0 9
			Dudley and Matthews Interest		9 16 9
		9,834 18 9			9,834 18 9
			Bal. brought down		8,068 1 8

*Richard Smith in Account with Park Head Colliery
from 31 December 1836 to 31 December 1837*

Dr   Cr

	Tons Cwts	£ s d		£ s d
Sales			*Bailiff for Getting*	
To Best Coal—			*Mines etc*	
ready money	11,002 12	4,932 16 11	By Joseph Robinson	
„ credit	6,179 8	2,881 4 5	(Bailiff)	
„ fire coal	341 5	— — —	Disbursements	9,016 17 11
	17,523 5	[sic] 7,814 1 4	On account of	
			Blackwell and Jones	453 16 4

Dr

	Tons	Cwts	£	s	d
To Common Coal—					
ready money	2,183	19	873	1	6
,, credit	24,697	16	9,567	7	5
	26,881	15	10,440	8	11
To Slack—					
ready money	9,685	—	1,989	1	6
,, credit	27,047	—	5,026	15	6
,, engine	1,567	—	—	—	—
,, schools	32	14	—	—	—
	38,331	14	7,015	17	0
To Coke					
ready money	4,017½ (qtrs)		381	19	4
,, credit	29,204 (qtrs)		2,768	14	4
,, to Priory	21½ (qtrs)		—	—	—
	33,243		3,150	13	8
To Ironstone—credit	7,937	18	5,840	4	9
Bricks	9,400		11	15	6
	1,500		1	19	0
To Sundries—ready money					
Manure	17	13	4	17	1
			18	11	7

Cr

	£	s	d
On account of			
Evers and Martin	2,544	13	4
On account of			
Benj. Gibbons	581	5	10
On account of			
J. Pearson and Sons	306	18	0
	12,903	11	5
Getting Ironstone			
By John Hickman	1,508	15	5
James Teague	885	4	6
E. & J. Skelding	92	17	2
Castings			
By Evers and Martin	106	4	1
Oil	83	17	11
Rates	431	2	10
Damages of land	9	15	0
Timber	47	0	8
Bank charges			
(Dixon & Co)	118	0	0
Sundries	64	14	6
By Thos Hughes for			
making bricks	394	3	5

	Tons Cwts	£	s	d		£	s	d
To Sundries—credit John Bradley & Co					By Blackwells & Sons			
use of Railway		281	0	10	for sales of coal	845	19	7
M. & W. Grazebrook					Allowances	357	4	2
water ease		70	7	7				
To Sundries—credit								
John Bradley for bricks		6	17	6				
Various								
Estate for bricks		22	18	9				
„ „ 42,000 bricks		53	0	0				
Limestone Works for 48,550 bricks		60	13	9				
Lessees for bricks		165	12	10				
		660	11	3				
Valuations of Pit Shafts and								
Underground Workings								
To Benj. Gibbons		470	0	0				
Evers and Martin		495	1	10				
Blackwell and Jones		54	8	6				
Jos. Pearson and Sons		607	3	4				
Izons and Co		29	17	6				
Blackwell and Jones for disbursements								
during time the trustees carried on								
the Colly. for them		477	5	5				
Deduct overcharge of Robinson's Salary		8	16	8				
		37,069	19	3		37,069	19	3
					By balance	19,221	8	7

In such a complex administrative structure—necessitated by the trustees' decision not to lease all the minerals but to continue to exploit the more valuable seams—confusion and friction might easily develop between those sections worked by the estate and those by the lessees. That this did not occur was the result of the carefully worded leases and plans introduced by Smith which clearly stated the mutual rights and obligations of the lessor and lessee and the royalties charged on the various types of minerals.

A typical lease for an undeveloped mining property, including thick coal, was that concluded with Messrs Philpotts and Plant on 31 December 1839.[69] The main recommendations of the mines report were all included in this lease together with more specific clauses added by Smith; the lease ran for twenty-one years and, to secure efficient control of operations, quarterly accounts were drawn up, both the accounts and the workings were open to inspection by Lord Ward's agents without notice, and all operations were to be conducted only after consultation with the mineral agent. Royalties payable on the various minerals, and standard weights and measures were clearly set out; these were all linked to the selling price and the royalty was as high as 33 per cent on the best thick coal. A significant number of the leases[70] negotiated after December 1836 were taken out by ironmasters—as the mines report had anticipated.

In order to encourage maximum output, a minimum royalty of £350 per quarter was paid whether or not thick coal to that amount had been sold, and a minimum of £150 was paid for heathen coal. Penalty clauses were inserted for selling thick coal as heathen coal (in order to pay a lower royalty), for surface damage, the late rendering of accounts, and the sale of coal which did not conform to the scale of weights laid down in the lease. As late as 1864 there were three different weights in use in the Black Country, each called a 'ton'. These were, the statute weight of 2,240lb, the long hundred of 2,400lb (20cwt x 120lb) and the 'boat load' or 'lease weight' of 2,880lb (24 long hundreds); some coal was 'sold land sale ... at statute weight, a greater portion is sold by the fair lease weight of 2,880 lbs.[71] To avoid confusion and loss of revenue, Smith laid down his own standard ton: this was 2,280lb for land sales and 2,520lb for 'water sale'. Presumably the former would attract custom, being larger than the statute ton, while the latter, although smaller than the usual 'water sale' ton, would consist entirely of good coal without the usual high proportion of slack.

Agents on the Dudley estate used these measurements until Frederick Smith introduced the use of the statute ton only in 1868. Surface damage was penalised where the surface was estate property; however, under the terms of the enclosure Acts, the Dudley estate was not liable to pay compensation for surface damage to former commons and waste—whoever owned the surface! To ensure the efficient working of the coal, all slack not required in the pits, for supporting the roof, was to be raised to the surface. As this fetched the lowest selling price—and, therefore, the lowest royalty per ton—the lessees would be persuaded to work the thick coal as carefully as possible so as to reduce the quantity of slack produced. As the minerals were situated in the area drained by the Pensnett engine, an annual payment was made for 'water ease' calculated on the total mineral royalty paid. At the end of the term, lessees were to leave all the machinery and equipment installed by them and to receive fair compensation—this would enable the estate to lease or work the pits without delay or further capital outlay; in the mines report, Smith had suggested that lessees might be allowed to remove their own machinery. Lord Hatherton had estimated[72] in September 1836 that leases would increase the mineral revenue by £7,000 per annum. Smith raised a substantial proportion of this figure from rents alone and the real extent of his success is indicated by the increase in revenue after 1836.

	Total Rent	Total Royalty
1834	£1,669	£ 4,765
1837	3,484	14,839
1847	4,116	74,955

Within a year, he had exceeded Hatherton's expectations on the royalty account alone and, by the end of the trust, had increased the royalty income many times over. Moreover, the expense to the estate was marginal and only involved the payment and cost of clerks, bailiffs and weighing machines. Working costs were all met by the lessees themselves. The total mineral royalty received by Smith between 1 January 1837 and 27 July 1846 was £314,650 18s 2d;[73] over the same period, rent for land and premises amounted to £29,909 8s 11d. Apart from the effect of the depression in the local iron trade in 1841-2, there was a steady increase in annual receipts, especially after 1843 when the railway boom produced highly favourable conditions for the Black Country iron and mineral trades. This phenomenal increase in the income from leased mineral properties was exceeded in the long run by an even greater expansion in the activity and income from mineral enterprises worked directly by the estate.

Throughout the trust period, the large collieries, and the most lucrative pits and sections within each colliery, remained part of estate enterprise, with lessees contributing to the cost of drainage where an engine served parts of the colliery worked both by the estate and by lessees. This complex structure was inevitable because of the extensive area and mineral rights owned by the estate which enabled larger units of production to be developed than was usual in the Black Country. Generally, pits in the area did not exceed three acres, and an acre

> may sell on the average at £1,000, but sometimes even £1,500 . . .
> and . . . The sinking of the two shafts in a mine 300 feet below
> the surface . . . providing the steam engine and all the other parts
> of the moving power, may require a capital of £6,000 and very
> often it is much more.[74]

Where estate engines could relieve neighbouring mines of flooding, the estate was paid an annual sum for 'water ease'—usually calculated on the quantity of minerals raised, not on the volume of water. In the latter half of the nineteenth century, attempts were made to establish adequate drainage in the Black Country by agreements amongst neighbouring coal owners to erect and maintain pumping engines by common subscription. This development was foreshadowed as early as 1838 when, under the leadership of the trustees, fifteen mine owners in the Deepfield area of Sedgley contracted with the trustees to erect a steam pumping engine to relieve their properties 'from a great accumulation of water therein called the Deepfield Pound and which prevented the working of the Mines'.[75] Because of non-payment of subscriptions, the original agreement was given up in 1847, the subscribers received back their capital and the engine remained the sole property of the estate which received an income from neighbouring mines. By 1838, there were thirty-eight pumping engines on the Dudley estate. These provided a regular source of income from the local canals, from estate mine tenants and from neighbouring mineral owners. Typical of such payments was that made to the estate by the Dudley Canal Company in 1834, 'for one years water raised by the Pensnett Engine £200'. In 1847, the Birmingham Canal Company paid £694 10s for water supplied by the new Deepfield Engine. In the same year 'sundry persons' paid £201 14s 5d for 'water ease' provided to neighbouring collieries by the Park Head engine. Mine lessees also paid for this service as a condition of their leases. In 1847 three lessees, Johnson and Cochrane, William Izon, and Philpotts and Plant paid a total of £810 7s 4d for drainage provided by the Pensnett engine. The total income from all the pumping engines was considerable and would have exceeded by far the working costs of the engines which remained under the direct control of the estate. As the engines also served the large collieries owned and worked by the estate on its own account, working costs of draining these pits were more than offset by receipts from lessees, neighbouring pits and canal companies.

Estate mineral enterprise expanded after 1836 as a result of Smith's activities. Average net profit was £45,563 14s per

P

annum which fully vindicated Smith's advice on the desirability
of leasing sections of the existing collieries while continuing to
retain easily-worked seams of thick coal and ironstone under the
direct management of the estate. Towards the end of the trust
period, total net income tended to rise in response to the boom in
the local iron trade during the mid-1840s, and the income from
estate-operated pits tended to increase more rapidly and exceeded
the royalty from leased pits.

	1836			1847		
	£	s	d	£	s	d
Receipts	92,251	9	2	246,753	14	4
Payments	81,570	10	3	174,506	19	2
Net profit (estate enterprise)	11,381	18	11	83,045	1	5
Royalties	13,623	9	5 (Broken mines)	74,945	4	4 (Leases)
Total net profit	25,005	8	4	157,990	5	9

On the basis of these figures, a comparison of the net and gross
income from estate colliery enterprise, excluding leases, indicates
an increase in the rates of net income to gross income from 12.3
per cent in 1836 to 33.6 per cent in 1847. This greater cost
efficiency resulted from Smith's decision that the estate should
work only those seams which yielded easy profits—where working costs would be low because of the shallow depth of the seam
and from the proximity of the working faces to the shafts. This
general expansion in the scale and production of mineral enterprise was accompanied by an extension of the transport facilities[76]
owned by the estate, and an increase in the activities of the Store
Yard at the Level.

The Store Yard at the Level, on the banks of the Dudley
Canal in Kingswinford manor, had developed at the time of the
enclosure awards of the 1780s. By 1822 its function was not only
to supply timber to estate pits, ironworks and farms, but also
castings, and machinery. The tithe survey of 1822 described the
site as containing an

Iron Foundry, Saw Mill, Boring Mill, Steam Engine Manufactory, Carpenters' Shop, Pattern Rooms etc.[77]
It remained in the occupation of the estate for much of the trust
period and was essentially an aspect of mineral enterprise. At the
time of their report, Smith and Liddell considered it to be one
of the few well-run enterprises on the estate.

Shortly before the death of the first earl in 1833, a second
store-yard had been opened in Tipton, at Castle Mill. Because of
its more central position at the Tipton end of the Dudley Canal
Tunnel, this site was in a more convenient position to serve and
maintain estate properties throughout the Black Country. Smith
extended the activities and facilities of the Fitting Shops at the
Tipton site after 1836 while the Level Store Yard resumed its
original function as a timber yard until 1858, when Smith erected
the Round Oak Iron Works on the site.

There is no doubt that, after 1833, mineral enterprise became
more profitable as a result of the trustees' policies—particularly
after Smith's appointment in December 1836. This was in spite
of the fact that, by 1844, the market for Black Country coal had
'been diminished ... owing to the introduction of the Derbyshire coals down the line of the Gloucester Railway'.[78] By that
time the expansion of the Black Country iron trade had produced
a market for 4,212,000 tons of minerals of which the Dudley
estate, because of its relatively large reserves compared with
certain parts of the region, supplied 1,400,000 tons. In contrast
with the static outlook and low profitability at the commencement
of the trust, mineral enterprise on the Dudley estate had expanded in terms of scale, output and real profits. In terms of net
profit on capital invested, there was a dramatic increase in
mineral and industrial income from 37.3 per cent in 1836 to
71.75 per cent in 1847.

	Net Profit	Dead and Convertible Stock[79]
1836	£25,005 8s 4d	£66,956
1847	£157,990 5s 9d	£219,990

The fortunes of mineral enterprise on the Dudley estate after

1845 were influenced by additional regional and national factors. Primarily, the decline in the Black Country wrought-iron trade, which reduced the local market for minerals, was not replaced by a comparable expansion of the steel industry. To some extent, the decline in the iron trade was related to, but was not directly the result of, the decline in local mineral production. Minerals were still available but production costs were increasing as a growing proportion of minerals came from deeper or thinner seams after the exhaustion of the more productive seams. Another important local factor was the growing problem of drainage. During the twentieth century, labour problems, the question of mineral royalties, and the threat of impending nationalisation all influenced the policies adopted by the Dudley estate.

Coal was never in short supply—particularly after the opening of Baggeridge Colliery in 1912—although local production fell by 50 per cent between 1872 and 1900, from 9 million tons to 4.5 million tons. Ironstone was available in the district but, as early as 1860 when 785,000 tons were mined locally, 500,000 tons had to be transported from north Staffordshire and Northamptonshire. On the Dudley estate, production from estate enterprises alone declined from 1,189,980 tons of coal and 101,382 tons of ironstone in 1871, to 705,000 tons and 17,028 tons in 1899. Pits at work on the estate declined from 109 (out of 243) in 1867 to 31 in 1890. Limestone was quarried at the Wren's Nest until 1924 but local demand was increasingly met by material imported from other districts. The total of men and boys employed at the mines throughout the area fell from 25,000 in 1865 to 14,000 in 1900.[80] During the boom years of 1871-2, employees in the Dudley pits totalled 10,000 men and boys out of the total Black Country labour force of 28,000. This declining trend in the Black Country contrasted with the national increase in coal output from 133 million tons in 1875 to 287 million tons in 1913. Within this period there were several sharp depressions —especially in 1885. It was at this time that the Dudley estate began to reduce the scale of mineral enterprise on its own account

and increase the proportion of estate pits leased on royalty. Drainage problems increased in the latter decades of the nineteenth
century. In a report to the Select Commission on Coal Supply in
1871, the local commissioner, J. Hartley, referred to his report of
3 March 1868 in which he observed that

> ... the subdivision ... into numerous small collieries ... has ren-
> dered difficult the acquisition of accurate statistics ... and the
> large volumes of water ... until drained by some voluntary system
> ... must continue.[81]

Compulsory action was at last taken when a Mines Drainage Act
was passed in 1873 which established a Drainage Commission to
levy money from mine owners and undertake the drainage of the
pits. Lack of co-operation and refusal to pay the levy on pits
temporarily closed by a slump in the trade, led to the failure of
the scheme and, by 1900, 40 million tons of coal were waterlogged.
In 1920, the Drainage Commission wrote off Tipton as a 'waterlogged rabbit warren'[82] and mining virtually ceased in that area.

With declining demand for coal, considerable hardship and
unrest resulted amongst the miners. In 1851,[83] the thick-coal
miner earned £1 to £1 10s per week and the thin-coal collier
£1 to £1 4s per week: the former always earned higher wages
because of the greater dangers and higher output. When the
butties reduced the miners' daily wage by 1s in 1858, because of
the depression in the iron and mineral trades following the boom
of the Crimean War period, strikes and riots were widespread
throughout the district.[84] The men remained on strike from July
to October: Richard Smith wrote to Hatherton on 4 October
that he hoped

> most of the Colliers will be at work tomorrow on the West side
> of Dudley [where estate pits were numerous]. Many of them are
> not mixed up with the strike, and but for the Oldbury men, the
> Kingswinford men would have remained quiet, and have been
> satisfied with the reduced wages.[85]

Along with the trade in general, wages in the estate pits had also been reduced but, because of the provision of benefits and the absence of truck, Lord Dudley's miners were more likely to comply peacefully.

Further developments were the decision to work an eight-hour day after 1 July 1872 and the introduction of a sliding-scale in 1874[86] whereby wages were linked to coal prices, with a minimum wage of 3s 6d per day for thick-coal miners. Before the system began in 1874, the local pits had been enjoying the tail-end of the boom created by the Franco-Prussian War. However, the price of furnace coal fell from 19s in March 1873 to 16s in March 1874. Thick-coal wages were reduced from 5s 6d to 4s 6d per day and thin-coal wages from 4s to 3s 3d (west of Dudley), and from 3s 9d to 3s east of Dudley. The miners began a strike which ended on 16 July 1874 in a victory for the masters. The sliding-scale was introduced on 24 July and by 5 October the price of coal had fallen to 13s and wages to 4s 6d, 3s 3d and 3s per day respectively. As demand for coal fell with the decline in iron production, the owners renounced the sliding-scale, in 1877, by taking out the minimum wage agreement. By May 1879 with the price of coal at 8s per ton, wages had fallen to 2s 9d, 2s 4½d and 2s 1½d per day respectively, a reduction of 40-50 per cent since March 1873. It was against this background that the Dudley estate tried to maintain the level of profits attained before 1845 and, after 1883, began to dispose of its mining property.

A major decision of the trustees had been to work the mines vigorously after 1836. By 1890 the question of royalties had become a matter for parliamentary concern and rates charged on royalty tended to fall after 1850. By the 1880s, royalty rates were beginning to fall on the Dudley estate also and royalty based on selling price, the practice established by Richard Smith, was being replaced by other arrangements.[87] The growing variety in royalties reflected the varying conditions under which leases were taken out: some related to unworked seams, others to broken mines of thick coal, or to 'pickings'. This last form concerned the lease of pits after the pillars of thick coal had been removed by a lessee. The remaining coal was then removed, after a period of time to allow for subsidence. Many of the conditions inserted in the large leases negotiated by Smith after 1836 were also omitted: minimum rents, inspection of accounts, supervision of the workings by estate agents, and so on, were superfluous in terms of many of the leases after 1870. Leases granted were for periods ranging from four to twenty-one years and, increasingly, until the pit or section was totally exhausted.[88]

The falling demand for coal as the local iron trade declined —as well as the growing number of totally exhausted pits—is reflected in the number of new leases granted by the estate after 1875. Up to 1880, approximately ten per year were negotiated; from 1881 to 1897 this fell to four per year; and, from 1898 to 1917, approximately one only per year. Most of them concerned the working of ribs, pickings or the clay which lay under the lower seams of coal. By the 1930s royalty rates on the Dudley estate had fallen still further but the rate still depended on the working conditions of the seam and its market value as these examples indicate:

28 Nov 1931. J. Clarke and Sons, Park Head, 7 acres 2 roods 16 perches: minimum royalty £50, Brooch Coal £50 per foot per acre: Ironstone 1/6 per ton.

20 July 1929. F. C. Dyke, Saltwells, 16 acres 1 rood: minimum royalty £100, Thick Coal pickings £75 per acre, Heathen Coal £30 per foot per acre.

10 Nov 1926. S. Bagley, Upper Gornal, Sandstone £12 per perch.

24 March 1932. Gibbons Ltd, Upper Gornal, 21 years minimum royalty £170, 39 acres. Top Fire Clay £300 per acre, Stinking Coal £120 per acre.

1 Oct 1926. King Bros Ltd, Stourbridge, minimum royalty £600, 8 acres 3 roods. Fireclay £160 per acre.

10 July 1930. E. J. and J. Pearson, Delph, 30 years, minimum royalty £500, 42 acres. Old Mine Clay £450 per acre. New Mine Clay £100 per foot per acre.

1 June 1931. Midland Slag Co Ltd, Barrow Hill, £1000 minimum royalty, 21 years. 42 acres 3 roods. Ragstone 6d per ton.[89]

As coal became scarcer on the estate and production costs

increased, the number of pits worked by the estate was reduced. By 1923, income from mineral leases was more than double that from estate-operated pits. Net receipts were £13,704 and £5,604 respectively.[90] As part of the general reorganisation of the estates in 1924, the direct operation of pits ceased and, thereafter, for the first time since Beaumont's work in 1798, mineral income came entirely from leased properties.

Income from leased mineral properties did not exceed revenue from estate-operated pits until about 1900. Leased pits produced a total royalty of £70,542 12s 3d in the boom year of 1854; of this, minimum royalties accounted for £15,059 18s 11d. The scale of the boom is indicated by the extensive difference between minimum royalties from negotiated leases, and actual receipts. Pits managed by the estate produced a net profit of £98,554 3s 5d in the same year. Royalty receipts had fallen to £26,146 3s 2d in 1871, in spite of the boom conditions at that time. As total mineral income was £167,826 17s 3d it is evident that the increase in local demand was met by an increase in the output of pits managed by the estate rather than leased properties. Mineral leases continued to decline in value, and by 1886, minimum royalty due had fallen to £6,855 16s 9d per annum.[91] After 1889, the estate steadily reduced the number of pits managed by the Mines Department—as production costs increased—and leased or sold them while a demand for local minerals still existed.

The last phase in the mineral history of the Dudley estate followed a report compiled by R. A. S. Redmayne in 1924.[92] This assessed current and future output of the pits and recommended a course of action which resulted in the cessation of mining activities by the estate itself and a reorganisation of the remaining leased mineral properties. It is likely that growing drainage problems, together with the mounting labour troubles of the mining industry in general, occasioned the report which provided a detailed analysis of the various sources of mineral income in 1924. The largest unit of production was the Baggeridge Colliery Co Ltd which began production in 1912. Although the total minimum royalty was £8,000 per annum, individual royalties indicate that the Dudley estate could no longer command such exceptionally high royalties as one-third of the selling price for thick coal which had been received in the 1840s and 1850s. Royalties were:

thick coal—$\frac{1}{12}$ of the selling price

all other coal—£30 per acre per foot thickness

gubbin ironstone—£40 per acre

other ironstone—6d per ton raised

fireclay—6d per ton raised.

Only 120 acres had been worked with an annual production of 188,000 tons. With additional facilities, Redmayne estimated that if production increased to 1 million tons per annum, 'a not unlikely eventuality', the resources of thick coal would last for over 100 years. In 1924 the estate held 2,000 of the 25,000 shares issued by the Baggeridge Colliery Co Ltd and debentures worth £1,900; income was also derived from royalties (minimum £8,000) and surface rents (£275). This enterprise was closed on 2 March 1968 by the National Coal Board, because of high production costs, leaving extensive deposits of minerals still untapped.

The remaining mineral areas still active in 1924 were at Himley and the Saltwells near Brierley Hill. In addition to Himley and Saltwells, there were small leased pits and quarries scattered throughout the Black Country mining coal, clay and stone producing a total royalty of £5,704 in 1923. This sum added to the minimum royalty from Baggeridge and the current income from Himley and Saltwells produced a total mineral income of £19,308.

A report by W. F. Clark in 1931,[93] mine agent since 1923, indicated that mineral income had in fact increased temporarily to £25,179 10s, largely due to increased output at Baggeridge and Himley. Production had ceased at Saltwells and the two pits at Himley would be worked-out by the end of the year. The report also considered the action to be taken in view of an unpublished circular issued on 21 November 1929 by the

Mineral Owners' Joint Committee, concerning the government's proposals for 'the Acquisition of Minerals'. The circular advised that, as the proposed Bill would leave lessors free to enjoy existing royalties until the termination of leases, all mineral owners should ensure that 'the lengths of their leases are sufficient to secure the working of the coal'. Any coal not let would be valued by the state and the owner would be compensated. Clark feared that

> with a Socialistic majority the mines will be acquired on some short cut-and-dried system of valuation, which may mean that the Baggeridge Colliery royalty may be acquired upon a basis of the royalties paid to the other lessees, something less than 3d a ton compared with 1s 1d the present Baggeridge royalty to Lord Dudley.
>
> Is it possible to make provision against such a catastrophe?

The estate's response was to speed up the sale of mineral land which had already been partially worked, so that current market values would be received rather than the compensation price to be offered by government valuation, which it was assumed would be lower. By 1942, total income had fallen to £8,602 14s 9d, and the 'Damaged Land and Royalty Accounts' finally ceased in 1950.

After 1845, the earls of Dudley—along with a minority of large landowners—continued to operate pits on their own account. By 1869, not more than five per cent of the collieries in England were owned and managed by landowners and most of these belonged to estates such as those of the Duke of Devonshire, the Earl of Lonsdale, the Bridgewater Trustees, the Marquess of Londonderry, the Earl of Durham and the Earl of Dudley. This situation represented a late stage in a long decline, but the Dudley estate was unusual in continuing to work collieries into the twentieth century, and the last colliery to be worked—at Himley—was not leased until 1924. However, to the extent that production in estate-operated mines declined in the last three decades of the nineteenth century, the trend was typical of other comparable aristocratic estates. Nevertheless, production remained relatively high until 1908 when estate enterprises sold a total of 423,395 tons of coal, 6,094 tons of ironstone, 17,708 tons of fireclay and 37,048 tons of limestone. Throughout the nineteenth century, Lord Dudley's mineral income compared favourably with the larger estates of other aristocratic coal owners.

	Dudley Estate			Duke of Norfolk	Earl Fitzwilliam	Earl of Durham[94]
1834	£28,133	7	11	—	£2,576 (1831)	£31,438
1847	83,045	1	5	—	8,991 (1850)	11,695
1854	98,554	3	5	—	—	84,207 (1856)
1871	141,680	14	1	—	37,210	—
1872	394,750	0	0	231,354 (1873)	—	380,000 (1873)
	(8,007 acres)			(15,270 acres)	(19,164 acres)	

Not only did the Dudley estate continue to work collieries on its own account long after comparable estates had begun to lease all minerals—such as the leasing of the Whitehaven collieries by the Earl of Lonsdale in 1888—but, after 1845, an increasing proportion of total net income was derived from estate pits rather than pits leased on royalty. This trend was probably maintained until the mid-1880s when the estate began to sell or lease many of the pits which it currently worked.

One of the more significant developments of the late nineteenth century as the more productive coal seams neared exhaustion—even on the Dudley estate—was growing speculation that thick coal could be found at a workable depth below the sandstone measures west of the boundary fault. As early as 1871, a paper delivered at Dudley Mining Institute considered the question 'Does Coal Exist Under the Red Sandstone Between the South Staffordshire and the East Shropshire Coalfields?'[95] Under the direction of John Hughes, mining engineer to the Dudley estate, a trial borehole was sunk in 1896 by Vivian's Boring and Exploration Co of Whitehaven. The site chosen was in Baggeridge woods on the northern edge of Himley Park in Sedgley parish; this was relatively remote from the traditional areas where the thick coal outcropped or lay at shallow depths—within

a four-mile radius of Dudley castle—and was approximately
half a mile east of the western boundary fault.

Throughout the area, this 'act of faith' was hailed as a beneficial development:

> at last . . . an extension of the famous coalfield is an accomplished
> fact. This event, the importance of which can scarcely be over-
> estimated . . . [is] . . . one of the most important . . . in the history
> of the Black Country . . . The extension and prosperity of nearly
> all the varied manufacturers for which the Black Country is
> famous depends upon a continuance of a plentiful supply of cheap
> fuel.[96]

A second shaft was begun in 1910 and production commenced in
1912. The scale of the undertaking is indicated by the cost of
plant installed—£150,000: this included ten steam boilers, supplied by Danks of Oldbury, and four electricity generating plants.
After the presence of the coal had been proved, a public company was formed to follow up the successful initiative taken by
the estate. The terms of the lease taken out by the Baggeridge
Colliery Co Ltd in September 1911 and the earl's minimum
royalty have already been indicated, together with the estimate of
the colliery's true potential given in Redmayne's report of 1924.
However, the main outlet for the transport of Baggeridge coal,
the Pensnett Railway, remained an estate enterprise. This was
extended from Shut End to Baggeridge so that coal could be
transported not only to the main individual customer—Round
Oak Steel Works—but also to the thirteen landsale wharves
throughout the Black Country and to the main canals. In 1913,
the Baggeridge branch was linked to the GWR at Gornal.

After 1923, the estate's connection with mineral production
ceased to be primarily that of entrepreneur and assumed the role
of supplier of capital—along with others—in the vast undertaking at Baggeridge. However, there was increasing investment in
the quarrying of sand, gravel and slag (for roadstone), as the
estate expanded its activities in this sector until the disposal of
property in 1947. This development is probably explained by the

relatively low production costs involved—unlike the coal seams
there was no drainage problem and materials could be worked
by surface quarrying. Moreover, there was no threat of nationalisation and local demand for these materials was expanding. Net
income from these sources and from estate timber was:

	1930			1935			1942			1946			1947		
	£	s	d	£	s	d	£	s	d	£	s	d	£	s	d
Timber	1,427	2	6	1,337	13	2							3,194	11	0
Sand and gravel	420	1	9	1,499	11	1	3,529	7	7	2,003	8	7	—		
Slag	4,650	12	2	235	18	4	—			—			—		
Tockey ashes etc	349	17	10	96	9	11	204	1	6	—			—		
Scrap	182	6	0	148	9	8	28	18	0	—			—[97]		

These figures reflect not only the growing value of the sand and
gravel quarries as an asset, but also the last stages of decline in
the mineral and industrial activities of the estate as a falling
income was drawn from the sale of old machinery and buildings,
slag, and other industrial waste from a former era of high prosperity. On the other hand, while the estates were capable of
yielding profit from a variety of sources, they were exploited to
the full. When the extensive sand quarries at Hinksford were
worked out, the plant and machinery were sold in 1940; only
Blackhills Quarry remained operative. This was sold as a going
concern in 1947 and is still active.

The last enterprise to be established by the estate after
1923 was the Baggeridge Brick Company which commenced
operations in 1936 as a private company. The site was adjacent
to the colliery and was intended to utilise the shale and
marl which were deposited on the spoil heaps at Baggeridge. The
first of the three large kilns was constructed in 1936 by F. B.

Clark—who had established the Aldridge Brick and Tile Company. The present earl still retains an interest in this concern, now a public company, which remains active despite the closure of the colliery. Clay is brought to the works from Himley in lorries along the line of the former Pensnett Railway—a unique link between the earliest and the most modern industrial activities of the Dudley estate.

The Dudley Estate: Net Income from Minerals and the Quantities of Minerals Sold, 1704-1942

	Pits Worked by the Estate			Royalties			Total		
	£	s	d	£	s	d	£	s	d
1704	—			—			1,941	0	0
1804	—			—			17,684	0	0
1834	28,123	7	11	4,765	1	8	32,888	9	7
1836	11,381	18	11	13,623	9	5	25,005	8	4
1847	67,044	15	8	74,955	4	4	142,000	0	0
1854	98,554	3	5	70,542	12	3	169,096	15	8
1859	—			—			110,734	4	3
1871	141,680	14	1	26,146	3	2	167,826	17	3
1872	394,750	0	0	22,507	0	0	417,257	0	0
1890	52,141	0	0	—			—		
1896	37,087	0	0	—			—		
1899	49,461	0	0	—			—		
1908	36,696	0	0	—			—		
1923	5,604	0	0	13,704	0	0	19,308	0	0
1930	None worked			20,861	0	0	20,861	0	0
1936	„ „			19,057	0	0	19,057	0	0
1942	„ „			8,602	0	0	8,602	0	0

Quantity of Minerals Sold—Excluding Leased Pits

	Coal Tons	Slack Tons	Ironstone Tons	Fireclay Tons	Limestone Tons
1800	—	—	—	—	85,000
1834	—	—	—	—	77,625
1837	—	—	—	—	104,004 (to iron-works only)
1845	1,400,000 (inc slack and ironstone)			—	92,164
1847	—	—	—	—	187,613
1871	1,189,980	(inc slack)	101,832	14,868	102,201
1877	268,306	390,310	50,958	10,679	—
1880	289,098	453,962	64,765	6,929	80,000 (1882)
1890	624,828	(inc slack)	15,005	19,237	65,126
1893	916,974	„ „	13,710	17,301	62,784
1899	705,000	„ „	17,028	12,073	60,395
1905	525,182	„ „	8,661	13,790	37,661
1908	423,395	„ „	6,094	17,708	37,048
1911	345,488	„ „	—	—	—
1923	158,000	„ „	—	—	—

After 1923, mineral production and profits came only from leased pits.

*Steam Engines Erected at Mines and Ironworks
Owned and Worked by the Dudley Estate*

	Mines	Blast	Forge	Total
1712	1	—	—	1
1731	3	—	—	3
1740	4	—	—	4
1797	4	2	1	7
1802	16	3	1	20
1839	38	6	4	48
1844	— (including leased ironworks)	19	1	20
1867	92 (excluding engines at the iron-works)	—	1	93
1882	84	2	1	87

Stock Account	Dead			Convertible			Total		
	£	s	d	£	s	d	£	s	d
1833	56,000								
1837	66,956	9	8						
1847	177,344	14	0	42,646	0	11	219,990	14	11
1854	254,399	1	5						
1871	586,173	1	9	119,604	13	6	705,777	15	3
1887	658,971	15	8	74,484	12	8	733,456	8	4

This list includes stock invested in ironworks and mines owned
and worked by the estate: valuations represent current estimates
after taking account of depreciation.

Notes to Chapter 6 are on pages 257-63

CHAPTER SEVEN

Estate Administration

Agents

Along with other estates possessing agricultural, industrial and mineral interests, the Dudley estate was faced with the problem of finding suitable agents to administer its affairs and it was not until the trust period that the 'management revolution' took place.

Agents for the great estates[1] were drawn from the landed gentry, attorneys, clerks, and accountants: such men, especially landowning gentry, managed the industrial and mineral interests of the Dudley estate between 1774 and 1833. Richard Mee, steward of Kingswinford manor, was both a local landowner and an attorney who had acted as attorney to the Ashwood Hay enclosure commissioners. As chief land agent, his duties included the supervision of the manor courts—in his capacity as steward of Lord Dudley's local manors—the management of the agricultural properties, and the collection of cottage and great rents. Lord Dudley held manor courts in Belbroughton, Dudley, Himley, Kingswinford, Rowley Regis, Sedgley, and Swindon where his stewards supervised the transfer of coyphold farm and cottage properties and collected the fines or heriots due. Minor manorial officials were also appointed by the courts, such as supervisors of highways for the various liberties. By the end of the eighteenth

Q

century, Lord Dudley had constructed large inns, known as the 'Court House', where the manor courts were held and where tenants came to pay their rents to his agents. After 1788, Mee was succeeded as chief steward or land agent by members of the Brettell family, Richard and Thomas, both of whom were local landowners and attorneys.

On the death of his steward, John Keelinge in 1823, Lord Dudley was forced to break with the traditional pattern because Francis Downing, who then succeeded to the position of chief land agent (and, in 1826, mineral agent), lacked the professional training necessary to administer the work of the manor courts. Accordingly, Joseph Bourne, a Dudley solicitor and landowner in Kingswinford, became chief steward.[2] However, the growing volume of business necessitated the employment of a London solicitor and after 1800 John Benbow[3] of Lincoln's Inn handled major legal transactions for the Dudley estate, and gradually assumed a general supervisory position over all estate activities.

Edward Cockshutt, a local landowner, was the mineral agent who, for a salary of £200, undertook the organisation and development of industrial and mineral enterprise during the period of expansion initiated by the second viscount after 1774. He was ultimately dismissed in 1797—for incompetence—and this phase of rapid but inefficient expansion was followed by an attempt to secure rationalisation and efficiency under the direction of the Newcastle mining engineer, Charles Beaumont. After he was dismissed by Lord Dudley for his radical measures, mineral and industrial enterprise on the estate continued to benefit from Beaumont's activities, and profitability was maintained for much of the period down to 1826 under the management of a local man, Charles Roberts. There is no indication as to whether or not Roberts was a professionally trained mining engineer—in view of subsequent developments, it is unlikely that he was. His salary was the same as that negotiated by Beaumont: £200 per annum plus 'poundage' or commission calculated on profit at 1s per £1.

A permanent staff of officials and agents existed by 1804 and they were collectively referred to as the Mines Department.[4]

The Staff Employed by the Mines Department, November 1804

Charles Roberts	Principal Mine Agent
George Rhodes	Travelling Clerk
Richard Bissell	Superintendent of the Works
Francis Downing	Office Clerk
Samuel Chavasse	Office Clerk
William Robinson	Engineer and Carpenter
Edward Jones	Ground Bailiff
James Price	Ground Bailiff
Samuel Hartshorne	Ground Bailiff
Edward Robinson	Bailiff
Edward Wilmot	Bailiff
John Witt	Bailiff. Weighing Machine Keeper (Coal) at Brierley Hill
John Shakspear	Bailiff
George Johnson	Bailiff
Richard Adie	Bailiff
Simeon Bissell	Bailiff
Richard Bissell Junior	Bailiff
Benjamin Bissell	Gauger of Boats
Samuel Lister	Engineer
Joseph Fereday	Weighing Machine Keeper (Coal)
Joseph Robinson	Weighing Machine Keeper (Coal)
James Holcroft	Bailiff
John Wall	Weighing Machine Man
John Pearce	Weighing Machine Man
Edward Harley	Weighing Machine Man
Joseph Parson	Superintendent of the Lime Works
John Collins	Bailiff
Richard Rhodes	Weighing Machine Keeper (Lime)
John Johnson	Weighing Machine Man (Limestone)
Thomas Fellows	Ground Bailiff
John Whick	Weighing Machine Keeper (Lime)
Richard Collins	Weighing Machine Keeper (Lime)
Thomas Wainwright	Gauger of Boats

These men had the responsibility for the management, organisation, and supervision of all forms of mineral and industrial enterprise on the estates and it is probable that the department was set up in this form by Charles Beaumont. In the 1830s the department moved into offices at The Priory, Dudley; before this, Lord Dudley's mineral affairs were administered from offices at the Level Store Yard. After 1826 when Francis Downing succeeded Roberts as principal mineral agent, mineral enterprise declined and the inefficient management which Beaumont had eradicated returned to the Dudley pits. Downing, designated as an office clerk in 1804, came from a local landowning family, and lacked the professional knowledge required by a principal mineral agent. His errors of judgement were revealed in the report by Smith and Liddell who observed that the only way to secure efficient control 'is to place the responsibility of this Department on a professional Mine Engineer'.[5] Downing's salary was £500 per annum in addition to the £500 he received as principal land agent.

Absolute financial control, exercised from a London office by experts combining the skills of land agency and accountancy and able to impose techniques of cost control on total estate expenditure, was not available until the last quarter of the nineteenth century, although not even then widely used.[6] Up to a point, the Dudley estate enjoyed this advantage during the period of the trust to the extent that there was a general manager of the estate's affairs—Benbow—and an auditor—Loch—whose duty it was to analyse and report on the profitability of all aspects of estate interests. Other developments of the trust period were the consolidation and identification of specific areas of responsibility on the part of a number of sub-agents under the overall control of Benbow. In general, land agency had come to be regarded as a distinct profession by the 1840s as seen in the career of men such as Henry Morton, chief agent of the Earl of Durham, and it was during the trust period that the first professional land agents were employed on the Dudley estate. Downing was prevailed upon to give up the land agency in 1834 so that he could concentrate on his duties as trustee.

Since 1823, a special appointment had been made of steward of all the manors whose sole responsibility was manorial affairs, but it seems that Bourne had the traditional lazy approach of the local Dudley officials. In 1848, Benbow observed that he had 'never been able to procure Mr Bourne's Account—It embraces professional Charges—and his Transactions as Steward of the Manor'.[7]

After Downing's fingers had been prised off the land agency in 1834, he was also forced to give up the mineral agency in 1836 by his fellow trustees. Thereafter, Richard Smith brought unsurpassed administrative efficiency and technical expertise to the conduct of mineral and industrial affairs. This success was reflected in his salary of £1,200 per annum plus a payment of $2\frac{1}{2}$ per cent on net profit above £35,000.[8] He quickly established a favourable reputation not only with his employers, but also with his employees, with the population of the district as a whole, and with the various commissions of inquiry, one[9] of which described him as an 'upright and humane' employer. These qualities persisted on the Dudley estate after 1864 under Richard Smith's successors: first of all under his younger son, Frederick, 1864-70 and later under his grandson, Edward Fisher Smith, 1870-86.

Systems of Accounts

Systems of book-keeping and accounts remained primitive and inefficient on the Dudley estate down to 1833. Rentals were the most significant accounts in this period. Until 1788, all rents received from estate properties were recorded in volumes designated as 'Lord Dudley's Rental', but, after this date, rents were recorded in separate volumes known as the 'Cottage Rental' or the 'Great Rental'. After 1788 there was also a change in the nature of the items included in the rentals which, before that time, had been 'really a statement of income'.[10] Until 1791 the rentals remained general statements of income including interest on loans and profit from turnpike and canal investments. After this date, a more systematic form of accounts was introduced to record items in separate accounts. Whatever the deficiencies of Lord Dudley's administration between 1774 and 1833, systems of accounts were never so primitive as those which prevailed on the Wentworth Woodhouse estate of the earls Fitzwilliam where collieries had begun as a department of household administration and colliery accounts were kept in the household account books.[11]

Professor S. Pollard[12] has shown that the master and steward system of accounts persisted until the end of the eighteenth century, and was based on a double-entry form whereby the debit side was the 'charge', representing all the receipts of the agent on behalf of his master, and the credit, or 'discharge' side, recorded all payments made, leaving the balance of cash held by the agent. The 'Cash Account of Thomas and Messrs Brettell to the Right Honourable Lord Viscount Dudley and Ward' for 1789[13] followed this pattern. On the 'charge' side of the account were dividends from canal shares, interest on loans, sales of timber, manorial fines, and rents received. The 'discharge' side contained a wide variety of payments including subscriptions to clubs, repair bills, gratuities, and agents' salaries. One notable absence from the account is any reference to mining profits or outlay: this suggests that a division already existed between estate business in general and mineral and industrial enterprise in particular.

One of the tasks assigned to Smith and Liddell by the trustees in 1835 was to improve the systems of accounts used by Lord Dudley's mineral and industrial agents:

> Although there is a profit upon the whole Concern ... it is necessary to ascertain whether upon individual portions of it, the reverse is not the case.[14]

James Loch commented that in Downing's mine accounts, items 'are put down in the order of the date of payment without any classification'.[15] This recalls the form used by Brettell in 1788 and the continued use of traditional accounts may be explained by the fact that Downing, like Brettell, was a product of the local landed gentry and was unable to adapt the traditional account used for landed estates in spite of its inadequacy for industrial affairs. Loch observed that 'no matter of accounts ever occupied so much of my personal labour and consideration and that of my clerks'.

The departmental allocation of costs was a development of the late eighteenth century. The Dudley estate partially operated this system before 1833 but the true profitability of individual branches of enterprise remained a mystery because of the absence of individual accounts for each enterprise. Timber was purchased from Lord Dudley's store-yard in Kingswinford, for use in his mines, and these transactions were recorded in the rentals for 1790 and 1791 as payments to the estate by the mine agent. The mining and industrial concerns run by the estate also paid a land rent to the estate. It was during the trust period that other improvements were introduced including double-entry forms, capital accounting, and the break-down of accounts to provide specific information such as net profit on individual concerns, administrative expenses, debts outstanding, or receipts from investments.

In 1835 Loch proposed that, in future:

the accounts should present a statement Dr. and Cr. of each separate pit or work carrying to the credit side of the account the quantity of Mine got . . . with the expence of getting the same, supported by monthly vouchers of payments . . . to be signed by two of the clerks in the office whose duty it shall be to ascertain at the monthly settlement of accounts, that the men have been paid by the Mine Bailiff. The Debit side . . . should confirm the manner in which the Mines so got have been disposed of under such heads as . . .

To sold for ready money
To sold on credit

To delivered to furnaces

To remaining in stock

The furnace account must be made out on a similar principle.

There are some payments and transactions ... which must be charged to the works generally. In this way (as payments on account ... cannot be dispensed with) the money so advanced will be ... at the personal risk of the Mine Agent, who will of course look to his own security in granting such accommodation and the care of keeping the necessary memorandums ...

The account should contain a summary ... of all persons who have purchased Mines (minerals) on credit arranged ... thus.

1. The arrears due at the end of the preceding year
2. Debts contracted during the current year
3. Sums received during the year
4. Amount of arrears due.

A separate Stock Book must be kept showing the receipts and disposal of the same.[16]

These recommendations were not fully implemented until after December 1836 when Smith became the mine agent and added his support to Loch's campaign for a more efficient system of book-keeping and accounts. One final complication in securing an accurate statement of the estate's total income and expenditure was the fact that the mine accounts terminated in December, the landed accounts at Ladyday, and the executor's accounts 'somewhat later'.

The Ledgers were too numerous in consequence of the Old Ledgers not being closed at the end of every year ... and the Journal, which ought to be the Principal Book and the foundation of the whole system is a mere memorandum Book ... Any person connected with Book keeping must know that the real nature of every transaction should be entered in the Journal of which the Ledger shows the result.[17]

As the main source of income came from mineral exploitation, Loch proposed that all accounts should be closed annually at the end of December. His final proposal was an attempt to establish an accurate record of capital invested in the various enterprises:

> An Account of the value of all the Articles and Machinery, including the Cost or Value of the Pits themselves at each work should also be taken annually with such additions or the contrary as may have occurred ... and a certain sum per cent should be written off yearly on Account of the loss for Tear and Wear.

Loch's visit to Himley in 1835 was a traumatic experience which led him to propose that his head clerk, Hathorn, should stay there in order to examine all the estate books and accounts so as to introduce a complete 'new system of Books'. This mammoth task occupied Hathorn and Loch until August 1835, but Loch was determined to 'have the Accounts kept in the way I think best for the right understanding of the Concerns, the benefit of the Remainder Men and the security of the Trustees'. By 1836, the records of the estate reveal that all Loch's proposals were in operation.

Similar weaknesses existed in the administration of the landed estates, and the purchase of distant properties increased the need for accurate and full accounts. Loch criticised the practice whereby the land agents remitted 'only Balances, after paying for Repairs etc instead of remitting the entire Rents'. This left expenditure too much to the discretion of sub-agents. Within the vicinity of Dudley, the various land agents 'did not show any Account of the Timber cut on the estate and applied to repairs'.[18] Moreover, he condemned the local agents because

> large sums for timber, ironmongery, glass, plant etc ... are carried to the Account of the Level Timber and Iron Store Yard ... but no Statement of the application of any of these Materials could be furnished.

Loch remedied this by introducing a stock book for the Level Store Yard, which recorded stock in hand and all transactions with estate enterprises. This was to be kept at the chief land agent's office at the Priory, and stock could only be drawn from the store-yard by an order from the Priory office. Durose, the surveyor in charge of the store-yard, was condemned for his lax conduct of affairs in supplying goods and materials without adequate records, and, in Loch's opinion, his function should be merely that of 'an executive Servant'. He was subsequently dismissed.

Additional accounts and practices were introduced as the scale and variety of estate operations increased. For example, after Smith introduced the practice of extensive leasing of the pits in 1836, two new accounts were opened by him to show receipts from rents and royalties; he also opened accounts to record the income from various estate pumping engines. These accounts enabled him to discover which lessees had failed to produce the minimum royalty assessed for each leased pit and whether or not a particular engine should be kept in operation in the interests of the estate and its tenants.

During the trust period, the systems of book-keeping and accounts had been radically overhauled, brought up to date, and efficiently administered. Most of the practices introduced by Loch were continued after 1845 to the long-term benefit of the estate. An auditor's report on estate accounts in 1871 observed that 'The Ledgers, Journals and Cash Books required in the business are all that can be desired both as to detail as well as in accuracy and neatness'.[19]

The Lords Dudley

By the mid-nineteenth century, the aristocracy in England were probably more closely involved in the administration of their estates than ever before. In the case of the Dudley estate, the lords Dudley continued to exercise general control of policy throughout the period 1774-1833, but only the second viscount and, for a few years after his death in 1788, his successor, were personally involved in everyday administration.

Broad questions of policy were undoubtedly decided by the

second viscount between 1774 and 1788. He was responsible for
the introduction into Parliament of all the local enclosure Bills,
which extended his personal estate and consolidated his rights in
the area, and for most of the local canal Bills. Rentals and accounts
were also examined and passed by him. In the early years after
acceding to the title in 1788, William, third Viscount Dudley and
Ward, remained active in exercising general control of estate
policy but ceased to involve himself in the day-to-day conduct of
affairs such as the passing of rentals and accounts. After 1790,
these were signed by Thomas Brettell. It may be that William's
disinclination to attend to routine administration led him in 1797
to ask an old friend, the Reverend Thomas Jeans of Paddington,
to 'superintend my concerns'.[20] This was the position assumed by
Benbow in 1802. The third viscount involved himself less and
less in the direction of affairs and he has been described as

> One of those ordinary mortals on whom capricious fortune takes
> a pleasure in lavishing worldly advantages. The obscure existence
> of the old lord was passed in the society of those who, like himself,
> preferred port wine and fiddling to the pursuits either of politics
> or literature.[21]

This may explain the deterioration in the state of affairs on the
Dudley estate after 1800. His son, John William, who inherited
the title as fourth viscount in 1823, was even less active in the
management of the estate. He was frequently abroad, and was
involved in politics after becoming an MP in 1802. Illness in-
capacitated him during the last two years of his life when he
was under constant medical care:

> Unsteadiness of purpose ... unwillingness to risk, and reluctance
> to assent—incapacity to make up his mind either as to the
> measures of others or his own conduct ... chequered his exist-
> ence ... during the latter years.[22]

This pattern of growing isolation between the lords Dudley and
their estates contrasts with the general trend among aristocratic
landowners and probably explains the degree to which inefficiency

and corruption flourished in the latter years of the period 1774-1833. Because of the late earl's state of mind, the validity of the will was questioned by his cousin, William, who inherited only the title. His sanity was also impaired, and he was disappointed at not inheriting the estates. His hostility was increased when his son William, heir to the estate, and his two other children were removed from his care and placed under the guardianship of E. J. Littleton by the Court of Chancery.

Young William made things more difficult when he wrote to his mother, Lady Amelia:

> I think you decided rather hastily upon sending me here [Petherwyn], as indeed I think most things are about me . . . I am sure the circumstances in our family are disagreeable enough, without adding to them . . . I think too that all the correspondence about my not receiving Papa's letters is highly unjust and foolish . . . I know what the state of his mind is, and I read and consider the letters accordingly.[23]

This provides an early insight into William's character—he was sixteen years old at the time: his forthright manner, perceptive qualities, and his sense of justice were to provoke many clashes with the trustees before the end of the trust. After inheriting the title on the death of his father in 1835, William played a significant part in the conduct of estate and regional affairs. Opinion was divided over what to do with William, especially after he left his tutor's house in March 1834 without permission. Littleton wrote at the time:

> I think I know Ward well and that anything said in the tone of a Sermon . . . will be laughed at by him. His lessons must be of a practical sort to do him any service. For instance, to disabuse his mind of false notions about himself and his prospects, I would show him finer Houses than he will possess, and better company than he will find about Himley. I made him go to Lansdowne House with this view the other night . . . and did all I could in the way of raillery to take the conceit out of him. He was greatly pleased with his Evening.[24]

He also insisted that William should take a degree and face up
to his responsibilities to others and to the estate: 'in matter of
duty, he must be made to feel that obedience will be expected, if
not requested'.

One of William's main weaknesses was gambling and, although
gambling debts during the nineteenth century ceased to be the
serious charge on landed estates that they had been before 1800,
Lord Ward's gambling debts embarrassed the trustees and put
the whole future of his estates in hazard. While a student at
Christ Church, Oxford, William incurred a gambling debt of
£1,100 which he asked Benbow to pay, and gave his 'word of
honour' not to play again.[25] All warnings went unheeded and
Ward's 'word of honour' not to gamble was continually broken:

> Lord Ward is frequenting the Low Hells in Town and losing
> hundreds ... to a Class of the lowest Swindlers ... I lament this
> Propensity to low Society and to such ruinous Courses: if he had
> lost his money among Gentlemen one might have forgiven his
> Folley.[26]

At his mother's request, William's tutor at Oxford was T. L.
Claughton. He had to negotiate with the Dean of Christ Church
in defence of William when the dean complained to Hatherton
in June 1836:

> I do not find in his Lordship that disposition to conform with
> academical discipline and regulations which is necessary to make
> residence here advantageous. Nor ... from the habits he has
> contracted [will] ... any material improvement take place.[27]

Foreign travel was, in his opinion, the 'fittest mode of completing
his Lordship's education'. However, the dean relented and
allowed him to continue his studies with the warning that 'Habits
of indulgence, fostered by an unlimited supply of money will not
easily be checked in this place'.[28] Six months later, he wrote to
Hatherton: 'I have the painful duty to acquaint you that I have
been compelled to rusticate Lord Ward till after the long
vacation'[29]—this followed incidents at a race meeting attended

by Lord Ward at Cottesford. However, like Hatherton, the dean was beginning to discern another side to William's character, and he added that 'His Lordship has many good qualities which if properly directed, will lead him to honour and distinction'. William returned to Oxford in October 1837 and subsequently took a first-class degree.

There are some indications that William did make a conscious effort to reform, particularly after graduating in the summer of 1838 when, accompanied by Claughton, he spent many weeks at one of Lord Francis Egerton's shooting lodges in northern Scotland:

> I am reconciling myself for the last four years I have foolishly spent in late Hours and useless Habits, with the severest north eastern breezes that ever searched through so lathy a being as myself. The breezes in the South are toxicated with dissipation. We have them here pure and unsullied from the foundery in Greenland.[30]

By the mid-nineteenth century, administrative matters probably took up more of a landowner's time than ever before.[31] In the case of the Dudley trust, the trustees tended to consult Lord Ward on major decisions—particularly those relating to the purchase of estates—while he himself undertook to express his opinions on the conduct of affairs in general and revealed a considerable mastery of essentials. Writing from Scarborough in August 1837, he stated his opinions on the question of large purchases of land and, incidentally, on the Bishop of Exeter:

> I have no doubt the Bishop of Exeter would like a tour into Herefordshire via Cheltenham, Himley etc and at the Trustees' expense but I will not if I can help it give him the option of so doing—nor do I wish for a place in that County. My wishes are these ... that it should be large enough to make Himley a second place. Therefore I should like one about 30 or 40,000 Acres. You will smile perhaps but I would rather wait and buy a good one, that will sink some years accumulation, than be laying out a

yearly Income on small places ... That is what I should call turning the old coal Pits to some Account.[32]

It was his suggestion that the new agricultural leases[33] should include a clause that the tenant must 'keep and leave'[34] the property in good repair. Throughout the trust, William was constantly informed of the conduct of affairs. When John Benbow died in 1855, certain matters relating to the trust were still outstanding, and, as 'A new "Administrator de bonis non" was required ... Lord Ward was ... clothed with that character'[35] in order to secure the outstanding estate.

Lord Ward's relationship with his employees and tenants was benevolent and paternalistic. On the occasion of his being created Earl of Dudley in February 1860, tenants in the Quarry Bank area of Brierley Hill presented him with a congratulatory address:

this evidence of a Royal Favour has been most judiciously conferred upon a nobleman, the management of whose property throughout this entire district justly entitles him to be ranked amongst the kindest, most liberal and best of England's landlords in whom an industrious and well-conducted tenantry always find a protector, friend and patron ... [and] your Lordship proves by great liberality your anxiety for the religion and moral welfare of the people ... granting, in this mining country where land is so valuable, ground for the erection of a church, churchyard, parsonage and gardens.[36]

Pensions were regularly paid throughout the period 1833-45—a practice inherited from the first earl.[37] Evidence submitted by Smith to the Midlands Mining Commission in 1843[38] revealed the extent of these payments.

	Thick-coal miners			Ironstone and thin-coal miners			Limestone			Total		
	£	s	d	£	s	d	£	s	d	£	s	d
Sick relief paid	105	17	6	64	14	6	178	13	6	349	5	6
by estate	80	18	6	32	7	3	59	11	2			
by miners' club	24	19	0	32	7	3	119	2	4			

	Thick-coal miners	Ironstone and thin-coal miners	Limestone	Total
Widows' Pensions (379)	51 3 0	59 16 6	132 17 0	243 16 6
Superannuated Miners' Pensions	96 17 6	—	270 10 0	367 7 0
			Total (for 1842)	960 9 0

This was in addition to pensions paid to employees on the landed estates: in 1836 these amounted to £405 3s 4d.

One of the major causes of social distress in the Black Country was the truck system—even after the Truck Act of 1831. It was probably because the Dudley estate, and Lord Ward himself, condemned the truck system that the Reverend C. Girdlestone, vicar of Kingswinford, published a pamphlet in April 1855, dedicated to Lord Ward who had

> so often responded nobly to the local demands on your pre-eminent position ... and the interest you have often proved yourself to feel in the welfare of that large number of our fellow creatures to whom you stand in a relation so pregnant with each kind of privilege, both rights and duties, as that of Lord of the Soil.[39]

He urged Lord Ward to use his influence to persuade other owners to ban truck and adopt similar practices to those in operation on the Dudley estate.

The estate did a great deal to promote education in the area at all levels. Even the majority of the mine agents were illiterate, as indicated in the mines report of 1850; perhaps with this in mind, Lord Ward and Smith sponsored the establishment of a Mechanics' Institute at Dudley in 1848. By 1835, the estate was paying annual subscriptions for the maintenance of local church schools at Himley, Kingswinford, Redhall Hill, Brierley Hill, Coseley, Dudley, and Sedgley—all of which had been built on land donated by Lord Ward. Free coal was conveyed to the

schools from estate collieries, and new schools were erected on
the newly acquired estates:

Erecting new school (Kidderminster)	£189	0	0
One year's salary to Rushock Schoolmaster	5	10	0
Annual subscription to Martley School	10	0	0[40]

Land and money were also donated for church construction.

The estate also became involved in town improvements and
local government development after a special inquiry—instituted
by the Central Board of Health in 1852 following a particularly
severe cholera epidemic—found that the average age of death in
Dudley was 16 years 7 months and that 69.8 per cent of the
population died before reaching the age of 20. These figures were
far worse than the national average. Apart from the overcrowded
tenements of the central areas in Dudley, a major health hazard
was the absence of clean, piped water; many Black Country
families took their water from the canals. It was to remedy this
deficiency that Lord Ward and Smith actively worked for the
foundation of the South Staffordshire Waterworks Company in
1856. Full acknowledgement of the earl's contribution to local
improvements was included in his obituary:

> nearly all the land on which church property now stands in
> Dudley, Sedgley, Cosely, Tipton, Kingswinford and Wordsley
> has been freely given to the public ... in educational matters,
> Lord Dudley was always ready to lend a helping hand, when he
> saw that a good reason for his aid was established ... He presided
> at a public meeting in Dudley (3 Feb 1853) and complained of
> 'the general want of a spirit of progress in the town' and also
> dwelt on the want of a proper system of sewerage: it may be
> assumed that the establishment of a Board of Health later in the
> same year, as well as the subsequent town improvements ...
> owed their achievement to the speech in question.[41]

On his death in May 1885, he was succeeded by his son William
Humble Ward whose interest lay mainly in national politics and
administration.[42]

The late earl, who succeeded to the title in 1932 and died in

1969, also participated in national affairs but his connections with industry were extensive.[43] As Viscount Ednam he became chairman of the new company in 1924[44] when Round Oak Iron Works Ltd was reorganised, and he negotiated the reorganisation and resettlement of the estates in 1923 and the consolidation of its interests into a public company—the Himley Estates Ltd—in 1926. The second earl sold the bulk of his estates to his son, Viscount Ednam, including £25,000 of 5 per cent debentures and 10,021 £5 shares in the Round Oak Works Ltd, 5,000 £5 shares and 112,200 5 per cent debentures in the Baggeridge Colliery Ltd. In order to raise capital and to meet the costs of reorganisation, Lord Ednam sold the freehold of the property to the Round Oak Works Ltd. He then formed a public limited company in March 1926 registered under the name of the Himley Estates Ltd. Lord Ednam was its Governing Director and he sold to it the life interest of Lord Dudley for £167,140 and his own reversionary life interest in the Dudley Settled Estates and investments—for £332,820. Excluded from this arrangement were Lord Ednam's 20,000 shares in the Baggeridge Colliery Co Ltd. Thereafter, as income from local enterprise fell, investment income increased:

1930	£26,346	15s	6d
1932	£29,207	1s	4d
1935	£25,929	4s	6d
1942	£39,257	6s	6d

This broadened the basis of the economic interests both of the Himley Estates and the family, and safeguarded them in the event of a collapse in the local economy.

Long before the decision to dispose of the family estates was taken in 1947, the late earl had precipitated the transformation of the family's main economic interests from an entrepreneurial role to that of rentier. After 1947, income was drawn from a number of public companies in which the Earl of Dudley held investments. Further diversification followed when much of the capital raised by the disposal of landed property was eventually invested in the Tribune Investment Trust Ltd which has United Kingdom and overseas interests. This phase marked the last in a long process of change and adjustment to changing circumstances. Nevertheless, the Dudley estate was unusual in the extent to which it pursued an entrepreneurial role in the iron and coal industries throughout the nineteenth century, and the Earl of Dudley was perhaps the most successful of the landed aristocratic entrepreneurs to survive into the twentieth century.

Notes to Chapter 7 are on pages 263-5

Notes

INTRODUCTION

1 Jevons, W. J. *The Coal Question,* VIII (1865).
2 Taylor, A. J. *Victoria History of the County of Stafford,* II (1967), 69.
3 See Court, W. H. B. *The Rise of the Midland Industries, 1600-1838* (1938). Also Chapter I, part two.
4 Richards, E. S. 'James Loch and the House of Sutherland, 1812-1855' (PhD thesis, University of Nottingham, 1967).
5 *Burke's Peerage IV,* 491.
6 He died in December 1969.
7 *Dudley Herald,* 30 April 1949.

CHAPTER ONE

1 Court, 22.
2 Gale, W. K. V. *The Coneygre Story* (1954), 4.
3 Taylor, 73.
4 The Ward family was the fifth to hold the Barony of Dudley. After the Norman Conquest, William Fitz-Ansculf received over eighty manors in the Midlands and South which together constituted the Barony of Dudley. About 1100 he was succeeded in the title by Fulk Paganel. In 1190, John de Somery

NOTES45

assumed the title by marriage, and it passed to John de Sutton in 1322, again by marriage. Edward Lord Dudley, the last of the Sutton Dudleys, died in 1643 and his estates passed to Frances, his granddaughter. Her husband, Humble Ward, was created Baron Ward in 1644 and their descendants held the estate and the title of Lord Viscount Dudley and Ward in 1774.

5 Chandler, G. and Hannah, I. C. *Dudley As It Was and As It Is To-day* (1949), 20.
6 Ibid, 21.
7 Dudley MSS.
8 Schubert, C. H. R. *The History of the British Iron and Steel Industry* (1957), 181.
Gornal Wood is located between Dudley and Himley.
Halesowen lies between Stourbridge and Birmingham.
9 Dud Dudley. *Metallum Martis: or, Iron made with Pit Coak, Sea Coale, and with the same Fuell to Melt and Fire Imperfect Mettals and Refine perfect Mettals* (1665).
10 Ibid. Pensnett Chase was in the manors of Kingswinford and Dudley.
11 Ibid, 30-2, for an account of the price and quantities of iron made.
12 William Salt Library, Stafford, 417/37.
13 Ibid.
14 Allen, J. S. 'The 1712 and Other Newcomen Engines of the Earls of Dudley', *Transactions of the Newcomen Society*, XXXVII (1964-5).
15 PRO C12/1436/12 as quoted in Allen, op cit.
16 Ibid.
17 Rolt, L. T. C. *Thomas Newcomen: the Prehistory of the Steam Engine* (1963), 58-60.
18 Harris, J. R. 'The Employment of Steam Power in the Eighteenth Century', *History*, LII (June 1967).
19 Morton, G. R. and Mutton, N. 'The Transition to Cort's Puddling Process', *Journal of the Iron and Steel Institute*

(July 1967), 205.

20 See Rostow, W. W. *The Stages of Economic Growth* (1961).

21 See Deane, P. *The Industrial Revolution* (1965).

CHAPTER TWO

1 Tate, W. E. 'The Cost of Parliamentary Enclosure in England', *Economic History Review*, II (1952-3).

2 Dudley MSS 21/3, Printed copies of original documents. Lord Dudley was lord of the manor in every case except Wombourne (Lord Wrottesley).

3 Brierley Hill Public Library H3.1, Ashwood Hay Enclosure Act, 1776 and Award, 1777. Brierley Hill Public Library H3.1, Pensnett Chase Enclosure Act, 1784 and Award, 1786.

4 Dudley MSS 21/3, 1.

5 Ashwood Hay Enclosure Act, 15.

6 Ashwood Hay Enclosure Award, Second Schedule, sheet 1.

7 See pp91-4.

8 The commissioners were—for Ashwood Hay—Samuel Wyatt of Burton, Edward Palmer of Coleshill, Harry Court of Stourbridge and Thomas Hanson of Birmingham; for Pensnett Chase—as above; for Wombourne and Swindon—John Bishton of Kilsall, Salop, William Callow of Tardebigge (Birmingham) and Harry Court; for Rowley Regis—John Bishton and William Roberts of Dudley.

9 Dudley MSS, Pensnett Chase Enclosure Act, 21/3, 1.

10 See below.

11 Beresford, M. W. 'Commissioners of Enclosure', *Economic History Review* (1946), as quoted by Parker, R. A. C. *Historical Association* (1960), 8.

12 Taylor, A. J. *Victoria History of the County of Stafford*, II, 94.

13 Pensnett Chase Enclosure Act, 15.

14 Brierley Hill Public Library. *The Morning Leader and*

County Express, November 1902.

15 Ibid, 18 September 1897.

16 Dudley MSS 12/1, W. F. Taylor to Sir Gilbert H. Claughton, 16 February 1915. Claughton was agent to the estate.

17 Dudley MSS 12/d, Clulow (representing Hale) to E. F. Smith (the earl's mineral agent), 13 March 1876.

18 Ibid, Bourne and Owen to E. F. Smith, 2 March 1876.

CHAPTER THREE

1 Dudley Public Library LD/625. Minutes of Evidence Taken Before the Select Committee on the Oxford, Worcester and Wolverhampton Railway, 1845. Appendix. Subsequently referred to as Railway Sel Com 1845.

2 At Dudley Public Library.

3 Staffordshire County Record Office D1778/v/708. See map, p56.

4 Brierley Hill Public Library, H15.2, Printed copy of the Stourbridge Canal Act.

5 Ibid. A Plan for a Navigable Canal from Netherton to the Black Delph.

6 Dudley Canal Proprietors' Minute Book, 5 September 1785.

7 It is appropriate that the proposed Black Country Industrial Museum is being developed alongside this canal at Castle Mill.

8 Of the canal Acts passed 1758-1802, 90 out of 165 had as their motive the exploitation of the coal trade: Ashton, T. S. *An Economic History of England in the Eighteenth Century*, 74.

9 Hatherton, Col. D260/M/F/5/19/4, 17.

10 See pp117-22.

11 Hatherton, Col. Loch's Fifth Report for year ending June 1839.

12 Ibid, D260/M/F/5/19/11, Hatherton to Benbow, 27 Jan-

uary 1839.

13 An area of Pensnett Chase to the south of Dudley. As the shallow thick-coal deposits were nearing exhaustion on the slopes of Brierley Hill, deeper deposits were opened up during the 1830s in the Shut End area which lacked a canal link at this time.

14 A steam railway built by the estate from Shut End on Pensnett Chase to Ashwood on the Staffs-Worcs Canal. See below.

15 *Dudley Herald,* 25 July 1868.

16 Dudley MSS 10/H.

17 Hatherton, Col. Lord Ward to Lord Hatherton, February 1841.

18 Ibid, January 1840.

19 Railway Sel Com 1845, Q.397.

20 See pp183-93.

21 PRO C/110/170, Beaumont to Jeans, 22 June 1797.

22 See below.

23 Dudley MSS 10/1, Mr Foster's Proposals for a Railroad, 24 February 1825. See map, p72.

24 Dudley MSS 10/1, Terms and Conditions of a Proposed Railway from the Staffordshire and Worcestershire Canal to Shut End, 17 January 1827.

25 *Mechanic's Magazine,* 20 June 1829.

26 The *Agenoria,* a beam engine type of locomotive, is now in the Railway Museum at York. The name may well reflect the third viscount's classical and literary interests. A second engine constructed at the time, *The Stourbridge Lion,* is attributed with the distinction of being the first steam locomotive to run in the USA.

27 Scott, W. *Stourbridge and its Vicinity* (1832), 364.

28 Hatherton, Col. D260/M/F/5/19/4. Loch's Final Report on the trust accounts.

29 See pp152-3.

30 Railway Sel Com 1845, appendix.

31 Ibid, Q.4474.

32 Hatherton, Col. D260/M/E/430/261. Smith to Hatherton, 13 September 1844.

33 Railway Sel Com, Q.6903.

34 Ibid. An Act for the Making of a Railway from the Great Western Railway at Oxford to Worcester and to Join the Grand Junction Railway at Wolverhampton, para 44.

35 See pp219-20.

CHAPTER FOUR

1 Mingay, G. E. *The Landed Estate in the Eighteenth Century* (1963), 90.

2 Dudley MSS 23/6, Abstract of a farm lease, 20 August 1783. This is typical of leases granted for established properties on the Dudley estate before 1815.

3 Dudley MSS 19/27, Lord Dudley with James Moor, Benjamin Skidmore and John Aston: Booty Colliers: Articles for renting New Inclosures at Pensnett, 27 February 1790.

4 Thompson, F. M. L. *English Landed Society in the Nineteenth Century* (1963), 229-30.

5 Dudley MSS 19/27, Lord Dudley to Mr George Campion, Lease of Mill Lands and Hereditaments at Wildmoor in Belbroughton, Lady Day 1802.

6 Dudley MSS 6/A, Statement of Properties on which Land Tax was purchased by Lord Dudley and Ward in Staffordshire, 30 April 1799.

7 Eleven steam engines were purchased in this period.

8 Dudley MSS 32/6, Report and Observations on Lord Dudley's Agricultural Property: John R. Roberts, 1 December 1824.

9 Ibid.

10 Dudley MSS 32/6, John Bradley in Account with Lord Dudley, 1797-1816. Subsequently referred to as Bradley's Accounts.

11 Hatherton, Col. D260/M/F/5/19/11. Francis Downing in

Account with the Trustees of the Late Earl of Dudley. Great rents were paid on farming property, as distinct from cottage rents.

12 Dudley MSS 620/20, Lord Dudley's Great Rental, 1800.

13 Thompson, F. M. L., 'English Great Estates in the Nineteenth Century', *International Conference of Economic History* (1960), 393.

14 Mingay, op cit, 381.

15 Dudley MSS 5/10, Papers relating to a chancery case, 1788: Honourable William Ward, Complainant (heir to the estate) versus John, Lord Viscount Dudley and Ward, Defendant.

16 This came to be known as Round Oak Store Yard and, by 1822, it consisted of an 'iron foundry, saw mill, boring mill, steam engine manufactory, carpenters shop, pattern rooms etc'. Fowler, op cit, item 1,501.

17 Hatherton, Col. D260/M/F/5/19/2, p11. Report by Messrs Smith and Liddell on the Mines etc at Dudley, 1836.

18 White, W. *Directory of Staffordshire* (Sheffield, 1834).

19 Thompson, F. M. L. *English Landed Society in the Nineteenth Century* (1963), 230-1.

20 Hatherton, Col. D260/M/F/5/19/4. Loch's Second Report on the Trust Accounts (1835), 25.

21 Richards, E. S., op cit, 164.

22 Loch's Second Report (1835), 19.

23 Thompson, F. M. L. *English Landed Society*, 235.

24 Hatherton, Col. D260/M/F/5/19/11. Lord Hatherton to Lord Ward, 12 November 1838.

25 Dudley MSS 12/d, Lord Ward to William Perry: Lease of a Farm and Premises called Hickmear Lands in Sedgley, 25 March 1854.

26 White, W. *Directory of Staffordshire* (1851), 29.

27 Loch's Second Report (1835), 25.

28 Spring, D. *The English Landed Estate in the Nineteenth Century, Its Administration, 1830-1870* (Baltimore 1962), 95.

29 Purchased from Lord Foley in 1838: see below. Hatherton, Col. D260/M/F/5/19/5. Accounts of the Kidderminster, Witley and Welsh Estates from 1838 to 1845.

30 Loch's Second Report (1835), 26.

31 Loch's Third Report (1836), 76.

32 Dudley MSS 10/11, Jamaica Year Book, 1812.

33 Hatherton, Col. D260/M/F/5/19/11. G. W. S. Hibbert and Co to Benbow, 16 June 1835.

34 Dudley MSS 6/B, Himley Estate Accounts, 1930-42.

35 See below.

36 Dudley MSS 32/6, Survey of Himley Estates, the Property of the Earl of Dudley. Statistics given to the British Iron Trade Association, 24 February 1883.

37 Dudley MSS 23/6, Survey of the Himley Estates by Sir Richard Redmayne. Particulars of Security for a Loan of £252,000, 7 February 1924.

38 Dudley MSS 5/23.

39 Hatherton, Col. D260/M/F/5/19/11. Loch to Hatherton, 8 December 1841.

40 Ibid.

41 Dudley MSS 23/3, An Act for Enabling the Sale and Conveyance of certain Cottages, Gardens and other Improved Lands comprised in the Will of the Right Honourable John William, Earl of Dudley.

42 Dudley MSS 23/13, Circular Concerning the Sale of Cottage Properties, 30 October 1847.

43 Dudley MSS 9/L.

44 Ibid, Sales of Cottage Property, 1848-1946.

45 Ibid, Copyhold Enfranchisement Book, 1848-1926.

46 Thompson, F. M. L. 'English Landownership: The Ailesbury Trust', Econ Hist Rev, 2nd ser XI (1958), 128.

47 Richards, op cit, 198.

48 Spring, D. 'The English Landed Estate in the Age of Coal and Iron, 1830-1880', The Journal of Economic History, XI (1951).

49 Redmayne's Survey, 1924.

50 *Burke's Peerage,* IV, 491.

51 Dudley MSS 10/K. Particulars and Valuations of Welsh and Scottish Estates, 1824-7.

52 Hatherton, Col. D260/M/F/5/19/1, The Earl of Dudley's Will, 26 July 1831, 20.

53 Hatherton, Col. Loch's First Report on the Trust Accounts, July 1834, 8.

54 Loch's Fourth Report on the Trust Accounts, 11 May 1838.

55 See Chapter 7.

56 Thompson, F. M. L. 'The Land Market in the Nineteenth Century', *Oxford Economic Papers,* IX (1957), 291-3.

57 Hatherton, Col. Benbow to Littleton, 12 May 1834. Survey of the estate, by W. Fowler.

58 Hatherton, Col. D260/M/F/5/19/11. Exeter to Hatherton, 5 December 1835.

59 Ibid, Benbow to Hatherton, 7 December 1835.

60 Ibid, Summary and Valuation of a Freehold Manor and Estate called Hendwr in the Parish of Llandrillo in the County of Merioneth, 24 February 1836. By H. C. Wright, 40 Tavistock Street, Covent Garden. His fee was £49 14s.

61 Loch's Fourth Report on the Trust Accounts, 1838, 27.

62 Hatherton, Col. D260/M/F/5/19/9. Benbow to Hatherton, 15 April 1837.

63 Hatherton, Col. D260/M/F/5/19/11. Terms Proposed by John Hodgetts Foley for the Sale of the Witley Estate, 19 December 1837.

64 Ibid, Lord Warden to Hatherton, 16 February 1838.

65 See pp201-9.

66 Hatherton, Col. D260/M/F/5/19/11. Benbow to Hatherton, 13 February 1838.

67 Ibid, Mr Robins' Valuation of Witley Court.

68 Ibid, Benbow to Hatherton, July 1838.

69 Thompson, F. M. L. 'The Land Market in the Nineteenth Century', *Oxford Economic Papers,* Vol 9 (1957), 294.

70 See pp155, 168-70.

71 Thompson, F. M. L. *English Landed Society*, 283 et seq.

72 Dudley MSS 8/M, Particulars of Sale of the Broome and Hurcot Estates, 30 July 1918.

73 *Estates Gazette*, March 1919, and *The Times*, 19 May 1919, as quoted by Thompson, op cit, 330.

74 Thompson, op cit, 332.

75 Dudley MSS 8/M, Particulars of Sale of the Witley and Holt Estates, 27 September 1920.

76 *Dudley Herald*, 25 September 1920.

77 *Dudley Herald*, 2 October 1920.

78 Ibid, Witley Court itself together with 1,100 acres was purchased by Sir Herbert Smith, a Kidderminster carpet manufacturer. After a fire seriously damaged the house, he auctioned it, with the land, in September 1938.

79 After the re-settlement of the estates in 1923, all assets were consolidated into a public company in 1926, the Himley Estates Ltd. The second earl's son, Lord Ednam, was the Governing Director, see Chapter 7.

80 *Dudley Herald*, 23 October 1926.

81 Ibid, 20 July 1935.

82 Dudley MSS 8/M, Particulars of Sale of Lands, 14 January 1947.

83 *Dudley Herald*, 9 May 1964, Obituary.

84 *Dudley Herald*, 18 January 1947.

85 Dudley MSS 8/M, Particulars of Sale of Lands, 9 July 1947.

CHAPTER FIVE

1 William Salt Library, Stafford, 20/39, Executor's Account, 1788.

2 Dudley MSS 614/20, Lord Dudley's Great Rental, 1791.

3 Dudley MSS 32/6, Bradley's Accounts, 1796-1817.

4 Reverend Stebbing-Shaw, *The History and Antiquities of*

Staffordshire (1801), II.

5 Ibid, 237.

6 Dudley MSS 2/13, Lord Dudley to Mrs Sarah Grazebrook.

7 Dudley MSS 10/26, Lord Dudley to Messrs Grazebrook.

8 Dudley MSS 8/K, List of Mines Leases, October 1836.

9 Dudley Public Library, L.D/625, Minutes of Evidence taken before the Select Committee on the Oxford, Worcester & Wolverhampton Railway, 1845, 190 and 200. Subsequently referred to as Railway Sel Com 1845.

10 White, op cit (1834), 51.

11 Morton, G. R. and Le Guillou, M. 'The Rise and Fall of the South Staffordshire Pig Iron Industry', *The British Foundryman,* July 1967.

12 Timmins, S. *Report on the Iron Trade of South Staffordshire* (1865), 7.

13 Dudley MSS 15/8, Lord Dudley to Richard Croft of Stourbridge, Ironmaster, and William Croft of Wombourn, Ironmaster, 1 February 1774. Lease of Cradley Forge and Cradley Furnace in Rowley and Cradley together with Cradley Slitting Mills or New Mills and Pools and Workmen's Houses.

14 A cord was usually 128cu ft.

15 Dudley MSS 23/6, Lord Dudley to G. J. A. and B. Parker: Lease of Land in Tipton near Tipton Green to Manufacture Pig, Cast Iron and Other Branches of Iron Manufactuory, 1783.

16 Lones, T. E. *A History of Mining in the Black Country* (Dudley, 1898), 28. 'Each acre of good mine yields c.1,000-1,200 blooms.'

17 In Brierley Hill to the south of Dudley.

18 Dudley MSS 20/1, Lord Dudley to Thomas, William and Benjamin Gibbons. Lease of Lands and Mines at the Level, 25 March 1800.

19 Dudley MSS 609/20, Lord Dudley's Rental, 1789.

20 Dudley MSS 20/1, Gibbons' Lease.

21 Hatherton, Col. Mines Report, 1836, 39: Accounts for the period 31 March-31 December 1834.

22 Dudley MSS 6/K, Messrs Parkes. Observations on their Lease of Park Head Furnace, May 1795.

23 Administration of the pits was radically overhauled, 1797-8, by the Newcastle mining engineer, Charles Beaumont. See Chapter 6.

24 Dudley MSS 12/L, Lord Dudley to Messrs Attwood. Lease of Lands and Mines at Netherton, Lady Day, 1800.

25 Mines Report (1836), 28.

26 Railway Sel Com, 1845. Richard Smith [Lord Dudley's mineral agent] in answer to Q.4621.

27 Hatherton, Col. D260/M/F/5/19/11. Downing to Littleton, 17 October 1833.

28 Ibid, Loch to Hatherton, 17 December 1835.

29 White, op cit, 59.

30 Midland Mining Commission, 1843, para 41.

31 Ibid, para 55.

32 Mushet, R. *Papers on Iron and Steel* (London 1840), as quoted by Morton and Le Guillou, op cit, 272.

33 Mines Report, 1836, 18.

34 Hatherton, Col. D260/M/F/5/19/4. Smith to Benbow, 5 May 1836.

35 Dudley MSS 8/K. Ironworks leased from Lord Dudley. Downing to the trustees, 16 October 1836.

36 Railway Sel Com, 1845, Statistical tables.

37 Dudley MSS 8/L, Richard Smith's Mine Accounts, 1837-60.

38 Dudley MSS 8/K, Account of Steam Engines Belonging to the Trustees, Xmas 1839, W. Rollinson.

39 Dudley MSS 8/K, List of Blast Engines Employed at the Different Iron Works, 6 October 1844, D. Pearson.

40 Railway Sel Com, 1845, 6. Evidence of Mr B. Best.

41 Downing, although a trustee, was persuaded to renounce the mineral agency in favour of Richard Smith—just as he had been 'replaced' by Bateman as land agent. See Chapter 7.

42 Hawkes Smith, W. *Birmingham and South Staffordshire* (1838).

43 See p28. Dud Dudley, a natural son of Lord Dudley, took out a patent in 1621 to smelt iron ore with mineral fuel.

44 Railway Sel Com, 1845, Q.387. Evidence of Richard Smith.

45 Dudley MSS 8/K, List of Blast Engines Employed at the Different Iron Works, 6 October 1844.

46 Chambers, J. D. *The Workshop of the World* (1961), 33-41.

47 Railway Sel Com, 1845. Evidence of Richard Smith.

48 See pp75-6.

49 Scrivenor, H. *History of the Iron Trade* (1854), 299.

50 Allen, G. C. *The Industrial Development of Birmingham and the Black Country* (1929), 100.

51 Royal Commission on Depression of Trade, Q.10. Evidence given by Wolverhampton Chamber of Commerce.

52 Mineral agent, 1864-70: Richard Smith's son.

53 Dudley MSS 12/C, Auditor's Report Upon the Examination of the Earl of Dudley's Accounts, Mines Department, 1871-2.

54 Dudley MSS 7/A, Lease of Minerals Granted to the Earl of Dudley by Mr B. Round at Southrop, Hook Norton, 29 September 1899.

55 Dudley MSS 12/A, Mines Department's Statistics, 1875-86.

56 Ibid. An 'oliver' was the local name given to an arrangement of hammers for the manufacture of hand-wrought chains and nails.

57 *The Engineer,* 9 May 1856.

58 *The Dudley Herald,* 25 July 1868.

59 Allen, op cit, 205.

60 Dudley MSS 12/H, Profit and Loss Account, Mines Dept Accounts for Year Ending in December 1854.

61 Auditor's Report, 1871.

62 Dudley MSS 32/6, Statistics and Analyses, 1866-1915.

63 Brierley Hill Public Library, 8/1, Prospectus of the Earl of Dudley's Round Oak Iron and Steel Works Ltd, April 1890.

64 Brierley Hill Public Library, 8/1, First Report to the Direc-

tors of the Earl of Dudley's Round Oak Iron and Steel Works Ltd, 14 September 1892.

65 I am indebted to Mr W. H. B. Hatton of Broome House, Stourbridge, for this information. He worked at Round Oak from 1899 to 1950 and was secretary of the company 1924-36 and managing director 1936-50. The new processes were introduced by his father, Mr G. Hatton, managing director from 1897 to 1924.

66 See pp241-2.

CHAPTER SIX

1 See p23.

2 Dudley MSS 6/K, Brettell (land agent) to Cockshutt (mineral agent), 23 May 1795.

3 Ibid. Statement by Chas. Norton. Quarter here probably refers to a quarter of a ton: a Winchester Bushel was about 77lb. As late as 1864, there were three different ton weights used in the Black Country: the statute weight of 2,240lb, the 'long hundred' of 2,400lb (20cwt x 120lb) and the 'boat load' or 'lease weight' of 2,880lb (24 long hundreds). The Dudley estate used only the statute ton after 1868.

4 They were not concluded by Cockshutt but by Charles Beaumont—or modelled on his leases after his dismissal in 1798.

5 Dudley MSS 6/A, Articles of Agreement between Lord Dudley and Charles Norton of Birmingham, Samuel Fereday and William Turton, Lime Merchants of Sedgley, 24 March 1800.

6 Mines Report, 1836, 18.

7 Ibid, 21.

8 Hatherton Papers D260/M/F/5/19/4, Downing's Comments on the Mines Report, May 1836.

9 Mines Report, 1836, 22.

s

10 Dudley MSS 8/K, Particulars of Leases, Agreements etc Belonging to the Late Earl of Dudley. From Mr Downing, 16 October 1836.

11 Dudley MSS 9/J, Richard Smith's Accounts as Mine Agent, from 31 December 1846 to 31 December 1847.

12 See below.

13 Dudley MSS 8/K, Account of Steam Engines and Weighing Machines Belonging to the Trustees, Xmas 1839. W. Rollinson.

14 Dudley MSS 9/J, Account of Francis Downing, Mine Agent as amended by James Loch, December 1834.

15 Dudley Public Library, LD 625, Report of the Enquiry into the Oxford, Worcester & Wolverhampton Railway, 1845. Evidence of Richard Smith.

16 Dudley MSS 9/J, Richard Smith's Accounts as Mine Agent from 31 December 1846 to 31 December 1847.

17 Dudley MSS 23/6, Lord Dudley to Lord Dundonald and the Honourable Alexander Forrester Cochrane. Lease of Land and Mines at the Level, 6 October 1787.

18 Select Committee on Coal Supply, Parl Papers 1871, XVIII, 27. '... the early workings of the south Staffordshire ... coalfield were not conducted under any scientific system of management, nor (owing probably to the great thickness and value of the principal or 10-yard seam) with any view of economy.'

19 Beaumont, C. 'A Treatise on the Coal Trade' (1789), reviewed in the *Gentleman's Magazine,* vol LIX, no 2 (1789). This contains proposals to reorganise the coal trade in Newcastle and on a national basis.

20 Public Record Office, C110/170, Beaumont to Jeans, 11 September 1797, 4.

21 Ibid, Beaumont to Jeans, 22 June 1797.

22 Ibid. 'Collier' here means butty collier as the chartermaster system operated in Lord Dudley's pits at this time. Labour was not yet directly employed. Because of the methods used,

large quantities of cobbles or small, broken coal (relatively worthless) tended to be produced in working 30-foot seam. The method of cutting the coal, Staffordshire 'square-work', involved the undercutting of a mass of coal and at the sides, so that the 'square' rested on a small base. This mass was then brought down by the 'pricker' who unbalanced the coal by shaking it with a long pole.

23 Ibid, 6. See Ashton, T. S. and Sykes, J. *The Coal Industry in the Eighteenth Century* (Manchester, 1929), 226 et seq, for a discussion of the inland coal trade. The price of coal in Staffordshire was 4s 6d a ton in 1790; the price of coal in London was £2 10s per ton in 1800. Vested interests (Midlands industrialists fearing a decrease in their coal supplies, and Newcastle dealers) secured restrictive legislation and, after 1805, inland coal had to pay a duty of 10s per chaldron. The wider markets secured by Beaumont may have helped bring matters to a head.

24 Public Records Office C110/170, Beaumont to Jeans, 25 April 1797.

25 Ibid, Beaumont to Jeans, 2 June 1797.

26 Ibid.

27 In 1791, annual consumption of coal in Birmingham was 200,000 tons. Arthur Young, 'Tours in England and Wales', selected from the *Annals of Agriculture* (LSE reprint), 256, as quoted by W. H. B. Court, op cit, 165. National output was 10 million tons.

28 Public Records Office C110/170, Beaumont to Jeans, 10 June 1797.

29 Ibid, Dumaresq to Jeans, 16 August 1797.

30 Ibid, Beaumont to Jeans, 2 June 1797.

31 *SC on the Employment of Children,* 1842. Report on south Staffordshire, 2.

32 Public Records Office C110/170, Contract between Charles Beaumont and B. Cartwright and Co for Mining Lord Dudley's Coal, 8 September 1797. This concerned a pit at

Brierley Hill.

33 See Taylor, A. J. 'The Sub-Contract System in the British Coal Industry', *Studies in the Industrial Revolution* (1960), ed Pressnell, L. S., 217, for a discussion of the butty system.

34 Thompson, *Landed Society*, 264.

35 See pp70-1.

36 Public Records Office C110/170, Beaumont to Jeans, 29 July 1797.

37 Dudley MSS 12/1, Agreement 18 November 1797 between Samuel Fereday of Ettingshall Park, Sedgley, and William Turton, Upper Gornal, Coalmasters and Lord Dudley.

38 Ibid, Beaumont to Jeans, 4 January 1798, A Plan for Working Lord Dudley's Extensive Coal Mines to the Greatest Advantage; also 'A Report on Lord Dudley's Coal Mines'.

39 Ibid, Beaumont's Plan, 1.

40 Ibid. 'Collier' here means individual miner, not the butty. Beaumont calculated that by these methods, 200 miners could produce 300,000 tons per year. A daily wage of 3s 6d would probably exceed existing wages which have been estimated at 1s 8d in 1780 and 3s 4d in 1813, Ashton and Sykes, op cit, 137.

41 By the mid-nineteenth century, the butty system was challenged in the Black Country by the miners themselves and mine-owners such as James Foster who demonstrated that the abandonment of sub-contracting led to increased output and greater economy. Midland Mining Commission, 1843, 69 as quoted by Taylor, op cit, 219.

42 Public Records Office C110/170, Beaumont to Jeans, 22 February 1798. The number of men was actually 30.

43 Public Records Office C110/170, undated pamphlet.

44 Ibid, Lord Dudley to Jeans, 16 April 1798.

45 Dudley MSS 6/A, Alex Raby's Account for Steam Engines, November 1800. Raby succeeded Jeans as the London agent.

46 Dudley MSS 6/A, Account of the Profits of Lord Dudley's Mines, Lady Day, 1804.

47 Hatherton, Col. D260/M/F/5/19/2. A Short Statement Submitted to Messrs Smith and Liddell as Instructions for their Survey of the Mines and Works of the Late Earl of Dudley. Subsequently referred to as Instructions, 1835.

48 Mines Report, 1836, 26.

49 Ibid, 10.

50 Hatherton, Col. D260/M/F/5/19/4. Downing's Comments on the Mines Report, 7 June 1836.

51 *SC on the State of the Population in the Mining Districts,* 1850. Report on south Staffordshire, 33.

52 Ibid.

53 South Staffs Mines Drainage Act, 1873.

54 Mines Report, 1836, 15.

55 Hatherton, Col. D260/M/F/5/19/12. Smith to Hatherton, 13 April 1836.

56 Thompson, *English Great Estates,* 389.

57 Mines Report, 1836, 29.

58 Spring, D. 'The Earls of Durham and the Great Northern Coalfield, 1830-1880', *Canadian Historical Review,* XXXIII (1952), 239.

59 Ward, J. T. 'West Riding Landowners and Mining in the Nineteenth Century', *Yorks Bulletin of Economic and Social Research,* XV, 63.

60 Thompson, *English Landed Society,* 264.

61 Hatherton, Col. D260/M/F/5/19/4. Loch to Benbow, 6 June 1836.

62 Mines Report, 1836, 59.

63 Hatherton, Col. D260/M/F/5/19/11. Downing to Benbow, 30 May 1836.

64 Hatherton, Col. D260/M/F/5/26. Lord Hatherton's Diary, 29 September 1836.

65 A large mansion erected at Dudley in 1826 for the mineral and land agent.

66 Dudley MSS 8/L, Richard Smith's Accounts With the Trustees from 1 January 1837 to 6 March 1845 and With

Lord Ward from 6 March 1845 to 31 December 1859.

67 On average, an acre of unworked coal produced 10,000 tons; three acres of broken mines produced the same quantity. Mines Report, 1836, 9.

68 Dudley MSS 9/K, Mines Leases and Agreements Made by F. Downing, 16 October 1836.

69 Dudley MSS 9/K, Lease of Minerals in Pensnett to Messrs Philpotts and Plant, 31 December 1839.

70 Ibid, 10/L, Schedule of Documents in the Evidence Room at Himley Hall.

71 Brierley Hill Public Library, 554.24, Proceedings of the Dudley, Midland and Geological Society: a paper by R. Kettle, 1864.

72 At the time of the Witley purchase.

73 Ibid, 8/L, Richard Smith's Accounts with the Trustees, 1 January 1837 to 6 March 1845: and with Lord Ward, 6 March 1845 to December 1860.

74 *First Report of the Commissioners for Enquiring into the Employment of Children in Mines and Manufactories*, 1842; Report on South Staffs, 2.

75 Dudley MSS 6/A, Agreement Between the Subscribers to the Hercules Pumping Engine (Deepfield Engine) and the Trustees of the Late Earl of Dudley, 1838.

76 See pp62-8, 75-6.

77 Brierley Hill Public Library, H3/1, 'Survey of Kingswinford' by W. Fowler, 1822.

78 Railway Report, 1845. Q.1839, Evidence of W. Matthews.

79 Hatherton, Col. D260/M/F/5/19/4. Loch's Report on the Final Accounts.

80 Allen, op cit, 281.

81 *SC on Coal Supply*, No 5 (1871), XVIII.

82 *SC on Mines Drainage*, South Staffs (1920), 10-12, XXI.

83 White, W. op cit, 60.

84 Hatherton, Col. D260/M/F/5/6/a. Mayor of Wolverhampton to Deputy-Lieutenant of Staffs, 5 July 1858.

85 Ibid, Smith to Hatherton, 4 October 1858.

86 Ibid, Miners' Wages and Coal Prices in South Staffordshire, by Thomas Mansell, General Secretary of the Miners' Association, Great Bridge, Tipton.

87 Dudley MSS 9/L, Sales of Property, 1850-1948, Vol 1: printed memo inside cover.

88 Dudley MSS 11/G, Record of Mine Leases, 1867-1907.

89 Dudley MSS 12/A, List of Properties Subject to Succession Duty on Mineral Royalties, 1932.

90 Dudley MSS 9/F, Mineral Statistics, 1880-1923.

91 Dudley MSS 12/A, Mine Dept Statistics, 1873-1886.

92 Dudley MSS 11/G, Report on the Mineral Resources of Lord Dudley's Settled Estates in South Staffordshire and East Worcestershire, 11 April 1924, by R. A. S. Redmayne.

93 Dudley MSS 32/6, Report on the Earl of Dudley's Mines and Minerals by W. F. Clark, 1931.

94 Ward, op cit, 63.

95 Paper by Mr Parton, F.G.S. Reported in *The Engineer*, 3 February 1871.

96 *Birmingham Post*, 4 July 1902.

97 Dudley MSS 6/B, Himley Estates' Accounts.

CHAPTER SEVEN

1 Pollard, S. *The Genesis of Modern Management* (1965), 126.

2 Dudley MSS 10/K, Statement by John William, Viscount Dudley and Ward, 14 May 1823.

3 Benbow was a trustee, 1833-45.

4 Dudley MSS 6/A, The Staff Employed by the Mines Dept, November 1804.

5 Mines Report (1836), 59.

6 Thompson. *English Great Estates*, 168.

7 Hatherton, Col. D260/M/F/5/19/12. Benbow to Hatherton, 1 August 1848.

8 See p200.
9 Midland Mining Commission 1843, lv.
10 Court, op cit, 152, writing about the rent roll of Lord Dudley for 1701.
11 Spring, *The English Landed Estate*, 81-3.
12 Pollard, op cit, 209.
13 Dudley MSS 608/20, Lord Dudley's Rental, 1788-91.
14 Trustees' Instructions, 1835.
15 Hatherton, Col. D260/M/F/5/19/4. Report on the Trust Accounts.
16 Ibid, Loch's First Report on the Trust Accounts, 18 July 1834.
17 Ibid, Loch's Second Report, 1835, 56.
18 Loch's Third Report, 27 October 1836.
19 Dudley MSS 12/L, Report Upon the Examination of the Earl of Dudley's Account, Mines Department, for 1871.
20 Public Records Office C110/170, Lord Dudley to Jeans, 10 December 1797.
21 Romilly, S. H. *Letters to Ivy from the First Earl of Dudley* (1905), 6.
22 Lord Brougham. *Edinburgh Review*, I XVII, 79, as quoted by Romilly, op cit, 385.
23 Hatherton, Col. D260/M/F/5/19/11. William Ward to Lady Ward, 24 November 1833.
24 Ibid, Littleton to J. H. Foley, 8 March 1834.
25 Hatherton, Col. D260/M/F/5/19/11. Lord Ward to Benbow, May 1836.
26 Ibid, Benbow to Hatherton, 21 February 1837.
27 Ibid, Dean of Christ Church to Hatherton, 7 June 1836.
28 Ibid, Dean of Christ Church to Hatherton, 12 June 1836.
29 Ibid, 22 February 1837.
30 Ibid, Ward to Hatherton, November 1838.
31 Spring, *The English Landed Estate*, 53.
32 Hatherton, Col. D260/M/F/5/19/11. August 1837.
33 See pp98-9.

34 Hatherton, Col. D260/M/F/5/19/11. Ward to Hatherton, 8 November 1838.
35 Ibid, Final Remarks on the Accounts of the Trust, R. Craig and J. H. Benbow [Benbow's son], 22 January 1858.
36 Brierley Hill Public Library. *County Express*, 7 October 1911.
37 Hatherton, Col. D260/M/F/5/19/11. Opinion of Sir William Horne, Lincoln's Inn, 7 April 1836. There was some dispute as to whether legacy duty was payable.
38 Midland Mining Commission, 1843. Return of Medical Relief and Pensions Paid to Wounded and Superannuated Miners and Widows by the Trustees of the late Earl of Dudley, 1842, lviii.
39 Brierley Hill Public Library, H16/1. Pamphlet on the Social Condition of the Colliery District of South Staffordshire, Rev C. Girdlestone, April 1855.
40 Loch's Report on the Trust Accounts from 1838 to 1849, Matthews' Accounts for Kidderminster and Witley, 1839.
41 *Dudley Herald*, 9 May 1885, Obituary.
42 See p16.
43 Ibid.
44 See pp170-1.

Acknowledgements

I wish to thank Lord Hatherton for permission to publish extracts from the Hatherton Collection at Stafford Record Office and the Earl of Dudley for making documents available at Dudley Public Library; also Mr F. Stitt, the County Archivist, Mr J. Hoyle, Director of Dudley Public Library, and their staffs for all their willing assistance, and Wolverhampton Public Library for their assistance.

Index

267

Brindley, James, 32
British Association for the Advancement of Science, 181
British Iron Co, 149
Brockmoor, 66, 70
Brockmoor Colliery, 131
Broome, 123
Building land, 123, 127
Bumble Hole Colliery, 141
Butty, *see* Chartermaster

Cables, 143
Caldon Low, 152
Canals, 24, 32, 55, 68-9, *157*; and the Dudley estate, 68, *56*; impact of railways, 80-1; problems of construction, 24; purpose, 62n
Cannock, 15
Cannock Extension Canal, 55
Castle Mill, 125, 172-3, 211
Castle Mill Engineering Works, 76, 87, 160, 211
Chain trade, 143, 159, 169
Charcoal, 136
Chartermaster,   184n,   191,   198;
'booty' collier, 249n; challenge to, 260n; on Dudley estate, 188-9, 192, 196, 198
Church construction, 240
Clark, F. B., 222
Clark, W. F., 217
Claughton, Sir Gilbert, 168
Claughton, T. L., 237
Clay, 130ff, 215, 223
Coal trade, 10, 182ff, 188, 195, 208; Dudley estate, 182ff, 223, 239, 243; collapse of, 211-15; methods of exploitation, 191-2, 198-9; miners, 187, 212, 216, 240; prices, 184-6n, 188, 214; production, 27, 79-80, 143-4, 152, 154, 171, 211; wages, 191, 213-14
Cockshutt, Edward, 95, 182, 226
Collier, 258n, 260n
Coneygre Colliery, 30, 201
Coneygre Iron Works, 76, 141, 148; estate production, 151-2, 159, 164-5; sale, 160
Corbyn's Hall, 66
Corbyn's Hall Iron Works, 145
Cort, Henry, 31, 135

Cottage property, 107; location, 108; sale of, 110-12, 123
Coventry Canal, 61
Cradley Heath, 9
Cradley Iron Works, 136, 148
Crimean War, 11, 154, 163, 213
Croft, R. & W., 136
Crogen, 113, 116-17
Crystal Palace, 149

Darby, Abraham, 31; Abraham II, 31
Darlaston, 9
Deepfields, 108
Deepfields Iron Works, 148-9
Downing, Francis, 12, 143, 151n, 176, 194, 195, 199, 226, 228
Drainage, 208-9, 212-13
Drainage Commission (1873), 213
Dudley, 9, 110, 126
Dudley and Ward, John, 2nd Lord (1774-88), 11, 234-5; economic policies, 32-4, 182; limestone, 173-4; timber, 94-5
Dudley and Ward, John William, 4th Lord (1823-7) and 1st Earl of (1827-33), 11, 211, 235; purchase of land, 113; will, 113
Dudley and Ward, William, 3rd Lord (1788-1823), 11, 173, 234-5; timber, 94-5
Dudley Barony, 27n
Dudley Canal, 58, 153; and collieries, 59; and the Dudley estate, 60, 138, 190, 209; construction, 59; freight rates, 59
Dudley Castle, 10, 172, 220
Dudley Castle Canal Tunnel, 60, 141, 196, 211; advantages, 60; and the Dudley estate, 61, 71, 160, 172; inadequacy of, 79-80; opposition, 61; water supply, 175-6
Dudley Council, 125
Dudley, Dud, 28
Dudley Enclosure Act (1784), 43
Dudley estate, 10, 11, 15, 17, 182, 243; accounts, 229-34; agents, 225-9; agriculture, 89-107; area, 15, 106, 114, 130; bricks, 131ff, 221; canal shares, 62-3; capital, 158-9, 167-9, 170, 198, 211, 220, 224, 242; chainos, 159, 169; clay, 131-5, 215;